The British
Labour Movement
to 1970

Harold Smith's other publications include:

The libraries of Greater Manchester: a guide to resources and special collections
The Society for the Diffusion of Useful Knowledge 1826–1846: a social and
bibliographical evaluation
Remember 1926: a booklist

The British Labour Movement to 1970

A BIBLIOGRAPHY

compiled by Harold Smith
with a Foreword by Asa Briggs

MANSELL PUBLISHING

ISBN 0 7201 0924 8

Mansell Publishing, a member of Bemrose U.K. Limited,
3 Bloomsbury Place, London WC1A 2QA

First published 1981
© Harold Smith, 1981

British Library Cataloguing in Publication Data
Smith, Harold, *b. 1918*
The British labour movement to 1970.
1. Labor and laboring classes –
Great Britain – History – Bibliography
I. Title
016.335′1′0941   Z7165.G7
ISBN 0-7201-0924-8

Phototypeset in V.I.P. Bembo by
Western Printing Services Ltd, Bristol
Printed and bound in Great Britain
at The Pitman Press, Bath

Contents

Contents

Foreword

The study of labour history has been transformed in recent years both in scope and in scale. Four main tendencies have been apparent: the effort to strengthen its academic base; the quest to ferret out lost sources; the desire to relate national history to local history and, most recently, local history to a revised synthesis of national—and to a lesser extent international—history; and a broadening of concern to encompass not only individuals and institutions but whole ways of life.

The Society for the Study of Labour History is celebrating its twenty-first anniversary in 1981, and it is fitting that this bibliographical guide, the product of years of committed research, should appear in that year. The Society itself can now be placed in perspective as a historical product. There were significant changes of preoccupation and style during the 1960s, and during the 1970s as labour history has boomed inside and outside universities we have moved far from the situation which was described in the introduction to the second volume of *Essays in Labour History* (Asa Briggs and John Saville, eds., Macmillan, 1971). The circumstances of the late 1950s out of which the Society emerged will doubtless provide an important topic for labour historians of the 1980s. So, too, will the range of research interests expressed in the Society's *Bulletin*, published biannually since 1960.

The *Bulletin* is only one of the many periodicals which matter to labour historians: *History Workshop* (biannual, 1976–), reflecting a different current of opinion, is another. The study of labour history can only be pursued in depth through periodicals, past and present, and pamphlets and broadsheets. Thanks to John Saville and his colleagues, we now at last have a richer and deeper knowledge of labour biography. Thanks to Harold Smith we will now have at our disposal a fuller, though still selective, labour bibliography than we have ever had before. Even if it were complete, it would reveal gaps as well as effort, and since some of these gaps are always being filled in, it will require regular revision.

It is interesting to note how much material has been produced during the last twenty-five years. Yet there are earlier books which have the status of classics, and there are reminiscences of members of the labour movement in its various phases which have a freshness and directness which very few historians can completely re-capture. *The Dictionary of Labour Biography* (Macmillan, 1972–), has now made full use of these.

It must have been very difficult for Harold Smith to know where to draw necessary dividing lines round his selections. The National Association for Promoting the Political and Social Improvement of the People recommended during the 1840s that people's libraries should be of 'a hundred to two hundred volumes each, containing the most useful works on politics, morals, the sciences, history and such instructive and entertaining works as may generally be approved of'. Almost all of these—like many WEA (Workers' Educational Association) lists of this century—would be relevant to an understanding of the changing culture of the developing labour movement. There are also biographies of people not directly connected with the labour movement which have a relevance to its history. Indeed, *Essays in Anti-Labour History* is as necessary a volume for the student of this subject as the three volumes of *Essays in Labour History*.

I have one final necessary reflection. Labour history now depends on the exploration and assessment of a whole range of materials besides books and pamphlets. Oral history is an essential approach, but so, too, is visual history—the capacity to treat things as messengers. Some of these things are collected in the National Museum of Labour History, London, a remarkable labour of love: others are scattered throughout the country. The vision of a single place, properly supported, where things and books could be placed together is surely no more Utopian than the original vision of a Society for the Study of Labour History.

ASA BRIGGS

Preface

This is a bibliography of books, pamphlets and periodical articles in the English language on the history of the British Labour movement published in the period 1945–1970.

The origin of the work lay in my belief that with the increasing interest in British Labour history, the formation of many Labour history societies and the phenomenal growth in the number of publications since the end of War there was a growing need for a comprehensive bibliography on the subject. I chose 1945 as the starting date and a quarter of a century as a reasonable period to cover. I hope to follow the present volume with decennial supplements, the first, 1971–1980, appearing, if all goes well, in 1982.

The bibliography is based on visits to the libraries listed below; visits to bookshops; constant scrutiny and checking of bibliographies, publishers' catalogues and booklists; and on my own collection. I have seen and checked all the items listed. I have excluded works on industrial relations, which are dealt with in the excellent bibliography by G. S. Bain and G. B. Woolven, *A bibliography of British industrial relations* (C.U.P., 1979); and government publications which are included in the H.M.S.O. *Daily Lists* and *Consolidated Guides*. Place of publication is London except where otherwise stated:

My thanks are due to many people and many organizations:

To the Social Science Research Council for their grant which made the work and, consequently, this book possible.

To the British Library; the British Library of Political and Economic Science; Kensington Public Library; Manchester Reference Library; the Marx Memorial Library; South Wales Miners' Library, Swansea; the University Library and Modern Records Centre, Warwick; and to the libraries of the Amalgamated Union of Engineering Workers; the Co-operative Union and Party, London and Manchester; the Fabian Society; the International Institute of Social History, Amsterdam; the Labour Party; Nuffield College, Oxford; Trades Union Congress; University of London; and University of London Institute of Historical Research.

To the following trade unions which sent me copies of their official histories and other publications: Amalgamated Textile Workers' Union; Associated Society of Locomotive Engineers and Firemen; Confederation of Health Service Employees; Educational Institute of

Scotland; Furniture, Timber and Allied Trades Union; Merchant Navy and Airline Officers' Association; National Association of Colliery Overmen, Deputies and Shotfirers (Midland Area); National Graphical Association; National Union of Domestic Appliance and General Metal Workers; National Union of Footwear, Leather and Allied Trades; National Union of Gold, Silver and Allied Trades; National Union of Teachers; Power Loom Carpet Weavers and Textile Workers' Association; Society of Graphical and Allied Trades; Union of Post Office Workers.

To Asa Briggs for his interest and encouragement and for his foreword; to Ruth and Edmund Frow who made their home and their library available to me; to the late James Klugman who placed his immense knowledge and extensive library at my disposal; to John Saville and Joyce Bellamy for their advice and guidance; and to all friends, Labour historians, fellow collectors and librarians who were patient with me in the preparation of this bibliography.

I hope that the users of the bibliography will let me know of any errors or omissions, particularly substantial Labour history collections which have escaped me, and suggest additional periodicals to be indexed. Such omissions, if located, will be included in the 1971–80 volume. It would be very useful to learn of the existence of any large collection of the publications of the smaller parties or groupings, which are very difficult to track down. The books, pamphlets and manifestos are normally printed in small editions and they vanish quickly from the bookshops of the Left which stock them. The publications are rarely, if ever, deposited in the British Library, or indeed in any library. I would naturally be happy to receive such publications (or to be told where they can be obtained), but their proper place is in the British Library for the use of students of British Labour history.

Finally I would like to add a personal note. To read of the lives and struggles of those who built the Labour movement is to be in the presence of people of heroic stature—political pioneers like George Julian Harney, Henry Hetherington, Ernest Jones, William Lovett, Feargus O'Connor and many others; devout men of conscience like George Loveless; social visionaries like Robert Owen and men of genius like William Morris —their story, the campaigns and battles, is a permanent inspiration and one of unfading glory. To reflect on the quiet courage of the men of Tolpuddle, on the national campaigns of Chartism when, in the words of Julius West, one of its historians, 'organized labour became for the first time a factor of importance in the life of the nation' and on the dramatic and colourful Dockers Strike of 1889 is to feel history come alive. This is a rich and priceless heritage which we do well to cherish.

So for me, despite the setbacks, the disappointments, the defections and the betrayals, the words of Walter Crane in his famous cartoon still hold good: 'The cause of Labour is the hope of the world'.

HAROLD SMITH

Periodicals indexed

*A	Agriculture
AE	Adult Education
AGHR	Agricultural History Review, 1953–
AH	Agricultural History
AHR	American Historical Review
AJPH	Australian Journal of Politics and History, 1955–
AJS	American Journal of Sociology
APSR	American Political Science Review
AR	Archives, 1949–
ARE	Arena, 1949–51
ASR	American Sociological Review
BA	British Academy. *Proceedings*
BCS	Board of Celtic Studies. *Bulletin*, 1946–
BH	Business History, 1958–
BHJ	Birmingham Historical Journal, 1947–
BHR	Business History Review
BJES	British Journal of Educational Studies, 1952–
BJIR	British Journal of Industrial Relations, 1963–
BJS	British Journal of Sociology, 1950–
C	Crossbow, 1957–
CH	Church History
CHJ	Cambridge Historical Journal, 1945–57
*CHR	Canadian Historical Review
CHS	Congregational Historical Society. *Transactions*
CJ	Cambridge Journal, 1947–54
CJEPS	Canadian Journal of Economics and Political Science, 1945–67
CJH	Canadian Journal of History, 1966–
*CJPS	Canadian Journal of Political Science, 1968–
CLJ	Cambridge Law Journal
CNR	Contemporary Review
CSSH	Comparative Studies in Society and History, 1958–
D	Daedalus
DR	Dublin Review
DWB	Dictionary of Welsh Biography
E	Economica
ECHR	Economic History Review
EHR	English Historical Review
EJ	Economic Journal
ELP	East London Papers, 1958–

EN	Encounter, 1953–
F	Fortnightly Review, 1946–
FA	Foreign Affairs
*FHS	Friends' Historical Society. *Journal*, 1946–
H	History
HAS	Halifax Antiquarian Society. *Transactions*
*HGS	Huguenot Society. *Proceedings*
HIST	Historian
HJ	Historical Journal, 1958–
HJU	Historica Judaica, 1945–61
HR	Human Relations, 1947–
HS	Historical Studies. Australia and New Zealand
HSI	Historical Studies. Irish Conference of Historians, 1958–
HSLC	Historic Society of Lancashire and Cheshire. *Transactions*
HST	History Studies (1968)
HT	History Today, 1951–
IA	International Affairs
IHR	Institute of Historical Research. *Bulletin*
*IHS	Irish Historical Studies
IRSH	International Review of Social History, 1956–
JBS	Journal of British Studies, 1961–
JCH	Journal of Contemporary History, 1966–
JEH	Journal of Economic History
JHI	Journal of the History of Ideas
JHSE	Jewish Historical Society of England. *Transactions*
*JIE	Journal of Industrial Economics
JMH	Journal of Modern History
JP	Journal of Politics
JPE	Journal of Political Economy
*JRH	Journal of Religious History, 1960–
JRL	John Rylands Library. *Bulletin*
*JSH	Journal of Social History, 1967–
JTH	Journal of Transport History, 1953–66
LCAS	Lancashire and Cheshire Antiquarian Society. *Transactions*
LHN	Local Historian, 1952–
LM	Labour Monthly
LQ	London Quarterly and Holborn Review, 1945–68
*LQR	Law Quarterly Review
M	The Month
MDQ	Modern Quarterly, 1945–53
MJPS	Midwest Journal of Political Science, 1957–
MLPS	Manchester Literary and Philosophical Society. *Memoirs and Proceedings*
MLR	Modern Law Review
MM	Mariners Mirror
MML	Marx Memorial Library. Quarterly Bulletin, 1957–
MQ	Marxist Quarterly, 1954–7
MS	Manchester School of Economic and Social Studies
MSS	Manchester Statistical Society. *Transactions*

Bibliographies

Allen, V. L. *International bibliography of trade unionism*. Merlin, 1968. viii, 180pp.

Althoz, J. L. *Victorian England 1837–1901*. CUP, for Conference on British Studies, 1970. xi, 100pp.

Bain, G. S. and H. Pollins. 'The history of white-collar unions and industrial relations: a bibliography'. SSLH, Autumn 1965, 11:20–65.

Bain, G. S. and G. B. Woolven. *A Bibliography of British industrial relations*. CUP, 1979. xxiv, 665pp.

Bernstein, S. 'Recent literature on Labor and socialism'. SAS, Fall 1960, Fall 1960, 24(4):334–53.

British National Bibliography, 1950– .

Brown, L.M. and I.R. Christie, eds. *Bibliography of British history 1798–1851*. Issued under the direction of the American Historical Association and the Royal Historical Society of Great Britain. OUP, 1977. xxxi, 759pp.

Canney, M.B.C., comp. *Robert Owen, 1771–1858. Catalogue of an exhibition of printed books held in the library of the University of London, Oct.–Dec. 1958*. The University, 1959. vii, 40pp.

Centerprise Bookshop. *Booklist compiled for the 'Remember 1926' Exhibition, July 1976*. The Bookshop, 1976. 36pp.

Chaloner, W.H. and R.C. Richardson. *British economic and social history: a bibliographical guide*. Manchester, University Press, 1976. xiv, 130pp.

Cohen, J. and J. Klugman. *A reader's guide to the study of Marxism*. Communist Party, 196?. 82pp.

Communist Party, Historian's Group. *Marxist and near-Marxist historical work available in English*. The Party, Historian's Group, ?1956. iii, 20 leaves.

Communist Party, History Group. *Select bibliography for the history of the British Labour movement, 1760–1939*. The Party, History Group, 1968 (first pub. 1961). 34pp.

Conway, E. and others. *Labour history of Manchester and Salford: a bibliography*. Manchester Centre for Marxist Education, 1977. 34pp.

Dowse, R.E. 'The I.L.P. 1914–32: a bibliographical study'. SSLH, Spring 1961, 2:3–8.

Doyle, M., comp. *Official trade union histories*. Workers' Educational Association, Service Centre for Social Studies, 1975. 5pp.

Economic History Review. 'List of publications on the economic and social history of Great Britain and Ireland, 1945– '. Published annually.

Elton, G.R. *Modern historians on British history, 1485–1945: a critical bibliography, 1945–1969*. Methuen, 1970. viii, 239pp.

The Essex Reference Index: British journals on politics and sociology, 1950–1973. Edited by K.I. Macdonald. Macmillan, 1975. vii, 397pp.

Foster, J. 'South Shields Labour movement in the 1830s and 1840s. Labour in South Shields 1800–1850: an interim bibliography'. NEG, Oct. 1970, 4:4–9.

Frow, R., E. Frow and M. Katanka. *The history of British trade unionism: a select bibliography*. Historical Association, 1969. 44pp.

Gard, R.M. 'Labour history of the railways in Durham and Northumberland to 1900: an introduction to sources and bibliography'. NEG, Oct. 1969, 3:17–23.

Garside, W.R. 'Labour problems in the Durham coalfield: a critical bibliography'. NEG, Oct. 1968, 2:18–22.

Gottschalk, A.W., T.G. Whittingham and N. Williams. *British industrial relations: an annotated bibliography*. Nottingham, The University, Department of Adult Education, ?1970. 72pp.

Gulick, C.A., R.A. Ockert and R. J. Wallace, comps. *History and theories of working-class movements: a select bibliography*. Berkeley, California, Bureau of Business and Economic Research and Institute of Industrial Relations, University of California, 1955. xix, 364pp.

Hammersmith Bookshop. *The general history of socialism and social struggles*. The Bookshop, 1964. 82pp.

Hanham, H.J., ed. *Bibliography of British history 1851–1914*. Issued under the direction of the American Historical Association and the Royal Historical Association of Great Britain. Oxford, Clarendon Press, 1976. xxvii, 1606pp.

Harrison, J.F.C. and D. Thompson. *Bibliography of the Chartist movement, 1837–1976*. [Hassocks], Sussex, Harvester Press, 1978. xvii, 214pp.

Havinghurst, A.F. *Modern England 1901–1970*. CUP, 1971. x, 109pp.

Hobsbawm, E.J. 'Trade union historiography'. SSLH, Spring 1964, 8:31–6.

Houlton, R. 'Two aspects of Guild Socialism—Penty and Hobson, and the Building Guilds: a select bibliography with commentary'. SSLH, Autumn 1963, 7:23–8.

Katanka, M. *Radicalism 1797–1969: together with other works of social, economic and political interest*. Katanka, ?1970. 48pp.

Katanka, M. *Scarce literature on reform and revolution, 1790 to the present day*. Katanka, ?1973. 66pp.

Kausch, D. 'George W.M. Reynolds: a bibliography'. *The Library*, Dec. 1973, Fifth series, XXVIII (4):319–26.

Kellaway, W., comp. *Bibliography of historical works issued in the United Kingdom 1957–1960*. Compiled for 7th Anglo-American Conference of Historians. University of London, Institute of Historical Research, 1962. xviii, 236pp.

Kellaway, W., comp. *Bibliography of historical works issued in the United Kingdom 1961–1965*. Compiled for the 8th Anglo-American Conference of Historians. University of London, Institute of Historical Research, 1967. xv, 298pp.

Kellaway, W., comp. *Bibliography of historical works issued in the United Kingdom 1966–1970*. Compiled for the 9th Anglo-American Conference of Historians. University of London, Institute of Historical Research, 1972. xv, 322pp.

Kolarz, W., ed. *Books on communism*. Ampersand, 1963 (first pub. 1959). viii, 568pp.

Labour Party. *Labour Party bibliography*. (Publications of the Party and associated and affiliated organizations.) The Party, 1967. 96pp.

Labour Party. *The Labour Party: a select reading list excluding Labour Party publications*. The Party, 1975. 24pp. (Supplements preceding entry.)

Lancaster, J.C., comp. *Bibliography of historical works issued in the United Kingdom 1946–1956*. Compiled for the 6th Anglo-American Conference of Historians. University of London, Institute of Historical Research, 1957. xxii, 388pp.

Leighton, M.E., comp. *Peterloo. Monday 16th August 1819: a bibliography*. Manchester, Libraries Committee, 1969. 32pp.

Lindsay, D.W. 'F.D. Maurice (1805–72)—a short bibliographical study'. NEG, Oct. 1970, 4:9–11.

MacDougall, I., ed. *A catalogue of some labour records in Scotland and some Scots records outside Scotland*. Edinburgh, Scottish Labour History Society, 1978 (An interim bibliography published 1965). xxxvi, 598pp.

Maehl, Jnr., W.H. '"Jerusalem deferred": recent writing in the history of the British Labor movement'. JMH, Sept. 1969, 41(3):335–67.

Marwick, W.H. 'The working class movement in Scotland: bibliographical notes'. SSLH, Spring 1963, 6:34–6.

Marx Memorial Library. *Trade union and Labour movement*. The Library, 1974. (Part 12 of general catalogue.) 29pp.

Mason, A. 'The General Strike in the North East: a bibliographical sketch'. NEG, Oct. 1969, 3:34–41.

Matthews, W., comp. *British autobiographies: an annotated bibliography of British autobiographies published or written before 1951*. Berkeley, University of California Press, 1955. xiv, 376pp.

Morgan, A. *The South Wales valleys in history: a guide to literature*. Aberfan, Ty Toronto, 1974. v, 74pp.

Mowat, C.L. 'The history of the Labour Party: the Coles, the Webbs, and some others'. JMH, June 1951, 23(2):146–53.

Mowat, C.L. 'Some recent books on the British Labor movement'. JMH, Dec. 1945, 17(4):356–66.

Munby, L. and E. Wangerman, eds. *Marxism and history: a bibliography of English language works*. Lawrence and Wishart, 1967. vii, 62pp.

National Book League. *T.U.C. Centenary 1868–1968; books reflecting the social changes of the last century*. N.B.L., 1968. 62pp.

Ottley, G., comp. *A bibliography of British railway history*. Allen and Unwin, 1965. (Railway Labour, pp.249–64.)

Owen, G.L. 'G.D.H. Cole's historical writings'. IRSH, 1966, 11(2):169–96.

Pearl, M.L. *William Cobbett: a bibliographical account of his life and times*. (Based on the Cole collection at Nuffield College.) OUP, 1953. vii, 266pp.

Peel, J. 'Birth control and the British working-class movement: a bibliographical review'. SSLH, Autumn 1963, 7:16–22.

Pettman, B.O. *Strikes: a selected bibliography*. (Period: 1950–75.) Bradford, M.C.B., 1976 (first pub. 1971). vii, 64pp.

Saville, J. 'Henry George and the British Labour movement: a select bibliography with commentary'. SSLH, Autumn 1962, 5:18–26.

Sheffield City Libraries. Department of Local History. *A bibliography of Edward Carpenter*. (Based mainly on the Edward Carpenter Collection in the Sheffield City Libraries.) Sheffield, City Libraries, 1949. ix, 83pp.

Silver, H. 'Education and the Labour movement'. History of Education, June 1973, 2(2):173–202.

Smethurst, J.B. *A bibliography of Co-operative Societies' histories*. Manchester, Co-operative Union, 1973. 122pp.

Smith, H. *Remember 1926: a booklist*. Remember 1926: General Strike 50th anniversary exhibition, 1976. 8pp.

Society for the Study of Labour History. *Bulletin*, 1960– . Bibliographies pub. periodically.

Stevenson, B., comp. *Reader's Guide to Great Britain*. National Book League/British Council, 1977. 558pp.

The Warwick Guide to British Labour Periodicals: a check list. Arranged and compiled by R. Harrison, G.B. Woolven and R. Duncan. Hassocks, Harvester Press, 1977. xxiii, 685pp.

Weisser, H.G. 'Chartist biography: a critical bibliographical essay'. *Rocky Mountain Social Science Journal*, Jan. 1972, 9(1):117–25.

Weisser, H.G. 'The local history of Chartism—a bibliographical essay'. *British Studies Monitor*, Winter 1973, 111, (2):18–30.

Westergaard, J., A. Weyman and P. Wiles. *Modern British society: a bibliography*. Pinter, 1977 (first pub. 1974). 199pp.

Williams, J.E. 'Labour in the coalfields: a critical bibliography'. SSLH, Spring 1962, 4:24–32.

Winkler, H.R. 'Bibliographical article. Some recent writings on Twentieth-Century Britain'. JMH, Mar. 1960, 32(1):32–47.

Woolven, G.B. *Publications of the Independent Labour Party 1893–1932*. Coventry, Society for the Study of Labour History, 1977. xiv, 38pp.

Writings on British History. All pub. by the Institute of Historical Research, University of London.

1946–1948. Munro, D.J., ed. 1973. xvi, 622pp.

1949–1951. Munro, D.J., ed. 1975. xix, 365pp.

1952–1954. Sims, J.M., ed. 1975. xix, 346pp.

1955–1957. Sims, J.M. and P.M. Jacobs, eds. 1977. xx, 362pp.

1958–1959. Creaton, H.J., ed. 1977. xxi, 229pp.

1960–1961. Philpin, C.H.E. and H.J. Creaton, eds. 1978. xxi, 279pp.

Young, J.D. 'A survey of some recent literature on the Labour movement'. PQ, Apr.–June 1968, 39(2):205–15.

The Bibliography

General

Anthologies

1 Anderson, M., comp. *Reformers and rebels: a calendar of anniversaries.* Cobbett, 1946. 146pp.
   Quotations from writings of radical authors for each day of the year.

2 Aspinall, A., ed. *The early trade unions: documents from the Home Office papers in the Public Record Office.* Batchworth, 1949. xxxi, 410pp.

3 Clarke, J.F. and D.J. Rowe. 'Local records for Labour history. Tape recordings'. NEG, Oct. 1968, 2:10–12.

4 Cole, G.D.H. and A.W. Filson, eds. *British working class movements: select documents 1789–1875.* Macmillan, 1965. xxii, 629pp.
   Designed to serve as a companion to G.D.H. Cole, *A short history of the British working-class movement* (*see* no.1183), and may be used with Cole and Postgate (*see* no.1184).

5 Communist Party, History Group. 'Prints of the Labour movement (James Klugman collection)'. OH, Spring 1965, 36–7:40pp.

6 Harrison, J.F.C. *Society and politics in England, 1780–1960: a selection of readings and comments.* New York, Harper and Row, 1965. xiv, 482pp.

7 Hobsbawm, E.J., ed. *Labour's turning point. Nineteenth century.* Vol. III, 1880–1900, in the *History in the making* series, Dona Torr, gen.ed. Lawrence and Wishart, 1948. xxvi, 166pp.
   Extracts from contemporary sources. *See also* nos.8 and 12.

8 Jefferys, J.B., ed. *Labour's formative years. Nineteenth Century.* Vol. II, 1849–79, in the *History in the making* series, Dona Torr, gen.ed. Lawrence and Wishart, 1948. 203pp.
   See also nos.7 and 12.

9 Lane, P., ed. *Documents on British economic and social history.* Book Three: 1945–67. Macmillan, 1969. 128pp.

10 Lenin, V.I. *British Labour and British Imperialism: a compilation of writings by Lenin on Britain.* Lawrence and Wishart, 1969 (first pub. 1934 as *Lenin on Britain*). viii, 316pp.

11 Longmate, N., ed. *A socialist anthology and the men who made it, compiled with an historical introduction.* Foreword by Michael Foot. Phoenix, 1953. 256pp.

12 Morris, M. ed. *From Cobbett to the Chartists. Nineteenth century*. Vol. I, 1815–48, in the *History in the making* series, Dona Torr, gen.ed. Lawrence and Wishart, 1948. 257pp.
    See also nos.7 and 8.

13 Pelling, H. *The challenge of socialism*. Black, 1968. xviii, 370pp.
    Selections from documents covering 1775–1952, illustrating the aims and ideals of British socialists.

14 Pike, E.R. *Human documents of the age of the Forsytes* [i.e. 1880–1900]. Allen and Unwin, 1969.
    Includes Dock Strike, Cradley Heath chain-makers, Matchgirls' Strike, pp.203–42, 271–9.

15 Pike, E.R. *Human documents of the Victorian golden age, 1850–75*. Allen and Unwin, 1967.
    Includes Workers Unite! Co-operation, pp.330–6, Trade Unions, pp.313–29.

Autobiographies, biographies, memoirs, obituaries

I GENERAL

16 Arnot, R.P. 'Lives of Labour leaders'. MQ, Jan. 1954, 1(1):57–61.

17 Arnot, R.P. 'Reminiscences of Labour history pioneers'. SSLH, Spring, 1961, 2:9–10.

18 Boyle, J.W., ed. *Leaders and workers*. Dublin, Mercier Press in association with Radio Telefis Eireann, 1966. 95pp.
    See nos.228, 266, 273, 480, 490, 753, 758, 1018, 1047, 1177.

19 Cole, M. *Makers of the Labour movement*. Longmans, 1948. xv, 319pp.
    Biographies of men who 'helped to prepare for the rise to political power of the British Labour and socialist movement'. *See* nos.39, 136, 201, 375, 400, 482, 631, 660, 760, 813, 835, 865, 1071, 1100.

19a Evans J.N. *Great figures in the Labour movement*. Pergamon, 1966. vii, 176pp.
    See nos.54, 113, 376, 483, 558, 587, 662, 711, 817, 1080

20 Goldsmith, M. *Who's who in the Attlee team*. Muse Arts, 1945. 33pp.
    Short biographies of Labour ministers

21 Saville, J. 'Dictionary of Labour movement biography'. SSLH, Autumn 1960, 1:27.

22 Saville, J. 'Dictionary of Labour movement biography'. SSLH, Spring 1961, 2:15–17.

II INDIVIDUAL

N. Ablett

23 Morris-Jones, H. 'Noah Ablett'. DWB, 1959, p.1113.

W. Abraham (Mabon)

24 Evans, E.W. *Mabon (William Abraham 1842–1922): a study in trade union leadership*. Cardiff, University of Wales Press, 1959. xii, 115pp.

25 Morris-Jones, H. 'W. Abraham (Mabon)'. DWB, 1959, p.1.

W.E. Adams

26 Adams, W.E. *Memoirs of a social atom*. New York, Kelley, 1968 (first pub. 1903; new introduction by J. Saville). 668pp.
    Two vols. in one.

27 Morton, A.L. Review of *Memoirs of a social atom*. SSLH, Autumn 1968, 17:32–5.
    See no.26.

Viscount Addison

28 Minney, R.J. *Viscount Addison: Leader of the Lords*. Odhams, 1958. 256pp.

J.B. Alderson

29 Boase, F. 'Joseph B. Alderson'. MEB, 1965 reprint, Vol. 4, Col. 69.

R. Allen

30 Clarke, J.F. 'Papers of Robert Allen (1883–1966)—Tyneside engineer'. NEG, Oct. 1969, 1:17–18.

R.C. Allen

31 Gilbert, M., ed. *Plough my own furrow: the story of Lord Allen of Hurtwood as told through his writings and correspondence*. Longmans, 1965. xiii, 442pp.

32 Marwick, A. *Clifford Allen: the open conspirator*. Oliver and Boyd, 1964. xii, 219pp.

33 Middleton, J.S. 'R.C. Allen'. DNB, 1931–40, 1970, reprint pp.6–7.

H.C. Anderson

34 Labour Monthly. 'Helen Crawfurd Anderson'. LM, May 1951, 36(5):231.

E. Andrews

35 Andrews, E. *A woman's work is never done: being the recollections of a childhood and upbringing amongst the South Wales miners and a lifetime of service to the*

Labour movement in Wales. Rhondda, Cymric Democrat Pub. Co., ?1949. viii, 43pp.

W.H. Andrews

36 Arnot, R.P. 'W.H. Andrews 1870–1950'. LM, Feb. 1951, 33(2):74.

N. Angell

37 Angell, N. *After all: an autobiography.* Hamilton, 1951. xii, 370pp.

R. Applegarth

38 Briggs, A. 'Robert Applegarth and the trade unions', *Victorian people: a reassessment of persons and themes 1851–67*, pp.176–204. Penguin, 1965 (first pub. 1954).

39 Cole, M. 'Robert Applegarth (1834–1924)', *Makers of the Labour movement*, pp.154–64 (*see* no.19). Longmans, 1948.

J. Arch

40 Arch, J. *Autobiography.* Preface by Frances, Countess of Warwick. MacGibbon and Kee, 1966 (first pub. 1898). 147pp.
    Much of the original material omitted from this edition.

41 Ashby, A.W. 'J. Arch'. DNB, 1912–21, 1968 reprint, pp.13–14.

R.P. Arnot

42 Dutt, R.P. 'Greetings to Robin Page Arnot'. LM, Dec. 1970, 52(12):540.

43 Labour Monthly. 'Open letter to Page Arnot'. LM, Jan. 1961, 43(1):26.
    Written on the occasion of his 70th birthday.

Sir W. Ashley

44 Semmell, B. 'Sir William Ashley as "Socialist of the Chair"'. E, Nov. 1957, 24(96):343–53.

C.R. Attlee

45 Attlee, C.R. *As it happened.* Odhams, 1956. 256pp.

46 Boardman, H. 'Attlee's achievement', *The glory of Parliament*, pp.147–50. Allen and Unwin, 1960.

47 Bridges, Lord. 'Clement Richard Attlee (1883–1967)', *Biographical Memoirs of Fellows of the Royal Society*, pp.15–36. RS, 1968, 14.

48 Broad, L. 'Clement Attlee', *The path to power; the rise of the premiership from Rosebery to Wilson*, pp.154–66. Muller, 1965.

49 Brome, V. *Clement Attlee.* Lincolns-Praeger, 1949. 92pp.
    Pictorial biography.

50 Clemens, C. *The man from Limehouse: Clement Richard Attlee.* Introduction

by Ellen Wilkinson. Missouri, International Mark Twain Society, 1946. xiv, 159pp.

51 Crossman, R.H.S. 'Mr. Attlee as Premier', *The charm of politics and other essays in political criticism*, pp.69–74. Hamilton, 1958.

52 Dutt, R.P. 'Earl Attlee'. LM, Nov. 1967, 49(11):512–13.

53 Elletson, D.H. 'The second Labour Prime Minister', *Chequers and the Prime Ministers*, pp.146–50. Hale, 1970.

54 Evans, J.N. 'Clement Attlee', *Great figures in the Labour movement*, pp.117–32. Pergamon, 1966.

55 Golant, W. 'The early political thought of C.R. Attlee'. PQ, July–Sept. 1969, 40(3):246–55.

56 Golant, W. 'The early political thought of C.R. Attlee'. PQ, July–Sept. 1970, 41(3):309–15.

57 Golant, W. 'The emergence of C.R. Attlee as leader of the Parliamentary Labour Party in 1935'. HJ, 1970, 13(2):318–22.

58 Granada Historical Records Interview. *Clem Attlee: the Granada historical records interview*. Panther, 1967. 87pp.
    Transcript of interviews, 16th and 17th September 1965.

59 Heasman, D.J. 'My station and its duties—the Attlee version'. PA, Winter 1967–8, 21(1):75–84.

60 Jenkins, R. 'Lord Attlee and his colleagues', *Essays and speeches*, pp.52–4. Edited by A. Lester. Collins, 1967.
    Review of no.68.

61 Jenkins, R. *Mr. Attlee: an interim biography*. Heinemann, 1948. viii, 266pp.
    Account ends 26th July 1945 with Attlee becoming Prime Minister.

62 Jensen, J.V. 'Clement R. Attlee and twentieth century parliamentary speaking'. PA, Summer 1970, 23(3):277–85.

63 Murphy, J.T. *Labour's big three: a biographical study of Clement Attlee, Herbert Morrison and Ernest Bevin*. Bodley Head, 1948. 266pp.

64 The Observer. 'Mr. Attlee', *A book of British profiles compiled from The Observer*, by S. Haffner, pp.37–41. Heinemann, 1954.

65 Pritt, D.N. 'The silence of Earl Attlee'. LM, June 1961, 43(6):283–5.
    Review of no.68.

66 Pritt, D.N. 'The world of Mr. Attlee'. LM, June 1954, 36(6):274–81.

67 Punnett, R.M. 'The parliamentary and personal backgrounds of British Prime Ministers 1812 to 1963'. QR, July 1964, 302(641):254–66.

68 Williams, F. *A Prime Minister remembers: the war and post-war memoirs of the Rt. Hon. Earl Attlee . . . based on his private papers and on a series of recorded conversations*. Heinemann, 1961. viii, 264pp.
    Period: 1945 General Election–1951 General Election.

69 Wyatt, W. 'Lord Attlee', *Distinguished for talent: some men of influence and enterprise*, pp.169–75. Hutchinson, 1958.

T. Attwood

70 Boase, F. 'Thomas Attwood', MEB, 1965 reprint, Vol. 1, Col. 105.

71 Briggs, A. 'The background of the Parliamentary reform movement in three English cities (1830–2)'. CHJ, 1950, 10(3):293–317.
Birmingham, Leeds, Manchester.

72 Briggs, A. 'Thomas Attwood and the economic background of the Birmingham Political Union'. CHJ, 1948, 9(2):190–216.

73 Carlyle, E.I. 'Thomas Attwood', DNB, 1967–8 reprint, Vol. 22, pp.86–9.

74 Cole, G.D.H. 'Thomas Attwood', *Chartist portraits*, pp.106–32 (*see* no.1411). Macmillan, 1965 (first pub. 1941).

S. Bamford

75 Bamford, S. *Autobiography of Samuel Bamford*. Vol. 1, *Early days,* viii, 363pp. Vol. 2, *Passages in the life of a radical*, Pt. 1, 296pp; Pt. 2, 282pp. Cass, 1967 (first pub. 1817 as *An account of the Arrest . . .*).

76 Bamford, S. *Passages in the life of a radical*. MacGibbon and Kee, 1967. 368pp.
Omits last five chapters of the book as originally published.

77 Boase, F. 'Samuel Bamford', MEB, 1965, reprint, Vol. 1, Cols. 149–50.

78 Lockett, T.A. 'Votes for men: Samuel Bamford (1788–1872)', *It happened around Manchester,* pp.9–23. University of London Press, 1968.

79 Smith, E. 'Samuel Bamford', DNB, 1967–8 reprint, Vol. 1, pp.1020–1.

J. Barker

80 Boase, F. 'Joseph Barker', MEB, 1965, reprint, Vol. 1, Cols. 164–5.

81 Grant, A.H. 'Joseph Barker', DNB, 1967–8 reprint, Vol. 1, pp.1124–6.

T. Barker

82 Barker, T. 'Lenin inspired us—a veteran's reminiscences'. LM, Apr. 1970, 52(4):158–63.

83 Dutt, R. P. 'Tom Barker'. LM, May 1970, 52(5):215.

84 Kaiser, T. 'Self-portrait of a revolutionary: the story of Tom Barker as told to Tom Kaiser (June 1967)'. SSLH, Autumn 1967, 15:18–27.

G.N. Barnes

85 Middleton, J.S. 'G.N. Barnes', DNB, 1931–40, 1970 reprint, pp.41–2.

N. Barou

86 Infield, H.F., ed. 'Noah Barou', *Essays in Jewish sociology, Labour and co-operation in memory of Dr. Noah Barou 1889–1955*, pp.1–52. Yoseloff, 1962.

Rev. J. Barr

87 Barr, Rev. J. *Lang Syne*. Glasgow, MacLellan, 1949. 384pp.

88 Johnston, T. 'Rev. J. Barr', *Memories*, pp.240–2 (*see* no.454). Collins, 1952.

M.M. Barry

89 Ward, J.T. 'Tory Socialist: a preliminary note on Michael Maltman Barry (1842–1909)'. SLH, April 1970, 2:25–37.

J. Beauchamp

90 Labour Monthly. 'Joan Beauchamp (Mrs. W.H. Thompson)'. LM, Oct. 1964, 46(10):446
(*See* no.1020).

E.S. Beesly

91 Harrison, R. 'E.S. Beesly and Karl Marx'. IRSH, 1959, 4(1):22–58.

92 Harrison, R. 'E.S. Beesly and Karl Marx'. IRSH, 1959, 4(2): 208–38.

93 Harrison, R. 'Professor Beesly and the working-class movement', *Essays in Labour history*, pp. 205–41. Edited by A. Briggs and J. Saville (*see* no. 1179). Macmillan, 1960.

B. Behan

94 Behan, B. 'Why I am an agitator'. TC, Spring 1963, 171(1017):33–6.

A.W. Benn

95 Bromhead, P. 'Mr. Wedgwood Benn, the peerage and the constitution'. PA, Autumn 1962, 14(4):493–506.

96 O'Leary, C. 'The Wedgwood Benn case and the doctrine of wilful perversity'. PS, Feb. 1965, 13(1):65–78.

97 Tapper, C. 'A case of privilege'. NLR, Nov.–Dec. 1961, 12:39–43.

L. Bennett

98 Fox, R.M. *Louie Bennett: her life and times*. Dublin, Talbot Press, 1958. 123pp.
Associated with the Irish Women Workers' Union for nearly 40 years.

J.D. Bernal

99 Snow, C.P. 'J.D. Bernal: a personal portrait', *The science of science*, pp. 19–31. Edited by M. Goldsmith and A. Mackay. Penguin, 1966.

C. Berridge

100 Labour Monthly. 'Claude Berridge'. LM, Aug. 1966, 48(8):372.

A. Besant

101 Banks, J.A. and O. Banks. 'The Bradlaugh-Besant trial and the English newspapers'. PPS, July 1954, 8(1):22–34.

102 Besant, A. 'Why I am socialist', *A selection of the social and political pamphlets of Annie Besant.* New York, Kelley, 1970 (first pub. 1886). 8pp.

103 Cole, M. 'Annie Besant', *Women of today,* pp.191–232. Nelson, 1946 (first pub. 1938).

104 Lovett, H.V. and P. Cadell. 'Annie Besant'. DNB, 1931–40, 1970 reprint, pp.72–4.

105 Nethercot, A.H. *The first five lives of Annie Besant.* Hart-Davis, 1961. 435pp.

106 Rubinstein, D. 'Annie Besant and Stewart Headlam: the London School Board election of 1888'. ELP, Summer 1970, 13(1):3–24.

107 Stafford, A. 'Annie Besant', *A match to fire the Thames,* pp.57–62. Hodder, 1961.

A. Bevan

108 Beaven, J. 'Bevan in perspective'. TC, Aug. 1960, 168(1002):108–14.

109 Bevan, A. *In place of fear.* New introduction by Jennie Lee. MacGibbon and Kee, 1961 (first pub. 1952). 203pp.

110 Brome, V. *Aneurin Bevan.* Longmans, 1953. viii, 244pp.

111 Connell, J. 'Aneurin Bevan', *World-famous rebels,* pp.240–50. Odhams, 1970.

112 Crane, P. 'Voice from the valleys: the career of Aneurin Bevan'. M, Jan. 1963, 29(1):5–9.

113 Evans, J.N. 'Aneurin Bevan', *Great figures in the Labour movement,* pp.150–66. Pergamon, 1966.

114 Foot, M. *Aneurin Bevan: a biography.* Vol. 1: 1897–1945. MacGibbon and Kee, 1962. 536pp.
    To his entry into the Cabinet (*see* no.118).

115 Fyvel, T.R. 'Bevan and Lee', *Britain between east and west,* pp.32–5. Contact, ?1946.

116 Harris, L. 'Aneurin Bevan', *The fine art of political wit,* pp.136–58. Cassell, 1965.

117 Jenkins, P. 'Bevan's fight with the B.M.A. Labour and nationalization', *Age of austerity,* pp.240–65 (*see* no.2084). Edited by M. Sissons and P. French. Penguin, 1964 (first pub. 1963).

118 Jenkins, R. 'Aneurin Bevan', *Essays and speeches,* pp.55–8. Collins, 1967.
Review of no.114.

119 Krug, M.M. *Aneurin Bevan: cautious rebel.* Yoseloff, 1961. 316pp.

120 Labour Monthly. 'Aneurin Bevan'. LM, Aug. 1960, 42(8):380.

121 Llewellyn, D. *Nye: the beloved patrician, glimpses of the greatness of Aneurin Bevan.* Cardiff, Western Mail and Echo, 1960. 31pp.

122 The Observer. 'Aneurin Bevan', *A book of British profiles compiled from The Observer,* by S. Haffner, pp.77–83. Heinemann, 1954.

123 Socialist Medical Association. *Aneurin Bevan: an appreciation of his service to the health of the people.* The Association, ?1961, 13pp.
Contributors: Somerville Hastings, David Kerr, D. Stark Murray, Arthur Blenkinsop.

124 Wyatt, W. 'Aneurin Bevan', *Distinguished for talent: some men of influence and enterprise,* pp.176–83. Hutchinson, 1958.

E. Bevin

125 Bullock, A. *The life and times of Ernest Bevin.* Vol. 1, *Trade union leader 1881–1940.* Heinemann, 1960, xv, 672pp. Vol. 2, *Minister of Labour 1940–5.* Heinemann, 1967. xiii, 407pp. (*see* nos. 126, 129).

126 Campbell, J.R. 'The history of Ernie Bevin, Labour leader'. LM, Apr. 1960, 42(4):184–7.
Review of no.125.

127 Crossman, R.H.S. 'Ernest Bevin's loyalty', *The charm of politics and other essays in political criticism,* pp.75–7. Hamilton, 1958.
Review of no.133.

128 Evans, T. *Bevin.* Allen and Unwin, 1946. 231pp.

129 Jenkins, R. 'Ernest Bevin', *Essays and speeches,* pp.43–6. Collins, 1967.
Review of no.125.

130 Murphy, J.T. *Labour's big three: a biographical study of Clement Attlee, Herbert Morrison and Ernest Bevin.* Bodley Head, 1948. 266pp.

131 The Observer. 'Ernest Bevin', *A book of British profiles compiled from The Observer,* by S. Haffner, pp.3–8. Heinemann, 1954.

132 Van Den Bergh, T. 'Ernest Bevin', *The trade unions—what are they?,* pp.75–91 (*see* no.3187). Pergamon, 1970.

133 Williams, F. *Ernest Bevin: portrait of a great Englishman.* Hutchinson, 1952. 288pp. (*see* no.127).

R. Blackburn

134 Blackburn, R. *I am an alcoholic.* Wingate, 1959. 218pp.

R. Blatchford

135 Barrow, L. 'The origins of Robert Blatchford's social imperialism'. SSLH, Autumn 1969, 19:9–12.

136 Cole, M. 'Robert Blatchford (1851–1944)', *Makers of the Labour movement*, pp.185–202 (*see* no.19). Longmans, 1948.

137 Ensor, R.C.K. 'R.P.G. Blatchford', DNB, 1941–50, 1967 reprint, pp.86–7.

138 Thompson, L. *Robert Blatchford: portrait of an Englishman*. Gollancz, 1951. vi, 242pp.

R. Bolt

139 Hayman, R. *Robert Bolt*. Heinemann, 1969. x, 88pp.

M. Bondfield

140 Bondfield, M. *A life's work*. Hutchinson, 1949. 368pp.

R. Boughton

141 Russell, T. 'Rutland Boughton (January 23, 1878–January 25, 1960)'. LM, Mar. 1960, 42(3):126–7.

142 Stevens, B. 'Rutland Boughton'. NR, Spring 1959, 8:74–81.

S. Box

143 Box, S. *The good old days: then and now*. Hereford, the author, 1954. ix, 110pp.
Trade unionism and Labour Party in Herefordshire, 1912–53.

B. Braddock

144 Toole, M. *Mrs. Bessie Braddock M.P. a biography*. Hale, 1957. 223pp.

J. and B. Braddock

145 Braddock, J. and B. *The Braddocks*. Macdonald, 1963, x, 244pp.

B. Bradley

146 Labour Monthly. 'Ben Bradley 1898–1957'. LM, Feb. 1957, 39(2):75.

J. Braine

147 Braine, J. *A personal record*. Monday Club, 1968. 11pp.
How he 'lost his faith in socialism'.

148 Coleman, T. 'John Braine: talk of the devil', *The only true history*, pp.100–4. Hutchinson, 1969.

J. Brent

149 Harrison, S. *Good to be alive: the story of Jack Brent*. Lawrence and Wishart, 1954. 96pp.

P. Brewster

150 Boase, F. 'Patrick Brewster', Vol. 1, Cols. 394–5, MEB, 1965 reprint.

151 Grant, A.H. 'Patrick Brewster', DNB, 1967–8 reprint, Vol. 2, p.1212.

R. Bridgman

152 Labour Monthly. 'Reginald Bridgman MVO, CMG (October 14, 1884–December 11, 1968)'. LM, Jan. 1969, 51(1):44.

H. Broadhurst

153 MacDonald, J.R. 'Henry Broadhurst', DNB, 1901–11, 1969 reprint, pp.228–30.

F. Brockway

154 Brockway, F. *Inside the left: thirty years of platform, press, prison and Parliament*. Allen and Unwin, 1947 (first pub. 1942). 352pp.

155 Brockway, F. *Outside the right: a sequel to 'Inside the left'*. Allen and Unwin, 1963. 231pp.

G. Brown

156 Connor, W. (Cassandra, *pseud.*) *George Brown: a profile and pictorial biography*. Pergamon, 1964. 96pp.

157 Harris, K. 'George Brown, 1966', *Conversations*, pp.89–95. Hodder, 1967.

W.J. Brown

158 Brown, W.J. *Brown studies*. Latimer House, 1949. 224pp.

159 Brown, W.J. *Jamaican journey*. Allen and Unwin, 1948. 201pp.
Diary: Dec. 1946–Jan. 1947.

160 Brown, W.J. *The land of look behind*. Latimer House, 1949. 220pp.
Diary: Dec. 1947–Jan. 1948.

G.S. Bull

161 Gill, J.C. *Parson Bull of Byerley*. S.P.C.K., 1963. xii, 163pp.

162 Gill, J.C. *The ten hours parson: Christian social action in the eighteen thirties*. S.P.C.K., 1959, xiv, 210pp.

I. Bulmer-Thomas

163 Crossman, R.H.S. 'The turn-coat—Ivor Bulmer-Thomas', *The charm of politics and other essays in political criticism*, pp.81–3. Hamilton, 1958.

J. Burns

164 Bell, P. 'The first socialist M.P.s' [i.e. Burns and Hardie]. MML, July-Sept. 1962, 23:5–8.

165 Cole, G.D.H. 'J. E. Burns', DNB, 1941–50, 1967 reprint, pp. 121–4.

166 Kapp, Y. 'John Burns library'. OH, Winter 1959, 16:21pp.

167 Kent, W. *John Burns: Labour's lost leader.* Williams and Norgate, 1950. xv, 389pp.

168 Stafford, A. 'John Burns', *A match to fire the Thames,* pp.52–5. Hodder, 1961.

169 Van Den Bergh, T. 'John Burns', *The trade unions—what are they?,* pp.29–42. Pergamon, 1970.

T. Burt

170 Straker, W. 'Thomas Burt', DNB, 1922–30, 1967 reprint, pp.143–4.

A. Bush

171 Corbett, J. 'Tribute to Alan Bush'. LM, Dec. 1970, 52(12):553.

172 Workers' Music Association. *Tribute to Alan Bush on his fiftieth birthday: a symposium.* The Association, 1950. 63pp.

C.R. Buxton

173 DeBunsen, V. *Charles Roden Buxton: a memoir.* Allen and Unwin, 1952. 187pp.

J.R. Campbell

174 Dutt, R.P. 'John Ross Campbell'. LM, Oct. 1969, 51(10):444.

E. Carpenter

175 Carpenter, E. (Dean of Westminster). *Edward Carpenter 1844–1929: democratic author and poet: a restatement and appraisal.* Dr. Williams' Trust, 1970. 31pp.

176 Pierson, S. 'Edward Carpenter, prophet of a socialist millenium'. VS, Mar. 1970, 13(3):301–18.

177 Smith, G.C.M. 'Edward Carpenter', DNB, 1922–30, 1967 reprint, pp.159–61.

178 Vanson, E. *Edward Carpenter: the English Whitman.* CNR, June 1958, 193: 314–16.

W. Carpenter

179 Boase, F. 'William Carpenter', MEB, 1965 reprint, Vol. 1, Cols. 555–6.

180 Watt, F. 'William Carpenter', DNB, 1967–8 reprint, Vol. 3, p.1074.

W. J. Carron

181 Wyatt, W. 'W.J. Carron', *Distinguished for talent: some men of influence and enterprise,* pp.133–40. Hutchinson, 1958.

J. Cartwright

182 Miller, N.C. 'John Cartwright and radical parliamentary reform, 1808–19'. EHR, Oct. 1968, 83(329):705–28.

183 Smith, E. 'John Cartwright', DNB, 1967–8 reprint, Vol. 3, pp.1133–4.

B. Castle

184 De'ath, W., comp. *Barbara Castle: a portrait from life.* Brighton, Clifton Books, 1970. 126pp.
    Contributors include Vic Feather, Michael Foot, Paul Johnson.

C. Cauldwell

185 Maxwell, D.E.S. 'Christopher Cauldwell and John Cornford; poets in the Party', *Poets of the thirties,* pp.43–82. Routledge, 1969.

H.H. Champion

186 *Dictionary of Australian Biography.* Sydney, Angus and Robertson, 1949. Vol. 1, p.158.

187 Pelling, H.M. 'H.H. Champion: pioneer of Labour representation'. CJ, Jan. 1953, 6(4):222–38.

V.G. Childe

188 Labour Monthly. 'V. Gordon Childe (April 14th 1892–October 19th 1957)'. LM, Nov. 1957, 39(11):498.

Lord Citrine

189 Citrine, Lord. *Men and work: an autobiography.* Hutchinson, 1964. 384pp.
    To 1939.
    Two careers. Hutchinson, 1967. 384pp. (*see* no.191).

190 Harris, K. 'Lord Citrine, 1961', *Conversations,* pp.11–25. Hodder, 1967.

191 Horner, A. 'Citrine and the T.U.C.'. LM, Feb. 1965, 47(2):88–90.
    Review of no.189.

J. Clunie

192 Clunie, J. *Labour is my faith: the autobiography of a house painter.* Dunfermline, the author, 1954. 95pp.

193 Clunie, J. *The voice of Labour: the autobiography of a house painter.* Dunfermline, the author, 1958. 168pp.

J.R. Clynes

194 Middleton, J.S. 'J.R. Clynes'. DNB, 1941–50, 1967 reprint, pp.161–3.

Z.K. Coates

195 Labour Monthly. 'Zelda Kahan Coates'. LM, July 1969, 51(7):301.

R.B.B. Cobbett

196 Boase, F. 'Richard Baverstock Brown Cobbett'. MEB, 1965 reprint, Vol. 1, Col. 658.

W. Cobbett

197 Cobbett, W. *The autobiography of William Cobbett, the progress of a plough-boy to a seat in Parliament.* Edited by William Reitzel. Faber, 1967. 272pp.

198 Cole, G.D.H. *The life of William Cobbett.* Home and Van Thal, 1947 (first pub. 1924). xii, 455pp.

199 Cole, G.D.H. 'Rural rides', *Persons and periods: studies*, pp.138–58. Penguin, 1945 (first pub. 1938).

200 Cole, G.D.H. 'William Cobbett (1762–1835)', *Persons and periods: studies,* pp.116–37. Penguin, 1945 (first pub. 1938).

201 Cole, M. 'William Cobbett (1762–1835)', *Makers of the Labour movement,* pp.23–39 (*see* no.19). Longmans, 1948.

202 Derry, J.W. 'William Cobbett: a sentimental radical', *The radical tradition, Tom Paine to Lloyd George,* pp.49–79. Macmillan, 1967.

203 Kegel, C.H. 'William Cobbett and Malthusianism'. JHI, June 1958, 19(3):348–62.

204 Martin, E.W. 'William Cobbett and the making of modern England'. HT, Jan. 1960, 10(1):44–50.

205 Osborne, J.W. 'William Cobbett and the Corn Laws'. HIST, Feb. 1967, 29(2):186–99.

206 Osborne, J.W. *William Cobbett: his thought and his times.* New Jersey, Rutgers University Press, 1966. x, 272pp.

207 Pemberton, W. *William Cobbett.* Penguin, 1949. 192pp.

208 Smith, E. 'William Cobbett'. DNB, 1967–8 reprint, Vol. 4, pp.598–601.

C. Cockburn

209 Cockburn, C. *In time of trouble: an autobiography.* Hart-Davis, 1956. 264pp.
First volume: to 1938.
Crossing the line: being the second volume of autobiography of Claud Cockburn. MacGibbon and Kee, 1958. 214pp.
View from the West, being the third volume of autobiography of Claud Cockburn. MacGibbon and Kee, 1961. 208pp.

210 Cockburn, C. *I, Claud . . . the autobiography of Claud Cockburn.* Penguin, 1967. 454pp.

G.D.H. Cole

211 Arnot, R.P. 'A memoir of G.D.H. Cole (September 25, 1889–January 14, 1959)'. LM, Feb. 1959, 41(2):66–70.

212 Bailey, S.K. 'What Cole really meant', *Essays in Labour history*, pp.20–4 (*see* no.1179). Macmillan, 1960.

213 Briggs, A. 'G.D.H. Cole: a tribute'. NR, Spring 1959, 8:38–9.

214 Brown, I. 'G.D.H. Cole as an undergraduate', *Essays in Labour history*, pp.3–5 (*see* no.1179). Macmillan, 1960.

215 Gaitskell, H. 'At Oxford in the twenties', *Essays in Labour history*, pp.6–19 (*see* no.1179). Macmillan, 1960.

216 Martin, K. 'G.D.H. Cole: a tribute'. NR, Spring 1959, 8:36–8.

217 Worswick, G.D.N. 'Cole and Oxford, 1938–58', *Essays in Labour history*, pp.25–40 (*see* no.1179). Macmillan, 1960.

M. Cole

218 Cole, M. *Growing up into revolution.* Longmans, 1949. viii, 244pp.

H. Collins

219 Fyrth, J. 'Dr. Henry Collins (1917–69)'. SSLH, Spring 1970, 20:9–10.

L.J. Collins

220 Collins, Canon L.J. *Faith under fire.* Frewin, 1966. 383pp.

J. Connolly

221 Davies, N. *Connolly of Ireland: patriot and socialist.* Caernarfon, Swddfa'r Blaid, 1946. 59pp.

222 Deasy, J. *James Connolly: his life and teachings.* Dublin, New Books, 1966. 14pp.

223 Deighan, J. 'James Connolly, and the British Labour movement'. LM, June 1968, 50(6):276–9.

224 Dooley, P. *Under the banner of Connolly.* Connolly Association, 1945. 24pp.

225 Greaves, C.D. *The life and times of James Connolly.* Lawrence and Wishart, 1961. 363pp.

226 Johnston, T. 'James Connolly', *Memories*, pp.238–40 (*see* no.454). Collins, 1952.

227 McLysaght, E. 'Larkin, Connolly and the Labour Movement', *Leaders and men of the Easter Rising: Dublin 1916*, pp.123–33. Edited by F.X. Martin. Methuen, 1967.

228 Ryan, D. 'James Connolly', *Leaders and workers,* pp.67–75 *(see* no.18). Edited by J.W. Boyle. Dublin, Mercier Press, 1966.

A. J. Cook

229 Middleton, J.S. 'A.J. Cook', DNB, 1931–40, 1970 reprint, p.192.

230 Morris-Jones, H. 'A.J. Cook', DWB, 1959, pp.81–2.

T. Cooper

231 Boase, F. 'Thomas Cooper', MEB, 1965 reprint, Vol. 4, Cols. 749–50.

232 Cole, G.D.H. 'Thomas Cooper', *Chartist portraits,* pp.187–217 *(see* no. 1411). Macmillan, 1965 (first pub. 1941).

233 Collins, P. *Thomas Cooper, the Chartist: Byron and the 'Poets of the Poor'.* Nottingham, University, 1969. 266pp.

234 Hobman, D.L. 'Thomas Cooper, Chartist and poet'. CNR, Oct. 1948, 174(994):233–6.

235 MacDonald, J.R. 'Thomas Cooper', DNB, 1967–8 reprint, Vol. 22, pp.483–4.

F. Copeman

236 Copeman, F. *Reason in revolt.* Blandford, 1948. 235pp.

J. Cornford

237 Maxwell, D.E.S. 'Christopher Cauldwell and John Cornford; poets in the Party', *Poets of the thirties,* pp.43–82. Routledge, 1969.

238 Stansky, P. and W. Abrahams. *Journey to the Frontier: Julian Bell and John Cornford: their lives and the 1930's.* Constable, 1966. xviii, 430pp.

F. Cousins

239 Burnett, H., ed. 'Frank Cousins: television interview by John Freeman', *Face to face,* pp.90–1. Cape, 1964.

240 Goodman, G. *Brother Frank: the man and his union.* Panther, 1969. 128pp.

241 Stewart, M. *Frank Cousins: a study.* Hutchinson, 1968. xiv, 210pp.

242 Wyatt, W. 'Frank Cousins', *Distinguished for talent: some men of influence and enterprise,* pp.141–51. Hutchinson, 1958.

J. Cowen

243 Boase, F. 'Joseph Cowen'. MEB, 1965 reprint, Vol. 4, Col. 779.

E.T. Craig

244 Boase, F. 'Edward Thomas Craig'. MEB, 1965 reprint, Vol. 5, Col. 789.

W. Crane

245 Bell, M.H. 'Walter Crane'. DNB, 1912–21, 1968 reprint, pp.133–5.

R. Cranston

246 Boase, F. 'Robert Cranston'. MEB, 1965 reprint, Vol. 4, Col. 792.

W. Crawford

247 Boase, F. 'William Crawford'. MEB, 1965 reprint, Vol. 4. Col. 797.

W.S. Crawford

248 Lee, S. 'William Sharman Crawford'. DNB, 1967–8 reprint, Vol. 5, p.59.

G. Crawshay

249 Boase, F. 'George Crawshay'. MEB, 1965 reprint, Vol. 4, Col. 799.

Sir W.R. Cremer

250 MacDonald, J.R. 'Sir William Randal Cremer'. DNB, 1901–11, 1969 reprint, pp.441–2.

C.A. Cripps (Baron Parmoor)

251 Mansbergh, N. 'Charles Alfred Cripps'. DNB, 1941–50, 1967 reprint, pp.186–7.

R. S. Cripps

252 Cooke, C. *The life of Richard Stafford Cripps*. Hodder, 1957. 415pp.

253 Estorick, E. *Stafford Cripps: a biography*. Heinemann, 1949. viii, 378pp.

254 Marquand, D. 'Sir Stafford Cripps: the dollar crises and devaluation', *Age of austerity*, pp.173–95 (*see* no.2084). Edited by M. Sissons and P. French. Penguin, 1964 (first pub. 1963).

255 Schuster, Sir G. 'Richard Stafford Cripps', *Biographical Memoirs of Fellows of the Royal Society*, pp.11–32. RS, 1955, 1.

W. Crooks

256 Cole, G.D.H. 'William Crooks'. DNB, 1912–21, 1968 reprint, pp.137–8.

257 Stafford, A. 'Will Crooks', *A match to fire the Thames*, pp.46–8. Hodder, 1961.

H. Dalton

258 Dalton, H. *Call back yesterday. Memoirs 1887–1931*. Muller, 1953. 330pp.
The fateful years. Memoirs 1931–45. Muller, 1957. 493pp.
High tide and after. Memoirs 1945–60. Muller, 1962. xiv, 453pp.

259 Jenkins, R. 'Hugh Dalton', *Essays and speeches,* pp.47–51. Collins, 1967.
Review of no.258, *High tide and after.*

J. Dash

260 Dash, J. *Good morning, brothers!* Mayflower, 1970 (first pub. 1969). 175pp.

261 Dash, J. 'My "obituary"'. LM, Feb. 1968, 50(2):85–6.
BBC TV programme.

262 Eighteen, J. 'Wakey! wakey!'. LM, Dec. 1969, 51(12):557–7.
Review of no.260.

A. Davenport

263 Harrison, R. 'Allen Davenport'. SSLH, Spring 1961, 2:14.

R. Davies

264 Davies, R. (Bob). 'Pages from a worker's life, 1916–26.' OH, Autumn,
1961, 23:18.

S.C. Davies

265 Davies, S.C. *North country bred: a working-class family chronicle.* Routledge,
1963. xiv, 256pp.

M. Davitt

266 Moody, T.W. 'Michael Davitt', *Leaders and workers,* pp.47–55 (*see* no.18).
Edited by J. W. Boyle. Dublin, Mercier Press, 1966.

267 Moody, T.W. 'Michael Davitt and the British Labour movement
1882–1906'. RHS, 1953, 5(3):53–76.

268 Sheehy-Skeffington, F. *Michael Davitt: revolutionary, agitator and Labour
leader.* MacGibbon and Kee, 1967. 234pp.

A. Deakin

269 Allen, V.L. *Trade union leadership, based on a study of Arthur Deakin.* Longmans, 1957. xiii, 326pp.

C. Despard

270 Fox, R.M. 'Charlotte Despard', *Rebel Irishwomen,* pp.99–103. Dublin,
Progress, 1967 (first pub. 1935).

271 Kamm, J. 'Charlotte Despard', *Rapiers and battleaxes; the women's movement
and its aftermath,* pp.156–60. Allen and Unwin, 1966.

Lady E.F. Dilke

272 Lee, S. 'Lady Emilia Frances Dilke'. DNB, 1901–11, 1969 reprint,
pp.507–8.

J. Doherty

273 Boyd, A. 'John Doherty', *Leaders and workers,* pp.17–25 *(see* no.18). Edited by J. W. Boyle. Dublin, Mercier Press, 1966.

D. Donnelly

274 Donnelly, D. 'Portrait of a political rebel'. TC, 3, 1968, 177(1038):11–12.

T. Driberg

275 Driberg, T. *Colonnade 1937–47.* Pilot, 1949. 384pp.
Selection from his journalism.

276 Driberg, T. *The best of both worlds: a personal diary.* Phoenix House, 1953. vi, 234pp.
Period: April 1951–Oct. 1952.

T.S. Duncombe

277 Barker, G.F.R. 'Thomas Slingsby Duncombe'. DNB, 1967–8 reprint, Vol. 6, pp.178–80.

278 Boase, F. 'Thomas Slingsby Duncombe'. MEB, 1965 reprint, Vol. 1, Col. 932.

279 Kingsford, P.W. 'Radical dandy: Thomas Slingsby Duncombe 1796–1861'. HT, June 1964, 14(6):399–407.

T. Dunning

280 Dunning, T. 'The reminiscences of Thomas Dunning (1813–1894) and the Nantwich Shoemakers case of 1834'. LCAS, 1947, 59:85–130.

E. Durbin

281 Brown, E.H.P. 'Evan Durbin 1906–48'. E, Feb. 1951, 18(69):91–5.

S.A. Dutt

282 Labour Monthly. 'S.A. Dutt. Obituary (August 30, 1888–August 30, 1964)'.LM, Oct. 1964, 46(10):465.

W.H. Dyson

283 Grimsditch, H.B. 'Will Dyson'. DNB, 1931–40, 1970 reprint, p.249.

G. Edwards

284 Edwards, G. *From crow-scaring to Westminster: an autobiography.* National Union of Agricultural Workers, 1957 (first pub. 1922). 240pp.

285 Wearmouth, R.F. 'George Edwards: the product and leader of the agricultural labourers'. LQ, Jan. 1952, 40–3.

H.T. Edwards

286 Edwards, H.T. *Hewn from the rock: the autobiography of Huw T. Edwards.* Cardiff, Western Mail and TWW, 1967. 238pp.

I. Edwards

287 Edwards, I. *No gold on my shovel.* Porcupine, 1947. 224pp.

W.J. Edwards

288 Edwards, W.J. *From the valley I came.* Angus and Robertson, 1956. viii, 263pp.
Covering the period up to 1926: Welsh Labour movement, Ruskin College.

C.H. Elt

289 Boase, F. 'Charles Henry Elt'. MEB, 1965 reprint, Vol. 1, Col. 990.

F. Engels

289a Cadogan, P. 'Harney and Engels'. IRSH, 1965, 10(1):66–104.

290 Carlton, G. *Friedrich Engels: the shadow prophet.* Pall Mall, 1965. ix, 235pp.

291 Coates, Z.K. *The life and teaching of Friedrich Engels.* Lawrence and Wishart, 1945. 99pp.

292 Fagan, H. 'Engels and the British working class'. MML, Oct.–Dec. 1970, 56:8–14.

293 Henderson, W.O. and W.H. Chaloner. 'Friedrich Engels and the England of the 1840's'. HT, July 1956, 6(7):448–56.

294 Henderson, W.P. and W.H. Chaloner. 'Friedrich Engels in Manchester'. MPLS, 1956–7, 98(2):13–29.

295 Jenkins, M. *Frederick Engels in Manchester.* Manchester, Lancashire and Cheshire District Committee Communist Party, 1951. 23pp.

J. Epps

296 Bettany, G.T. 'John Epps'. DNB, 1967–8 reprint, Vol. 6, pp.800–1.

297 Boase, F. 'John Epps'. MEB, 1965 reprint, Vol. 1, Col. 994.

D. Evans

298 Six Point Group. *Dorothy Evans and the Six Point Group.* Claire Madden for The Group, 1945. 74pp.
'Dorothy Evans: the story of a militant', by Monica Whately, pp.41–50.

J. Fielden

299 Cole, G.D.H. 'John Fielden', *Chartist portraits,* pp. 218–38 (*see* no.1411). Macmillan, 1965 (first pub. 1941).

J.H.B. Figgins

300 Labour Monthly. 'J.H.B. Figgins 1893–1956'. LM, Feb. 1957, 39(2):81.

J. Finch

301 Boase, F. 'John Finch'. MEB, 1965 reprint, Vol. 5, Col. 294.

302 Rose, J.B. 'John Finch, 1784–1857, a Liverpool disciple of Robert Owen'. HSLC, 1958, 109:159–84.

G.H. Fletcher

303 Connole, N. *Leaven of life: the story of George Henry Fletcher*. Lawrence and Wishart, 1961. ix, 211pp.

H. Foot

304 Foot, H. *A start in freedom*. Hodder, 1964. 256pp.

M. Foot

305 Blackburn, R. and A. Cockburn. 'Credo of the Labour left: interview with Michael Foot'. NLR, May-June 1968, 49:19–34.

G. Foulser

306 Foulser, G. *Seamen's voice*. MacGibbon and Kee, 1961. 192pp.
     Britain's seamen's strike, 1960.

J. Frost

307 Barker, G.F.R. 'John Frost'. DNB, 1967–8 reprint, Vol. 7, pp.728–9.

308 Boase, F. 'John Frost'. MEB, 1965 reprint, Vol. 1, Cols. 1109–10.

309 Cole, G.D.H. 'John Frost', *Chartist portraits*, pp.133–62 (*see* no.1411). Macmillan, 1965 (first pub. 1941).

H. Gaitskell

310 Boardman, H. 'Gaitskell as leader', *The glory of Parliament*, pp.151–4. Allen and Unwin, 1960.

311 Jenkins, R. 'Hugh Gaitskell', *Essays and speeches*, pp.59–72. Collins, 1967.

312 Klugman, J. 'Does Labour deserve Gaitskell?'. LM, Mar. 1956, 38(3):115–23.

313 Nairn, T. 'Hugh Gaitskell'. NLR, May-June 1964, 25:63–8.
     Review of no.315.

314 The Observer. 'Hugh Gaitskell', *A book of British profiles compiled from The Observer*, by S. Haffner, pp.65–9. Heinemann, 1954.

315 Rodgers, W.T., ed. *Hugh Gaitskell 1906–63*. Thames and Hudson, 1964. 167pp.
     Tributes from 14 friends and colleagues.

316 Wyatt, W. 'Hugh Gaitskell', *Distinguished for talent: some men of influence and enterprise,* pp.184–93. Hutchinson, 1958.

W. Gallacher

317 Carr, E.H. 'Mr. Gallacher and the C.P.G.B.', *Studies in revolution,* pp.166–80. Macmillan, 1950.

318 Communist Party. *Communist M.P.* The Party, 1945. 32pp.

319 Communist Party. *William Gallacher: a great working class leader.* The Party, 1965. 16pp.

320 Dutt, R.P. 'Greetings to William Gallacher: on his 80th birthday, December 25th 1961'. LM, Dec. 1961, 43(12):568–9.

321 Gallacher, W. *The last memoirs of William Gallacher.* Lawrence and Wishart, 1966. 320pp.

322 Gallacher, W. *Revolt on the Clyde: an autobiography.* Lawrence and Wishart, 1949 (first pub. 1936). ix, 301pp.

323 Gallacher, W. *'Rise like lions'.* Lawrence and Wishart, 1951. 253pp.
    Covers the period 1945–50.

324 Gallacher, W. *The rolling of the thunder.* Lawrence and Wishart, 1948. 229pp.

325 Gallacher, W. *The tyrants' might is passing.* Lawrence and Wishart, 1954. 104pp.
    Reminiscences, mainly from 1950 onwards.

326 Kemp-Ashraf, P.M. and Jack Mitchell, eds. *Essays in honour of William Gallacher.* Berlin, Humboldt-Universität, 1966. 354pp. *See* nos.2252, 2266.

327 Labour Monthly. 'William Gallacher. December 25th, 1881–August 12th, 1965'. LM, Sept. 1965, 47(9):408–10.

328 MacDiarmid, H. 'William Gallacher', *The company I've kept,* pp.126–61. Hutchinson, 1966.

329 MacKenzie, C. 'Memories of Gallacher'. LM, June 1966, 48(6):284–6.
    Review of no.322.

330 Zhak, L. 'The fighting Scotsman' [William Gallacher], *Lenin's comrades-in-arms: episodes from the lives of Lenin's foreign comrades-in-arms and contemporaries,* pp.10–33. Moscow, Progress Publishers, 1969.

R.G. Gammage

331 Boase, F. 'R.G. Gammage'. MEB, 1965 reprint, Vol. 1, Col. 1119.

332 Gonnor, E.C.K. 'R.G. Gammage'. DNB, 1967–8 reprint, Vol. 7, p.839.

E.M. Geldart

333 Downing, A.B. 'From Max Muller to Karl Marx: a study of E.M. Geldart, scholar of Balliol'. UHS, 1970, 14(4):171–89.

G. Gissing

334 Goode, J. 'Gissing, Morris and English socialism'. VS, Dec. 1968, 12(2):201–26.

335 Lelchuk, A. '"Demos": the ordeal of the two Gissings'. VS, Mar. 1969, 12(3):357–74.

336 Secombe, T. 'George Gissing'. DNB, 1901–11, 1969 reprint, pp.114–16.

P. Glading

337 Labour Monthly. 'Percy Glading (November 29, 1893-April 15, 1970)'. LM, May 1970, 52(5):206.

K.B. Glasier

338 McAllister, G. *Katharine Bruce Glasier 1867–1950*. Katharine Bruce Glasier Memorial Fund, ?1952. 4pp.
   Fund appeal leaflet.

W. Godwin

339 Woodcock, G. *William Godwin: a biographical study*. Porcupine Press, 1946. x, 266pp.

V. Gollancz

340 Burnett, H., ed. 'Victor Gollancz: television interview by John Freeman', *Face to face,* pp.34–5. Cape, 1964.

341 Gollancz, V. *More for Timothy: being the second instalment of an autobiographical letter to his grandson*. Gollancz, 1953. 390pp.

342 Gollancz, V. *My dear Timothy: an autobiographical letter to his grandson*. Penguin, 1969 (first pub. 1952). 443pp.

343 Gollancz, V. *Reminiscences of affection*. Gollancz, 1968. 287pp.
   In effect a third instalment of an autobiographical letter to his grandson.

344 Strachey, J. 'Victor Gollancz', *The strangled cry and other unparliamentary papers,* pp.217–21. Bodley Head, 1962.

H. Gosling

345 Sanders, W.S. 'Harry Gosling'. DNB, 1922–30, 1967 reprint, pp.352–3.

R. Gosling

346 Gosling, R. *Sum total*. Faber, 1962. 174pp.

A. Gossip

347 Harrison, S. *Alex Gossip*. Lawrence and Wishart, 1962. 64pp.

R.B.C. Graham

348 Bloomfield, P., ed. *The essential R.B. Cunninghame Graham*. Cape, 1952. 255pp.
Selections from his works and a biography, pp.13–27.

349 MacDiarmid, H. *Cunninghame Graham: a centenary study*. Glasgow, Caledonian Press, 1952. 40pp.

350 MacShane, F. 'R.B. Cunninghame Graham'. SAQ, Spring 1969, 68(2):198–207.

351 Tomlinson, H.M. 'R.B. Cunninghame Graham'. DNB, 1931–40, 1970 reprint, pp.354–6.

352 Tschiffeley, A.F. *Tornado cavalier: a biography of R.B. Cunninghame Graham*. Harrap, 1955. 151pp.

W. Graham

353 Graham, T.N. *Willie Graham: the life of the Rt. Hon. W. Graham*. Foreword by C.R. Attlee. Hutchinson, 1948. 207pp.

354 Middleton, J.S. 'William Graham'. DNB, 1931–40, 1970 reprint, pp.356–7.

V. Grayson

355 Groves, R. *The mystery of Victor Grayson*. Pendulum, 1946. 118pp.

H. Grenfell

356 Dutt, R.P. 'Harold Grenfell'. LM, April 1948, 30(4):111–13.

J. Griffiths

357 Griffiths, J. *Pages from memory*. Dent, 1969. ix, 213pp.

St. John B. Groser

358 Groser, Father St. John B. *Politics and persons*. S.C.M. Press, 1949. 175pp.
Largely East London's Labour movement.

J. Gutteridge

359 Chancellor, V.E., ed. *Master and artisan in Victorian England: the diary of William Andrews and the autobiography of Joseph Gutteridge*. Evelyn, Adams and Mackay, 1969. vii, 238pp.
Autobiography, pp.75–238.

C. Haldane

360 Haldane, C. *Truth will out*. Weidenfeld, 1949. x, 339pp.

J.B.S. Haldane

361 Clark, R. *J.B.S. The life and work of J.B.S. Haldane*. Hodder, 1968. 286pp.

362 Huxley, J. 'Haldane'. EN, Oct. 1965, 25(4):59–61.

363 Montagu, I. 'Filleted Haldane'. LM, Mar. 1969, 51(3):140–1.
Review of BBC TV programme, 'Last of the polymaths', 6th February 1960.

364 Pirie, N.W. 'John Burdon Sanderson Haldane (1892–1964)', *Biographical Memoirs of Fellows of The Royal Society*, pp.219–49. RS, 1966, 12.

M.A. Hamilton

365 Hamilton, M.A. *Up hill all the way: a third cheer for democracy*. Cape, 1953. 160pp.

T. Hancock

366 Yeo, S. 'Thomas Hancock, 1832–1903 "The Banner of Christ in the hands of the Socialists"', *For Christ and the people: studies of four socialist priests and prophets of the Church of England between 1870 and 1930*, pp.1–60. Edited by M.B. Reckitt. S.P.C.K., 1968.

W. Hannington

367 Hannington, W. *Never on our knees*. Lawrence and Wishart, 1967. 368pp.

368 Hill, (E.J.) 'Wal Hannington'. LM, Dec. 1967, 49(12):561–2.
Review of no.367.

369 Labour Monthly. 'Wal Hannington'. LM, Dec. 1966, 48(12):560.

J.K. Hardie

370 Bealey, F. 'Keir Hardie and the Labour groups—1'. PA, Winter 1956, 10(1):81–93.

371 Bealey, F. 'Keir Hardie and the Labour groups—2'. PA, Spring 1957, 10(2):220–33.

372 Bell, P. 'The first socialist M.P.s' [i.e. Burns and Hardie]. MML, July-Sept. 1962, 23:5–8.

373 Cockburn, J. *The hungry heart: a romantic biography of James Keir Hardie*. Jarrolds, 1956. 286pp.

374 Cole, G.D.H. 'James Keir Hardie'. DNB, 1912–21, 1968 reprint, pp.239–40.

375 Cole, M. 'James Keir Hardie (1856–1915)', *Makers of the Labour movement*, pp.203–16 (*see* no.19). Longmans, 1948.

376 Evans, J.N. 'Keir Hardie', *Great figures in the Labour movement*, pp.34–44. Pergamon, 1966.

377 Fagan, H. 'Keir Hardie and the Labour Party: 1856–1915', *The unsheathed sword: episodes in English history. Part 2, Champions of the workers,* pp.66–86. Lawrence and Wishart, 1959 (*see* no.1188).

378 Hughes, E. *Keir Hardie.* Lincolns-Praeger, 1950. 80pp.

379 Hughes, E. *Keir Hardie.* Allen and Unwin, 1956. 248pp.

380 Jemnitz, J. 'Correspondence of Keir Hardie with Viktor Adler'. SSLH, Autumn 1966, 13:22–5.

381 Lean, G. 'The damnedest aristocrat: Keir Hardie', *Brave men choose,* pp.161–84. Blandford, 1961.

382 Morgan, K.O. *Keir Hardie.* OUP, 1967. 64pp.

383 Morgan, K.O. 'The Merthyr of Keir Hardie', *Merthyr politics: the making of a working-class tradition,* pp.58–81. Edited by G. Williams. Cardiff, University of Wales Press, 1966.

384 Reid, F. 'Keir Hardie's biographers'. SSLH, Spring 1968, 16:30–33.
    Review of 9 books on Keir Hardie.

385 Shaw, G.B. 'Keir Hardie', *Pen portraits and reviews,* pp.100–14. Constable, 1949 (first pub. 1931).

G. Hardy

386 Hardy, G. *Those stormy years: memoirs of the fight for freedom on five continents.* Lawrence and Wishart, 1956. 256pp.
    Including his period of office as Secretary of Industrial Workers of the World, 1920–1.

387 Labour Monthly. 'George Hardy'. LM, Dec. 1966, 48(12):312.

T. Hardy

388 Barker, G.F.R. 'Thomas Hardy'. DNB, 1967–8 reprint, Vol. 8, pp.1241–2.

G.J. Harney

389 Black, F.G. and R.M. Black, eds. *The Harney papers.* Assen, Van Gorcum, 1969. xxx, 388pp.

390 Boase, F. 'George Julian Harney'. MEB, 1965 reprint, Vol. 5, Cols. 579–80.

391 Cadogan, P. 'Harney and Engels'. IRSH, 1965, 10(1)66–104.

392 Cole, G.D.H. 'George Julian Harney', *Chartist portraits,* pp.268–99 (*see* no.1411). Macmillan, 1965 (first pub. 1941).

393 Schoyen, A.R. *The Chartist challenge: a portrait of George Julian Harney.* Heinemann, 1958. viii, 300pp.

V. Hartshorn

394 Cook, W.L. 'Vernon Hartshorn'. DNB, 1931–40, 1970 reprint, pp.406–7.

395 Richards, T. 'Vernon Hartshorn'. DWB, 1959, pp.344–5.

Sir P. Hastings

396 Hastings, Sir P. *Autobiography*. Heinmann, 1948. vi, 302pp.

S. Headlam

397 Leech, K. 'Stewart Headlam, 1847–1924 and the Guild of St. Matthew', *For Christ and the people: studies of four socialist priests and prophets of the Church of England between 1870 and 1930*, pp.61–88. Edited by M.B. Reckitt. S.P.C.K., 1968.

398 Rubinstein, D. 'Annie Besant and Stewart Headlam: the London School Board election of 1888'. ELP, Summer 1970, 13(1):3–24.

D. Healey

399 Altman, D. 'What Denis Healey thinks'. CNR, Sept. 1960, 198:469–72.

A. Henderson

400 Cole, M. 'Arthur Henderson (1863–1935)', *Makers of the Labour Movement*, pp.248–67 (*see* no.19). Longmans, 1948.

401 Hamilton, M.A. 'Arthur Henderson'. DNB, 1931–40, 1970 reprint, pp.417–20.

402 Winkler, H.R. 'Arthur Henderson', *The diplomats*, pp.311–43. Edited by G.A. Craig and F. Gilbert. Princeton, University Press, 1953.

F. Henderson

403 Labour Monthly. 'Fred Henderson (February 25, 1867-July 18, 1957)'. LM, Sept. 1957, 39(9):397.

G. Henson

404 Boase, F. 'Gravener Henson'. MEB, 1965 reprint, Vol. 1, Col. 1434.

405 Church R.A. and S.D. Chapman. 'Gravener Henson and the making of the English working class', *Land, labour and population in the industrial revolution, essays presented to J.D. Chalmers*, pp.131–61. Edited by E.L. Jones and G.E. Mingay. Arnold, 1967.

406 Doubleday, W.E. 'Gravener Henson'. DNB, 1967–8 reprint, Vol. 9, pp.589–90.

M. Hess

407 Berlin, Sir I. *The life and opinions of Moses Hess*. Cambridge, Heffer (for the Jewish Historical Society of England), 1959. ii, 49pp.

408 Silberner, E. 'Moses Hess'. HJU, April 1951, 13(1):3–28.

H. Hetherington

409 Holyoake, G.J. 'Henry Hetherington'. DNB, 1967–8 reprint, Vol. 9, pp.750–1.

A. Heywood

410 Boase F. 'Abel Heywood'. MEB, 1965 reprint, Vol. 5, Cols. 647–8.

E.J. Hill

411 Labour Monthly. 'Ted Hill'. LM, Jan. 1970. 52(1):14.

S. Hill

412 Craik, W. *Sydney Hill and the National Union of Public Employees*. Allen and Unwin, 1968. 119pp.
   Hill was General Secretary of the Union, 1962–7.

L.T. Hobhouse

413 Shadwell, A. 'Leonard Trelawney Hobhouse'. DNB, 1922–30, 1967 reprint, pp.420–1.

J.A. Hobson

414 Brailsford, H.N. *The lifework of J.A. Hobson*. Cumberlege, 1948. 29pp.

415 Tawney, R.H. 'John Atkinson Hobson'. DNB, 1931–40, 1970 reprint, pp.435–6.

J. Hodge

416 Middleton, J.S. 'John Hodge'. DNB, 1931–40, 1970 reprint, pp.437–8.

G. Hodgkinson

417 Hodgkinson, G. *Sent to Coventry*. Introduction by R.H.S. Crossman. Maxwell, 1970. xxxi, 256pp.

T. Hodgskin

418 Halévy, E. *Thomas Hodgskin*. Benn, 1956 (first pub. 1903). 197pp.

J. Hole

419 Harrison, J.F.C. *Social reform in Victorian Leeds: the work of James Hole 1820–95*. Leeds, Thoresby Society, 1954. vii, 70pp.

G.J. Holyoake

420 MacDonald, J.R. 'George Jacob Holyoake'. DNB, 1901–11, 1969 reprint, pp.291–3.

A. Horner

421 Horner, A. *Incorrigible rebel*. MacGibbon and Kee, 1960. 235pp.
Horner was General Secretary of the National Union of Mineworkers, 1947–59.

422 Paynter, W. 'Tribute to Arthur Horner, 1894–1968'. LM, Oct. 1968, 50(10):469–70.

423 Romilly, G. 'Gentle revolutionary: a portrait of Arthur Horner', *The changing nation*, pp.36–41. Contact, 1947.

G. Howell

424 MacDonald, J.R. 'George Howell'. DNB, 1901–11, 1969 reprint, pp.308–9.

E. Hughes

425 Labour Monthly. 'Emrys Hughes M.P.'. LM, Nov. 1969, 51(11):496.

T. Hughes

426 Boase, F. 'Thomas Hughes'. MEB, 1965 reprint, Vol. 5, Cols. 722–3.

427 Briggs, A. 'Thomas Hughes and the public schools', *Victorian people: A reassessment of persons and themes, 1851–67*, pp.148–75. Penguin, 1965 (first pub. 1954).

428 Davies, J.L. 'Thomas Hughes', DNB, 1967–8 reprint, Vol. 22, pp.879–82.

429 Mack, E.C. and W.H.G. Armytage. *Thomas Hughes: the life of the author of Tom Brown's schooldays*. Benn, 1952. 302pp.

430 Vidler, A.R. 'Thomas Hughes and the National Church', *F.D. Maurice and company: nineteenth century studies*, pp.250–8. S.C.M. Press, 1966.

H. Hunt

431 Hamilton, J.A. 'Henry Hunt'. DNB, 1967–8 reprint, Vol. 10, pp.264–6.

432 Proctor, W. 'Orator Hunt, M.P. for Preston, 1830–32'. HSLC, 1963, 114:129–54.

D. Hurst

433 Communist Party. London District Committee. *Denny Hurst: a tribute*. The District Committee, 1958. 11pp.

D. Hyde

434 Hyde, D. *I believed: the autobiography of a former British communist*. Heinemann, 1951. 303pp.

H.M. Hyndman

435 Cole, G.D.H. 'Henry Mayers Hyndman'. DNB, 1912–21, 1968 reprint, pp.280–2.

436 Hobsbawn, E.J. 'Hyndman and the S.D.F.', *Labouring men: studies in the history of Labour*, pp.231–8 (*see* no.1191). Weidenfeld, 1968.

437 Rubinstein, D. 'Booth and Hyndman'. SSLH, Spring 1968, 16:22–4.

438 Shaw, G.B. 'Hyndman', *Pen portraits and reviews*, pp.125–30. Constable, 1949 (first pub. 1931).

439 Shaw, G.B. 'The Old Revolutionist and the New Revolution', *Pen portraits and reviews,* pp.130–41. Constable, 1949 (first pub. 1931).

440 Tsuzuki, C. *H.M. Hyndman and British socialism.* OUP, 1961. x, 304pp.

P. Inman

441 Inman, P. *No going back.* Williams and Norgate, 1952. 224pp.
    Author was Lord Privy Seal in Labour Government, 1947.

I. Ironside

442 Salt, J. 'Isaac Ironside and the Hollow Meadows Farm experiment'. YB, Mar. 1960, 12(1):45–51.

G. Isaacs

443 Eastwood, G.G. *George Isaacs: printer, trade-union leader, Cabinet minister.* Odhams, 1952. 223pp.

T.A. Jackson

444 Jackson, T.A. *Solo trumpet: some memories of socialist agitation and propaganda.* Lawrence and Wishart, 1953. ix, 166pp.

445 Labour Monthly. 'T.A. Jackson (August 21, 1879–August 18, 1955)'. LM, Oct. 1955, 37(10):446.

J. Jarvie

446 T[uckett], A. 'James Jarvie (1919–1970)'. LM, Nov. 1970, 52(11):527.

C. Jenkinson

447 Hammerton, H.J. *This turbulent priest: the story of Charles Jenkinson, parish priest and housing reformer.* Lutterworth, 1952. 192pp.

M. Jepps

448 London Young Communist League. *Malcolm Jepps Exhibition: a tribute and an example.* The League, 1954. 8pp.
    Catalogue of exhibition.

H. Johnson (Dean of Canterbury)

449 Arnot, R.P. 'Red Dean and yellow reviewers'. LM, Nov. 1968, 50(11):525–6.
    Review of no.450.

450 Johnson, H. *Searching for light: an autobiography*. Joseph, 1968. 446pp.

451 Labour Monthly. 'Dr. Hewlett Johnson, 1874–1966'. LM, Dec. 1966, 48(12):577.

452 The Observer. 'Dean of Canterbury', *A book of British profiles compiled from The Observer*, by S. Haffner, pp.16–19. Heinemann, 1954.

453 Richards, J. 'The Red Dean retires'. CNR, Mar. 1963, 203:152–4.

T. Johnston

454 Johnston, T. *Memories*. Collins, 1952. 255pp.
    (*See* nos.88, 226, 479, 561, 625, 972).

B. Jones

455 Jones, H.C. *Ben Jones: a great co-operator; his life*. C.P.S., 1945. 131pp.

E.C. Jones

456 Boase, F. 'Ernest Charles Jones'. MEB, 1965 reprint, Vol. 2, Col. 125.

457 Broadridge, S. 'Diary of Ernest Jones, 1839–47'. OH, Spring 1961, 21:21pp.

458 Cole, G.D.H. 'Ernest Jones', *Chartist portraits*, pp.337–57 (*see* no.1411). Macmillan, 1965 (first pub. 1941).

459 Communist Party. Lancs. and Cheshire District. History Group. *Ernest Jones (Chartist), a fighter for Manchester's working class*. Communist Party, 1953. 6pp.

460 Hamilton, J.A. 'Ernest Charles Jones'. DNB, 1967–8 reprint, Vol. 10, pp.987–9.

461 Saville, J. *Ernest Jones: Chartist; selection from the writings and speeches with introduction and notes*. Lawrence and Wishart, 1952. 284pp.

462 Thompson, D., ed. 'Letters from Ernest Jones to Karl Marx 1865–1868'. SSLH, Spring 1962, 4:11–23.

E.P. Jones

463 Jones-Evans, P. 'Evan Pan-Jones—land reformer (1834–1922)'. WH, Dec. 1968, 4(2):143–59.

J. Jones

464 Jones, J. *Give me back my heart: final chapters in the autobiography of Jack Jones*. Right Book Club, 1950. 272pp.

465 Jones, J. *Me and mine: further chapters in the autobiography of Jack Jones.* Hamilton, 1946. 428pp.

466 Jones, J. *Unfinished journey.* Foreword by D. Lloyd George. Bath, Chivers, 1966 (first pub. 1937). 303pp.

T.G. Jones

467 Communist Party. Welsh Committee. *Dr. T. Gwynn Jones: a great Welshman.* Communist Party. Welsh Committee, ?1945. 24pp.

F.W. Jowett

468 Brockway, F. *Socialism over sixty years: the life of Jowett of Bradford (1864–1944).* Preface by J.B. Priestley. Allen and Unwin for National Labour Press, 1946. 415pp.
    Planned as autobiography, completed by Fenner Brockway.

S.E. Keeble

469 Edwards, M.L. *S.E. Keeble; pioneer and prophet.* Epworth, 1949, xviii, 106pp.
    Christian socialist and supporter of the Church Socialist League.

Dr. W. King

470 Boase, F. 'William King'. MEB, 1965 reprint, Vol. 2, Col. 230.

471 Holyoake, G.J. 'William King'. DNB, 1967–8 reprint, Vol. 11, p.170.

472 Mercer, T.W. *Co-operation's prophet: the life and letters of Dr. William King of Brighton, with a reprint of The Co-operator, 1828–30.* Manchester, Co-operative Union, 1947. vi, 190pp.

473 Pollard, S. 'Dr. William King of Ipswich: a co-operative pioneer', Co-operative College Papers, No. 6, pp.17–33. Loughborough, Co-operative Union, 1959.

C. Kingsley

474 Boase, F. 'Charles Kingsley'. MEB, 1965 reprint, Vol. 2, Cols. 234–5.

475 Kendall, G. *Charles Kingsley and his ideas.* Hutchinson, 1946. 190pp.

476 Martin, R.B. *The dust of combat: a life of Charles Kingsley.* Faber, 1959. 308pp.

477 Pope-Hennessy, U. *Canon Charles Kingsley: a biography.* Chatto and Windus, 1948. x, 294pp.

478 Stephen, L. 'Charles Kingsley'. DNB, 1967–8 reprint, Vol. 11, p.175.

D. Kirkwood

479 Johnston, T. 'David Kirkwood', *Memories,* pp.224–8 (*see* no.454). Collins, 1952.

J.F. Lalor

480 O'Neill, T.P. 'James Fintan Lalor', *Leaders and workers,* pp.37–45 (*see* no.18). Edited by J.W. Boyle. Dublin, Mercier Press, 1966.

G. Lansbury

481 Blythe, R. 'The Dove', *The age of illusion: England in the twenties and thirties 1919–40,* pp.270–93. Penguin, 1964 (first pub. 1963).

482 Cole, M. 'George Lansbury (1859–1940), *Makers of the Labour movement,* pp.268–87 (*see* no.19). Longmans, 1948.

483 Evans, J.N. 'George Lansbury', *Great figures in the Labour movement,* pp.78–101. Pergamon, 1966.

484 Hamilton, M.A. 'George Lansbury'. DNB, 1931–40, 1970 reprint, pp.524–6.

485 Postgate, R. *The life of George Lansbury.* Longmans, 1951. xiii, 332pp.

J. Larkin

486 Deasy, J. *Fiery cross: the story of Jim Larkin.* Dublin, New Books Publications, 1963. 40pp.

487 Fox, R.M. *Jim Larkin; the rise of the underman.* Lawrence and Wishart, 1957. 183pp.

488 Larkin, E. *James Larkin; Irish Labour leader, 1876–1947.* Routledge, 1965. xviii, 334pp.

489 McLysaght, E. 'Larkin, Connolly and the Labour movement', *Leaders and men of the Easter Rising: Dublin 1916,* pp.123–33. Edited by F.X. Martin. Methuen, 1967.

490 Plunkett, J. 'Jim Larkin', *Leaders and workers,* pp.77–86 (*see* no.18). Edited by J.W. Boyle. Dublin, Mercier Press, 1966.

491 Wolfe, B.D. 'The Catholic Communist (James Larkin)', *Strange communists I have known,* pp.52–71. Allen and Unwin, 1966.

H.J. Laski

492 Beloff, M. 'The age of Laski'. F, June 1950, 167(1002):378–84.

493 Callard, K. 'The heart and mind of Harold Laski'. CJEPS, May 1954, 20(2):243–51.

494 Cincinnatus, *pseud.* 'Mr. Laski's act of faith'. TC, April 1945, 137(818):159–67.
    Review of *Faith, reason and civilisation.*

495 Cook, T.I. 'Harold J. Laski'. APSR, Sept. 1950. 44(3):738–41.

496 Daily Express. *Laski v Newark Advertiser Co. Ltd. and Darlby*. Daily Express, 1947. 398pp.
Legal action arising from a speech made on 16th June 1945 by Laski in the General Election campaign.

497 Deane, H.W. *The political ideas of Harold J. Laski*. New York, Columbia University Press, 1955. xiii, 370pp.

498 Hatch, S. 'Harold Laski: an Old Reasoner?'. NR, Autumn 1957, 2:67–76.

499 Hawkins, C. 'Harold J. Laski: a preliminary analysis'. PSQ, Sept. 1950, 65(3):376–92.

500 Kampelman, M.M. 'Harold J. Laski: current analysis'. JP, Feb. 1948, 10(1):131–54.

501 Martin, K. 'H.J. Laski'. DNB, 1941–50, 1967 reprint, pp.484–6.

502 Martin, K. *Harold Laski 1893–1950: a biographical memoir*. Cape, 1969 (first pub. 1953). xvi, 278pp.

503 Peretz, M. 'Laski redivivus'. JCH, 1966, 1(2):87–101.

504 Robson, W.A. 'Harold Laski: an appreciation'. PAD, Autumn 1950, 28:219–20.

505 Soltau, R.H. 'Professor Laski and political science'. PQ, July-Sept. 1950, 21(3)301–10.

506 Strachey, J. 'Laski', *The strangled cry and other unparliamentary papers*, pp.196–200. Bodley Head, 1962.

507 Watkins, J.W.N. 'Laski on conscience and counter-revolution'. TC, March 1949, 145(865):173–9.

508 Zylstra, B. *From pluralism to collectivism: the development of Harold Laski's political thought*. Assen, Van Gorcum, 1968. x, 236pp.

S. Lawrence

509 Norton, A.T. 'Susan Lawrence'. DNB, 1941–50, 1967 reprint, p.489.

J. Lawson

510 Lawson, J. *A man's life*. Hodder, 1959 (first pub. 1932). 191pp.

Sir W. Lawther

511 Clarke, J.F. 'An interview with Sir William Lawther'. SSLH, Autumn 1969, 19:14–21.

J. Leach

512 Frow, R. and E. 'James Leach'. MML, July–Sept. 1966, 39:12–14.

J.T. Leader

513 Lee, S. 'John Temple Leader'. DNB, 1901–11, 1969 reprint, pp.431–3.

J. Lee

514 Fyvel, T.R. 'Bevan and Lee', *Britain between east and west*, pp.32–5. Contact, ?1946.

515 Lee, J. *This great journey: a volume of autobiography, 1904–45*. MacGibbon and Kee, 1963 (first pub. 1940 as *Tomorrow is a new day*). 230pp.

P. Lee

516 Lawson, J. *Peter Lee*. Epworth, 1949. viii, 216pp.

517 Moyes, W.A. 'Peter Lee', *Mostly mining—a study of the development of Easington rural district since earliest times*, pp.120–33. Newcastle, Graham, 1969.

F.R. Lees

518 Boase, F. 'Frederick Richard Lees'. MEB, 1965 reprint, Vol. 6, Col. 33.

J. Lehmann

519 Lehmann, J. *The whispering gallery: autobiography 1*. Longmans, 1955. ix, 342pp.

J.B. Leno

520 Boase, F. 'John Bedford Leno'. MEB, 1965 reprint, Vol. 6, Col. 42.

M. Levinson

521 Levinson, M. *The trouble with yesterday*. Davies, 1947. iv, 193pp.

C. Day Lewis

522 Dyment, C. *C. Day Lewis*. Longmans (British Council and National Book League), 1969 (first pub. 1955). 45pp.

523 Lewis, C.D. *The buried day*. Chatto and Windus, 1960. 244pp.

524 Maxwell, D.E.S. 'C. Day Lewis: between two worlds', *Poets of the thirties*, pp.83–126. Routledge, 1969.

A. Lindsay

525 Communist Party. Writers Group. *Nothing is lost: Ann Lindsay 1914–1954*. Rickwood for Communist Party, 1954. 16pp.

W.J. Linton

526 Boase, F. 'William James Linton'. MEB, 1965 reprint, Vol. 6, Cols. 60–1.

527 Garnett, R. 'William James Linton'. DNB, 1967–8 reprint, Vol. 22, pp.972–4.

H. Lister

528 Cameron, A. *In pursuit of justice: the story of Hugh Lister and his friends in Hackney Wick*. S.C.M., 1946. 189pp.
    Church of England priest and trade unionist.

F. Longden

529 Longden, F. *The proletarian revolution*. Glasgow, Strickland Press, 1951. 181pp.

W. Lovett

530 Beckerlegge, J.J. *William Lovett of Newlyn: the Cornish social reformer*. Mousehole, the author, 1948. 19pp.

531 Boase, F. 'William Lovett'. MEB, 1965 reprint, Vol. 2, Cols. 507–8.

532 Cole, G.D.H. 'William Lovett', *Chartist portraits*, pp.31–62 (*see* no.1411). Macmillan, 1965 (first pub. 1941).

533 Hamilton, J.A. 'William Lovett'. DNB, 1967–8 reprint, Vol. 12, pp.178–80.

534 Lovett, W. *Life and struggles of William Lovett in his pursuit of bread, knowledge and freedom*. Preface by R.H. Tawney reprinted from 1920 edition. MacGibbon and Kee, 1967 (first pub. 1876). xxxiii, 334pp.
    Includes text of 'The People's Charter'.

535 Tawney, R.H. 'William Lovett', *The radical tradition: twelve essays on politics, education and literature*, pp.15–31. Allen and Unwin, 1964.

J. Lowe

536 Boase, F. 'James Lowe'. MEB, 1965 reprint, Vol. 2, Col. 512.

R. Lowery

537 Harrison, B. and P. Hollis. 'Chartism, Liberalism and the life of Robert Lowery'. EHR, July 1967, 82(324):503–35.

B. Lucraft

538 Boase, F. 'Benjamin Lucraft'. MEB, 1965 reprint, Vol. 6, Col. 87.

J.M.F. Ludlow

538a Allen, P.R. 'F.D. Maurice and J.M. Ludlow: a re-assessment of the leaders of Christian socialism'. VS, June 1968, 11(4):461–82.

539 Hadden, J.C. 'John Malcolm Forbes Ludlow'. DNB, 1901–11, 1969 reprint, pp.478–9.

540 Masterman, N.C. *John Malcolm Ludlow: the builder of Christian socialism*. CUP, 1963. vii, 299pp.

M.R. MacArthur

541 Cole, M. 'Mary MacArthur', *Women of today*, pp.89–129. Nelson, 1946 (first pub. 1938).

542 Mallon, J.J. 'Anderson (i.e. MacArthur) M.R.'. DNB, 1912–21, 1968 reprint, pp.7–8.

543 Markham, V. 'Mary MacArthur', *Friendship's harvest*, pp.83–100. Reinhardt, 1956.

M. McCarthy

544 McCarthy, M. *Generation in revolt*. Heinemann, 1953. vi, 276pp.

W.F.R. Macartney

545 Labour Monthly. 'Wilfred Macartney'. LM, Dec. 1970, 52(12):548.

H. MacDiarmid

546 Arundel, H. 'MacDiarmid and the Scottish tradition', *Essays in honour of William Gallacher*, pp.193–8 (*see* no.326). Edited by P.M. Kemp-Ashraf and J. Mitchell. Berlin, Humboldt Universität, 1966.

547 Glen, D. *Hugh MacDiarmid (Christopher Murray Grieve) and the Scottish renaissance*. Edinburgh, Chambers, 1964. ix, 294pp.

548 MacDiarmid, H. *The company I've kept*. Hutchinson, 1966. 288pp.

549 MacDiarmid, H. *Selected essays*. Edited by Duncan Glen. Cape, 1969. 252pp.

A. MacDonald

550 Boase, F. 'Alexander MacDonald'. MEB, 1965 reprint, Vol. 2, Cols. 580–1.

551 Challinor, R. 'Alexander MacDonald and the miners'. OH, Winter 1967–8, 48:34pp.

J.R. MacDonald

552 Boardman, H. 'Ramsay MacDonald', *The glory of Parliament*, pp.39–42. Allen and Unwin, 1960.
　　Review of no.1984.

553 Broad, L. 'James Ramsay MacDonald', *The path to power: the rise of the premiership from Rosebery to Wilson*, pp.112–26. Muller, 1965.

554 Crossman, R.H.S. 'Ramsay MacDonald—myths of 1931', *The charm of politics and other essays in political criticism*, pp.63–8. Hamilton, 1958.
　　Review of no.1984.

555 Dowse, R.E. 'A note on Ramsay MacDonald and direct action'. PS, Oct. 1961, 9(3):306–8.

556 Elletson, D.H. 'The first Labour Prime Minister', *Chequers and the Prime Ministers*, pp.72–6. Hale, 1970.

557 Elton, Lord. 'J. Ramsay MacDonald'. DNB, 1931–40, 1970 reprint, pp.562–70.

558 Evans, J.N. 'Ramsay MacDonald', *Great figures in the Labour movement*, pp.102–16. Pergamon, 1966.

559 Gibbon, L.G. 'The wrecker—James Ramsay MacDonald', *A Scots Hairst: essays and short stories . . .*, pp.108–22. Edited and introduced by Ian S. Munro. Hutchinson, 1967.

560 Iremonger, L. 'Ramsay MacDonald', *The fiery chariot: a study of English Prime Ministers and the search for love*, pp.256–88. Secker, 1970.

561 Johnston, T. 'Ramsay MacDonald', *Memories*, pp.215–17 (*see* no.454). Collins, 1952.

562 Lyman, R.W. 'James Ramsay MacDonald and the leadership of the Labour Party, 1918–22'. JBS, Nov. 1962, 2(1):132–60.

563 McKibbin, R.I. 'James Ramsay MacDonald and the problem of the independence of the Labour Party, 1910–14'. JMH, June 1970, 42(2):216–35.

564 Mowat, C.L. 'Ramsay MacDonald and the Labour movement: right-left-right'. SSLH, Spring 1967, 14:6–7.

565 Potts, A. 'MacDonald-Ritson letter—25 August 1931'. NEG, Oct. 1968, 2:27–8.

566 Sacks, B. *J. Ramsay MacDonald in thought and action: an architect for a better world*. Albuquerque, University of New Mexico Press, 1952. xviii, 591pp.

567 Venkataramani, M.S. 'Ramsay MacDonald and Britain's domestic politics and foreign relations, 1919–31: a study based on MacDonald's letters to an American friend'. PS, Oct. 1960, 8(3):213–49.

568 Williams, F. 'Ramsay MacDonald', *A pattern of rulers*, pp.61–134. Longmans, 1965.

P. McGeown

569 McGeown, P. *Heat the furnaces seven times more*. Hutchinson, 1968. xi, 192pp.

J. McGovern

570 McGovern, J. *Neither fear nor favour*. Blandford, 1960. 236pp.

L. McGree

571 Labour Monthly. 'Leo McGree'. LM, July 1967, 49(7):324.

A. Machen

572 Labour Monthly. 'Alwyn Machen'. LM, Apr. 1960, 42(4):180.

J.P. MacKintosh

573 MacKintosh, J.P. 'Forty years on?'. PQ, Jan.–March 1970, 41(1):42–55.

574 MacKintosh, J.[P.] 'A passion for politics'. TC, 2, 1967, 176(1033):10–11.

J. MacLean

575 Clunie, J. 'Portrait of John MacLean', *The voice of Labour*, pp.77–101 (*see* no.193). Dunfermline, the author, 1958.

576 John MacLean Society. *John MacLean and Scottish independence*. Bathgate, West Lothian, the Society, 1970. 20pp.

577 MacDiarmid, H. 'John MacLean', *The company I've kept*, pp.120–52 (*see* no.548). Hutchinson, 1966.

M. McMillan

578 Cresswell, D. *Margaret McMillan: a memoir*. Foreword by J.B. Priestley. Hutchinson, 1948. 160pp.

579 Lord, M. *Margaret McMillan in Bradford, with reminiscences*. University of London Press for Margaret McMillan Fellowship, 1957. 32pp.

580 Lowndes, G.A.N. *Margaret McMillan: 'the children's champion'*. Museum Press, 1960. 110pp.

581 Mansbridge, A. 'Margaret McMillan'. DNB, 1931–40, 1970 reprint, pp.587–88.

582 Stevinson, E. *Margaret McMillan: prophet and pioneer*. University of London Press, 1954. 15pp.

R. & M. McMillan

583 Greenwood, A. '*All children are mine*'. University of London Press for Margaret McMillan Fellowship, 1953. 16pp.

W. McQuilkin

584 Barratt, M. 'The McQuilkin interview'. LM, Jan. 1968, 50(1):15–18. BBC TV interview, 24 Hours, 25.10.1965.

T. Maguire

585 Thompson, E.P. 'Homage to Tom Maguire', *Essays in Labour history*, pp.276–316 (*see* no.1179). Edited by A. Briggs and J. Saville. Macmillan, 1960.

J. Mann

586 Mann, J. *Woman in Parliament*. Odhams, 1962. 256pp.

T. Mann

587 Evans, J.N. 'Tom Mann', *Great figures in the Labour movement*, pp.45–61. Pergamon, 1966.

588 Fagan, H. 'Tom Mann and the "Dockers Tanner" 1856–1941', *The unsheathed sword: episodes in English history. Part 2, Champions of the workers*, pp.87–106. Lawrence and Wishart, 1959.

589 Mann, T. *Tom Mann's memoirs*. MacGibbon and Kee, 1967 (first pub. 1923). xiv, 278pp.

590 Middleton, J.S. 'Tom Mann'. DNB, 1941–50, 1967 reprint, pp.568–70.

591 Pollitt, H. 'Tom Mann centenary'. LM, Apr. 1956, 38(4):167–71.

592 Stafford, A. 'Tom Mann', *A match to fire the Thames*, pp.55–7. Hodder, 1961.

593 Torr, D. *Tom Mann and his times*. Vol. 1 (1859–1890). Lawrence and Wishart, 1956. 356pp.

594 Torr, D. 'Tom Mann and his times, 1890–2'. OH, Summer–Autumn 1962, 26/7:38pp.

595 Torr, D. 'Tom Mann in Australasia—1902–9'. OH, Summer 1965, 38:18pp.

596 Van Den Bergh, T. 'Tom Mann', *The trade unions—what are they?*, pp.15–28. Pergamon, 1970.

Cardinal Manning

597 Boase, F. 'Cardinal Henry Edward Manning'. MEB, 1965 reprint, Vol. 2, Col. 722.

598 Leslie, S. 'Cardinal Manning'. M, Mar. 1951, 5(3):133–41.

599 Rigg, J.M. 'Cardinal Henry Edward Manning'. DNB, 1967–8 reprint, Vol. 12, p.947.

L. Manning

600 Manning, L. *A life for education: an autobiography*. Gollancz, 1970. 263pp.

M. Margarot

601 Roe, M. 'Maurice Margarot: a radical in two hemispheres, 1792–1851'. IHR, May 1958, 31(83):68–78.

Countess Markiewicz

602 Greaves, C.D. 'Rebel Countess: Countess C.G. Markiewicz and the women's struggle'. LM, Feb. 1968, 50(2):82–5.

C. Marston

603 Reckitt, M.B. 'Charles Marston, 1859–1914 and the real disorders of the Church', *For Christ and the people: studies of four socialist priests and prophets of the Church of England between 1870 and 1930*, pp.89–134. Edited by M.B. Reckitt. S.P.C.K., 1968.

K. Martin

604 Dutt, R.P. 'Review: Editor: autobiography 1931–45'. LM, July 1968, 50(7):285–7 (*see* no.606).

605 Jones, M., ed. *Kingsley Martin: portrait and self-portrait*. Barrie and Jenkins, 1969. vii, 166pp.
Sixteen short tributes and some selected articles by Kingsley Martin.

606 Martin, K. *Father figures: a first volume of autobiography 1897–1931*. Penguin, 1969 (first pub, 1966). 224pp.
Editor: a second volume of autobiography 1931–45. Penguin, 1969 (first pub. 1968). 355pp.

607 Woolf, L. 'Kingsley Martin'. PQ, July–Sept. 1969, 40(3):241–5.

E. Marx

608 Feuer, L.S. 'Marxian tragedies: a death in the family'. EN, Nov. 1962, 19(5):23–32.

609 Tsuzuki, C. *The life of Eleanor Marx 1855–1898: a socialist tragedy*. Clarendon Press, 1967. xi, 354pp.

K. Marx

610 Bell, P. 'The daughters of Karl Marx'. MML, Oct.–Dec. 1964, 32:2–6.
Jenny, Laura, Eleanor.

F. Mattison

611 Mattison, F. 'A veteran's voice for peace'. LM, Aug. 1953, 35(8):354–7.

F.D. Maurice

612 Allen, P.R. 'F.D. Maurice and J.M. Ludlow: a re-assessment of the leaders of Christian socialism'. VS, June 1968, 11(4):461–82.

613 Boase, F. 'John Frederick Denison Maurice'. MEB, 1965 reprint, Vol. 2, Cols. 804–6.

614 Dring, T. 'Frederick Denison Maurice: the greatest prophet of the nineteenth century'. LQ, Jan. 1948, 36–46.

615 Higham, F. *Frederick Denison Maurice*. S.C.M., 1947. 128pp.

616 Ramsey, A.M. *F.D. Maurice and the conflicts of modern theology*. CUP. 1951. 118pp.

617 Ranson, G.H. 'The Kingdom of God as the design of society: an important aspect of F.D. Maurice's theology'. CH, Dec. 1961, 30(4):458–72.

618 Stephen, L. 'Frederick Denison Maurice'. DNB, 1967–8 reprint, Vol. 13, pp.97–105.

619 Vidler, A.R. *F.D. Maurice and Company: nineteenth century studies.* S.C.M., 1966. 287pp.

620 Wood, H.G. *Frederick Denison Maurice.* CUP, 1950. viii, 171pp.

J. Maxton

621 Anand, V.S. and F.A. Ridley. *James Maxton and British socialism.* Medusa Press, 1970. 32pp.

622 Edwards, R., comp. *James Maxton 1885–1946.* Independent Labour Party, ?1946. 30pp.
Pp.6–14 brief outline of his life by John McNair; pp.15–30 individual tributes.

623 Gallacher, W. 'Maxton and the I.L.P.'. LM, June 1955, 37(6):281–5.
Review of no.626.

624 Johnston, T. 'James Maxton'. DNB, 1941–50, 1967 reprint, pp.581–2.

625 Johnston, T. 'James Maxton', *Memories*, pp.228–31 (*see* no.454). Collins, 1952.

626 McNair, J. *James Maxton: the beloved rebel.* Allen and Unwin, 1955. xiv, 337pp.

627 Marwick, A. 'James Maxton and his place in Scottish Labour history'. SHR, April 1964, 43(135):25–43.

628 Orr, Lord (Boyd). *The role of the rebel in society.* James Maxton Memorial Committee, 1951. 32pp.

C. Mayhew

629 Mayhew, C. *Party games.* Hutchinson, 1969. 176pp.

H. Mitchell

630 Mitchell, H. *The hard way up: the autobiography of Hannah Mitchell, suffragette and rebel.* Edited by Geoffrey Mitchell. Faber, 1968. 260pp.
Mainly Manchester—Labour Party, I.L.P. and suffragettes.

John Mitchell

631 Cole, M. 'John Mitchell (1828–1895)', *Makers of the Labour movement*, pp.131–44 (*see* no.19). Longmans, 1948.

J. Mitford

632 Mitford, J. *Hons and rebels.* Penguin, 1962 (first pub. 1960), 247pp.

A. Moffatt

633 Moffatt, A. *My life with the miners*. Lawrence and Wishart, 1965. 324pp.

W.N. Molesworth

634 Boase, F. 'William Nassau Molesworth'. MEB, 1965 reprint, Vol. 2, Cols. 916–17.

635 Hamilton, J.A. 'William Nassau Molesworth'. DNB, 1967–8 reprint, Vol. 13, p.572.

H. Molony

636 Fox, R.M. 'Helena Molony', *Rebel Irishwomen*, pp.65–72. Dublin, Progress House, 1967 (first pub. 1935).

I. Montagu

637 Montagu, I. *The youngest son: autobiographical sketches*. Lawrence and Wishart, 1970. 384pp.
     To 1927.

R. Moore

638 Boase, F. 'Richard Moore'. MEB, 1965 reprint, Vol. 2, Cols. 952–3.

639 Hamilton, J.A. 'Richard Moore'. DNB, 1967–8 reprint, Vol. 13, p.825.

E.D. Morel

640 Adams, W.S. 'E.D. Morel and his friends', *Edwardian portraits*, pp.174–219. Secker and Warburg, 1957.

641 Cline, C.A. 'E.D. Morel and the crusade against the Foreign Office'. JMH, June 1967, 39(2):126–37.

642 Goldring, D. 'E.D. Morel', *The nineteen twenties: a general survey and some personal memories*, pp.159–71. Nicholson and Watson, 1945.

643 Porter, B. 'Eugene Dene Morel', *Critics of empire: British radical attitudes in Africa, 1895–1914*, pp.254–66 and 274–90. Macmillan, 1968.

644 Reindeers, R.C. 'Racialism on the left: E.D. Morel and the "Black Horror on the Rhine"'. IRSH, 1968, 13(1):1–28.

645 Taylor, A.J.P. 'The Great War: the triumph of E.D. Morel', *The trouble makers: dissent over foreign policy 1792–1939*, pp.120–51. Panther, 1969 (first pub. 1957).

J.M. Morgan

646 Armytage, W.H.G. 'John Minter Morgan's schemes, 1841–1855'. IRSH, 1958, 3(1):26–42.

647 Boase, F. 'John Minter Morgan'. MEB, 1965 reprint, Vol. 2, Cols. 966–7.

648 Boase, G.C. 'John Minter Morgan'. DNB, 1967–8 reprint, Vol. 13, p.919.

W. Morris

649 Arnot, R.P. *Bernard Shaw and William Morris*. William Morris Society, 1957. 26pp.

650 Arnot, R.P. *Unpublished letters of William Morris*. Labour Monthly, 1951. 16pp.

651 Arnot, R.P. *William Morris: the man and the myth*. Lawrence and Wishart, 1964. 131pp.

652 Arnot, R.P. 'William Morris, Communist'. MQ, Oct. 1955, 2(4):237–45.

653 Boase, F. 'William Morris'. MEB, 1965 reprint, Vol. 6, Cols. 250–1.

654 Briggs, A., ed. *William Morris: selected writings and designs*. Penguin, 1962. 309pp.

655 Briggs, R.C.H. 'Morris and Trafalgar Square [i.e. 13 November 1887]'. WMS, Winter 1961, 1(1):28–31.

656 Bunge, M. 'On William Morris' socialism'. SAS, Fall 1956, 20(4):142–4.

657 Cole, G.D.H., ed. *William Morris: stories in prose; stories in verse; shorter poems; lectures and essays*. Nonsuch, 1934. xxiv, 671pp.

658 Cole, G.D.H. *William Morris as a socialist*. William Morris Society, 1960. 20pp.

659 Cole, M. 'The fellowship of William Morris'. VQR, Spring 1948, 24(2):260–77.

660 Cole, M. 'William Morris (1834–1896)', *Makers of the Labour movement*, pp.165–84 (*see* no.19). Longmans, 1948.

661 Dunlap, J.R. *William Caxton and William Morris; comparisons and contrasts*. William Morris Society, 1964. 30pp.

662 Evans, J.N. 'William Morris', *Great figures in the Labour movement*, pp.23–33. Pergamon, 1966.

663 Faulkner, P. 'Senghor and Morris: Socialists'. WMS, Summer 1970, 2(4):2–7.

664 Faulkner, P. 'William Morris and the two cultures'. WMS, Spring 1966, 2(1):9–12.

665 Faulkner, P. *William Morris and W.B. Yeats*. Dublin, Dolmen Press, 1962. 31pp.

666 Godwin, E. and S. *Warrior bard: the life of William Morris*. Harrap, 1947. 176pp.

667 Grennan, M.R. *William Morris: medievalist and revolutionary*. New York, Kings Crown Press, 1945. x, 173pp.

668 Grey, L.E., *pseud.* (Grennan, M.R.). *William Morris: prophet of England's new order*. Cassell, 1949. xiv, 386pp.

669 Henderson, P., ed. *The letters of William Morris to his family and his friends.* Longmans, 1950. lxvii, 406pp.

670 Henderson, P. *William Morris.* Longmans (for British Council and National Book League), 1963 (first pub. 1952). 46pp.

671 Henderson, P. *William Morris, his life, work and friends.* Thames and Hudson, 1967. xii, 388pp.

672 Hulse, J.W. 'William Morris: pilgrim of hope', *Revolutionaries in London: a study of five unorthodox socialists*, pp.77–110. Oxford, Clarendon Press, 1970.

673 Hutt, A. 'Morris, Marxism and typography'. LM, Oct. 1957, 39(10):467–8.

674 Jordan, R.F. *The medieval vision of William Morris.* William Morris Society, 1960. 31pp.

675 Lemire, E.D., ed. *The unpublished lectures of William Morris.* Detroit, Wayne State University Press, 1969. 331pp.

676 Lindsay, J. *William Morris, writer.* William Morris Society, 1961. 30pp.

677 London Borough of Waltham Forest. *Catalogue of the Morris Collection.* William Morris Gallery, 1969 (first pub. 1958). viii, 76pp.

678 Mackail, J.W. *The life of William Morris.* Introduction by Sir Sydney Cockerell. Cumberlege, 1950 (first pub. 1899). xxv, 767pp.

679 Mackail, J.W. 'William Morris'. DNB, 1967–8 reprint, Vol. 22, pp.1069–75.

680 Manchester Guardian. *Mr. William Morris on art matters.* William Morris Society, 1961. 8pp.
    Reprinted from Manchester Guardian, 21 October 1882.

681 Mansfield, B.E. 'The socialism of William Morris: England and Australia'. HS, Nov. 1956, 7(27):271–90.

682 Meynell, E. *Portrait of William Morris.* Chapman and Hall, 1947. x, 229pp.

683 Middlebro', T. 'Brief thoughts on "News from nowhere"'. WMS, Summer 1970, 2(4):8–12.

684 Morris, B. 'William Morris as designer'. LM, Feb. 1968, 50(2):75–7.
    Review of no.705.

685 Morris, M., comp. *William Morris; artist, writer, socialist.* 2 vols. Vol. 1, *The art of William Morris. Morris as a writer.* viii, 673pp. Vol. 2, *Morris as a socialist. Morris as I knew him, by Bernard Shaw.* xl, 661pp. New York, Russell and Russell, 1966 (first pub. 1936).

686 Morton, A.L. 'A scale model of the future', *Language of men*, pp.58–61. Lawrence and Wishart, 1945.

687 Morton, A.L. 'Utopias yesterday and today'. SAS, Summer 1953, 17(3):258–63.

688 Purkis, J. *The Icelandic jaunt: a study of the expedition made by Morris to Iceland in 1871 and 1873.* William Morris Society, 1962. 29pp.

689 Rothstein, A. 'The great pioneer'. LM, Mar. 1956, 38(3):133–9.
Review of no.702.

690 Rothstein, A. 'William Morris at Clerkenwell'. MML, Apr.–June 1966, 38:13–15.

691 Rothstein, A. 'William Morris belongs to the people', *Britain's cultural heritage*, pp.39–42. Arena, 1952.

692 Shaw, [G.] B. *Morris as I knew him.* Foreword by Stanley Morison. Introduction by Sir Basil Blackwell. William Morris Society, 1966. 42pp.

693 Shaw, [G.] B. 'William Morris', *Pen portraits and reviews,* pp.201–10. Constable, 1949 (first pub. 1931).

694 Shaw, [G.] B. 'William Morris as actor and playwright', *Pen portraits and reviews,* pp.210–17. Constable, 1949 (first pub. 1931).

695 Sotheby & Co. *The incomparable collection of Kelmscott (Press) formed by Sir Sydney Cockerell . . . together with his distinguished collections of the Ashendene Press and Doves Press with books by other esteemed printers.* Sotheby, 1956. 63pp.

696 Stokes, E.E., Jnr. 'Morris and Bernard Shaw'. WMS, Winter 1961, 1(1):13–18.

697 Stokes, E.E., Jnr. 'The Morris letters at Texas [i.e. University of Texas Library]'. WMS, Summer 1963, 1(3):23–30.

698 Swannell, J.N. *William Morris and Old Norse literature.* William Morris Society 1961. vi, 21pp.

699 Thompson, E.P. *The communism of William Morris.* William Morris Society, 1965. 19pp.

700 Thompson, E.P. 'The murder of William Morris'. ARE, April-May 1951, 2(7):9–28.

701 Thompson, E.P. 'William Morris and the moral issues today'. ARE, June-July 1951, 2(8):25–30.

702 Thompson, E.P. *William Morris: romantic to revolutionary.* Lawrence and Wishart, 1955. 908pp.

703 Thompson, P. *The work of William Morris.* Heinemann, 1967. xvi, 300pp.

704 Watkinson, R. 'William Morris and the Bauhaus'. LM, July 1967, 49(7):310–11.

705 Watkinson, R. *William Morris as designer.* Studio Vista, 1967. 84pp.+64pp. (illus.).

706 Wiles, H.V. *William Morris of Walthamstow.* Walthamstow Press, 1951. xvii, 115pp.

707 William Morris Society. *The work of William Morris: an exhibition arranged by the William Morris Society*. Times Bookshop for William Morris Society, 1962. 76pp.
 76 extensively annotated entries.

H. Morrison

708 Boardman, H. 'Morrison as Foreign Secretary', *The glory of Parliament*, pp.145–7. Allen and Unwin, 1960.

709 Burnett, H., ed. 'Herbert Morrison: television interview by John Freeman', *Face to face*, pp.86–9. Cape, 1964.

710 Edelman, M. *Herbert Morrison*. Lincolns-Praeger, 1948. 103pp.

711 Evans, J.N. 'Herbert Morrison', *Great figures in the Labour movement*, pp.133–49. Pergamon, 1966.

712 Knox, C. 'Herbert Morrison', *People of quality*, pp.35–54. Macdonald, 1947.

713 Morrison, Lord. *Herbert Morrison: an autobiography*. Odhams, 1960. 336pp.

714 Murphy, J.T. *Labour's big three: a biographical study of Clement Attlee, Herbert Morrison and Ernest Bevin*. Bodley Head, 1948. 266pp.

715 The Observer. 'Herbert Morrison', *A book of British profiles compiled from The Observer*, by S. Haffner, pp.84–7. Heinemann, 1954.

J. Mortimer

716 Mortimer, J. 'My father, my union'. TC, 1, 1968, 177(1036):38–41.

Sir O. Mosley

717 Benewick, R. *Political violence and public order: a study of British fascism*. Lane, 1969. 340pp.

718 Cross, C. *The fascists in Britain*. Barrie and Rockliff, 1961. 212pp.

719 Mandle, W.F. 'The leadership of the British Union of Fascists'. AJPH, Dec. 1966, 12(3):360–83.
 Role of Mosley discussed.

720 Mandle, W.F. 'The New Party'. HS, Oct. 1966, 12(47):343–55.

721 Mandle, W.F. 'Sir Oswald Mosley's resignation from the Labour government'. HS, May 1963, 10(40):493–510.

722 Mosley, Sir O. *My life*. Nelson, 1968. x, 521pp.

723 Skidelsky, R. 'Oswald Mosley', *European fascism*, pp.231–61. Edited by S.J. Woolf. Weidenfeld, 1968.
 'intellectual and political pilgrimage of Sir Oswald Mosley'—to 1932.

A.J. Mundella

724 Armytage, W.H.G. *A.J. Mundella, 1825—97: the Liberal background to the Labour movement*. Benn, 1951. 386pp.

725 Armytage, W.H.G. 'A.J. Mundella and the hosiery industry'. ECHR, 1948, 18(1 and 2):91–9.

726 Boase, F. 'Anthony John Mundella'. MEB, 1965 reprint, Vol. 6, Cols. 262–3.

727 Dictionary of National Biography. 'Anthony John Mundella'. DNB, 1967–8 reprint, Vol. 22, pp.1081–4.
    Author unknown to DNB.

J. Murdoch

728 Young, J.Y. 'John Murdoch: a Scottish land and Labour pioneer'. SSLH, Autumn 1969, 19:22–4.

Lord Nathan

729 Hyde, H.M. *Strong for service: the life of Lord Nathan of Churt*. Allen, 1968. xi, 280pp.

E.V. Neale

730 Boase, F. 'Edward Vansittart Neale'. MEB, 1965 reprint, Vol. 2, Cols. 1088–9.

731 Hewkins, W.A.S. 'Edward Vansittart Neale'. DNB, 1967–8 reprint, Vol. 14, pp.138–41.

E.D. Nesbit

732 Darton, F.J.H. 'Edith Nesbit'. DNB, 1922–30, 1967 reprint, p.84.

733 Moore, D.L. *Edith Nesbit*. Benn, 1967. 335pp.

H.W. Nevinson

734 Brailsford, H.N. 'Henry Woodd Nevinson'. DNB, 1941–50, 1967 reprint, pp.619–21.

W. Newton

735 Jefferys, J.B. and others. 'William Newton Born 1822–Died 1876'. Amalgamated Engineering Union, North London District, 1951. 9pp.

H. Nicolson

736 Harris, K. 'Sir Harold Nicolson, 1961', *Conversations*, pp.177–90. Hodder, 1967.

737 Hudson, D. 'Harold Nicolson'. QR, April 1967, 305(652):163–71.

738 Nicolson, H. *Diaries and letters*. Vol. 1, 1930–39, Collins, 1966, 448pp. Vol. 2, 1939–45, Collins, 1967, 511pp. Vol. 3, 1945–62, Collins, 1968, 448pp.

C. Noel

739 Ecclestone, A. 'Reg Groves: Conrad Noel'. SSLH, Spring 1968, 16:42–4. Review of no.740.

740 Groves, R. *Conrad Noel and the Thaxted movement: an adventure in Christian socialism*. Merlin, 1967. 334pp.

741 Noel, C. *An autobiography*. Edited by Sydney Dark. Dent, 1945. xi, 136pp.

742 Putterill, J. *Conrad Noel: prophet and priest 1869–1942*. 1962. 7pp. Broadcast in 'Men of vision' series—BBC Overseas Programme, 12 August 1962.

743 Woodifield, R. 'Conrad Noel, 1869–1942 Catholic Crusader', *For Christ and the people: studies of four socialist priests and prophets of the Church of England between 1870 and 1930, pp.135–79*. Edited by M.B. Reckitt. S.P.C.K., 1968.

Lord Noel-Buxton

744 Anderson, Mosa. 'Lord Edward Noel-Buxton'. DNB, 1941–50, 1967 reprint, pp.632–3.

745 Anderson, Mosa. *Noel Buxton: a life*. Allen and Unwin, 1952. 190pp.

R. Oastler

746 Boase, F. 'Richard Oastler'. MEB, 1965 reprint, Vol. 2, Cols. 1194–5.

747 Cole, G.D.H. 'Richard Oastler', *Chartist portraits,* pp.80–105 *(see* no.1411). Macmillan, 1965 (first pub. 1941).

748 Driver, C. *Tory radical: the life of Richard Oastler*. N.Y., OUP, 1946. ix, 597pp.

749 Hewkins, W.A.S. 'Richard Oastler'. DNB, 1967–8 reprint, Vol. 14, pp.738–40.

750 Porritt, A. 'Richard Oastler'. HAS, March 1965, 23–44.

751 Pringle, P. 'The factory king [i.e. Richard Oastler]', *Great ideas in social reform,* pp.109–22. Maxwell, 1968.

J.B. O'Brien

752 Boase, F. 'James O'Brien'. MEB, 1965 reprint, Vol. 2, Col. 1197.

753 Briggs, A. 'Fergus O'Connor and J. Bronterre O'Brien', *Leaders and workers,* pp.27–36 *(see* no.18). Edited by J.W. Boyle. Dublin, Mercier Press, 1966.

754 Cole, G.D.H. 'James Bronterre O'Brien', *Chartist portraits,* pp.239–67 *(see* no.1411). Macmillan, 1965 (first pub. 1941).

755 Wallas, G. 'James (Bronterre) O'Brien'. DNB, 1967–8 reprint, Vol. 14, pp.760–1.

N.C. O'Brien

756 Fox, R.M. 'Nora Connolly O'Brien', *Rebel Irishwomen*, pp.51–64. Dublin, Progress House, 1967.

F. O'Connor

757 Boase, F. 'Feargus O'Connor'. MEB, 1965 reprint, Vol. 2, Cols. 1206–8.

758 Briggs, A. 'Fergus O'Connor and J. Bronterre O'Brien', *Leaders and workers*, pp.27–36 (*see* no.18). Edited by J.W. Boyle. Dublin, Mercier Press, 1966.

759 Cole, G.D.H. 'Feargus O'Connor', *Chartist portraits*, pp.300–6 (*see* no.1411). Macmillan, 1965 (first pub. 1941).

760 Cole, M. 'Feargus O'Connor (1794–1855)', *Makers of the Labour movement*, (*see* no.19). Longmans, 1948.

761 Connolly Association. *'Lion of Freedom': life of Feargus O'Connor. 1855–1955. Centenary*. The Association, 1955. 12pp.

762 Read, D. 'Feargus O'Connor: Irishman and Chartist'. HT, March 1961, 11(3):165–74.

763 Read, D. and E. Glasgow. *Feargus O'Connor: Irishman and Chartist*. Arnold, 1961. 160pp.

764 Wallas, G. 'Feargus O'Connor'. DNB, 1967–8 reprint, Vol. 14, pp.845–7.

G. Odger

765 Armytage, W.H.G. 'George Odger (1820–97)'. UTQ, Oct. 1948, 18(1):68–75.

766 Boase, F. 'George Odger'. MEB, 1965 reprint, Vol. 2, Col. 1212.

767 Hewkins, W.A.S. 'George Odger'. DNB, 1967–8 reprint, Vol. 14, pp.865–6.

M. O'Flanagan

768 Greaves, D. *Father Michael O'Flanagan: republican priest*. Connolly Association, 1954. 20pp.

Lord Olivier

769 McLeary, G.F. 'Sydney Haldane Olivier'. DNB, 1941–50, 1967 reprint, pp.641–2.

770 Olivier, M., ed. Letters and selected writings (of Sydney Haldane Olivier). Edited with a memoir by Margaret Olivier. Allen and Unwin, 1948. 252pp.
    Some impressions, pp.9–20, by Bernard Shaw.

A.G. O'Neill

771 Boase, F. 'Arthur George O'Neill'. MEB, 1965 reprint, Vol. 6, Col. 326.

A.R. Orage

772 Grimsditch, H.B. 'Alfred Richard Orage'. DNB, 1931–40, 1970 reprint, p.659.

773 Mairet, P. *A.R. Orage: a memoir*. N.Y., University Press, 1966 (first pub. 1936). xxxvi, 140pp.

774 Martin, W. *The New Age under Orage: chapters in English cultural history*. Manchester, University Press, 1967. xiv, 303pp.
     Orage edited *The New Age,* 1907–22.

G. Orwell

775 Ashe, G. 'Second thoughts on "Nineteen eighty-four"'. M, Nov. 1950, N.S.4(5):285–300.

776 Brander, L. *George Orwell*. Longmans, 1954. vii, 212pp.

777 Braybrooke, N. 'George Orwell'. F, June 1951, 169(1014):403–9.

778 Dooley, D.J. 'The limitations of George Orwell'. UTQ, April 1959, 28(3):291–300.

779 Dunn, A. 'My brother—George Orwell'. TC, March 1961, 169(1009):255–61.

780 Fen, E. 'George Orwell's first wife'. TC, Aug. 1960, 168(1002):115–26.

781 Fyvel, T.R. 'A case for George Orwell?'. TC, Sept. 1956, 160(955):254–9.

782 Fyvel, T.R. 'George Orwell and Eric Blair: glimpses of a dual life'. EN, July 1959, 13(1):605.

783 Greenblatt, S.J. *Three modern satirists: Waugh, Orwell and Huxley*. New Haven, Yale UP, 1965. xi, 125pp.

784 Heppenstall, R. *Four absentees*. Barrie and Rockcliff, 1960. 206pp.
     Reminiscences of Eric Gill, George Orwell, Dylan Thomas, J. Middleton Murry.

785 Heppenstall, R. 'Orwell intermittent'. TC, May 1955, 157(939):470–83.

786 Heppenstall, R. 'The shooting stick'. TC, April 1955, 157(938):367–73.

787 Hollis, C. *A study of George Orwell: the man and his works*. Hollis and Carter, 1956. viii, 212pp.

788 Hopkinson, T. *George Orwell*. Longmans (for British Council and National Book League), 1969 (first pub. 1953). 33pp.

789 King, C. 'The politics of George Orwell'. UTQ, Oct. 1956, 26(1):79–91.

790 Lutman, S. 'Orwell's patriotism'. JCH, April 1967, 2(2):149–58.

791 Maddison, M. '1984: a Burnhamite fantasy'. PQ, Jan.–March 1961, 32(1):71–9.

792 Mander, J. 'George Orwell, one step forwards: two steps back', *The writer and commitment,* pp.71–110. Secker and Warburg, 1961.

793 Mander, J. 'George Orwell's politics: 1'. CNR, Jan. 1960, 197:32–6.

794 Mander, J. 'George Orwell's politics: 2'. CNR, Feb. 1960, 197:113–9.

795 Potts, P. 'Don Quixote on a bicycle', In memoriam. *Dante called you Beatrice,* pp.71–87. Eyre and Spottiswoode, 1960.
     George Orwell (1903–50) for Richard, his son.

796 Ranald, R.A. 'George Orwell and the mad world: the Anti-Universe of 1984'. SAQ, Autumn 1967, 66(4):544–53.

797 Rees, R. *George Orwell: fugitive from the camp of victory.* Secker and Warburg, 1961. 160pp.

798 Siepman, E.D. 'Farewell to Orwell'. TC, March 1950, 147(877):141–7.

799 Smith, W.D. 'George Orwell'. CNR, May 1956, 189:283–6.

800 Strachey, J. 'England', *The strangled cry and other unparliamentary papers,* pp.23–32. Bodley Head, 1962.

801 Thirlby, P. 'Orwell as a Liberal'. MQ, Oct. 1956, 3(4):239–47.

802 Thomas, E.M. *Orwell.* Edinburgh, Oliver and Boyd, 1965. viii, 114pp.

803 Voorhees, R.J. 'George Orwell, rebellion and responsibility'. SAQ, Oct. 1954, 53(4):556–65.

804 Voorhees, R.J. *The paradox of George Orwell.* Lafayette, Ind., Purdue University, 1961. 127pp.

805 Wain, J. 'The last of George Orwell'. TC, Jan. 1954, 155(923):71–8.

806 Walsh, J. 'George Orwell'. MQ, Jan. 1956, 3(1):25–39.

807 Willison, I. 'Orwell's bad good books'. TC, April 1955, 157(938):354–366.

R. Owen

808 Boase, F. 'Robert Owen'. MEB, 1965 reprint, Vol 2, Cols. 1291–2.

809 Briggs, A. 'Robert Owen in retrospect', *Co-operative College Papers No.6,* pp.3–16. Loughborough, Co-operative Union, 1959.

810 Chaloner, W.H. 'Robert Owen, Peter Drinkwater and the early factory system in Manchester'. JRL., Sept. 1954, 37(1):78–102.

811 Cole, G.D.H. *The life of Robert Owen.* Cass, 1965 (first pub. 1925). xxii, 350pp.

812 Cole, G.D.H. 'Robert Owen and Owenism', *Persons and periods: studies,* pp.158–73. Penguin, 1945 (first pub. 1938).

813 Cole, M. 'Robert Owen (1771–1858)', *Makers of the Labour movement*, pp.62–85 (no.19). Longmans, 1948.

814 Cole, M. *Robert Owen of New Lanark*. Batchworth, 1953. vii, 231pp.

815 Davies, Sir A.T. *Robert Owen (1771–1858). Pioneer social reformer and philanthropist*. C.W.S., 1948. 84pp.

816 Derry, J.W. 'Robert Owen: a radical in business', *The radical tradition: Tom Paine to Lloyd George*, pp.119–54. Macmillan, 1967.

817 Evans, J.N. 'Robert Owen', *Great figures in the Labour movement*, pp.7–22. Pergamon, 1966.

818 Fagan, H. 'Robert Owen and his vision of the future: 1771–1858', *The unsheathed sword: episodes in English history. Part 2, Champions of the workers*, pp.7–23. Lawrence and Wishart, 1959. (*See* no.1188).

819 Feuer, L.S. 'The influence of the American communist colonies on Marx and Engels'. WPQ, Sept. 1966, 19(3):456–74.

820 Gorb, R. 'Robert Owen as a business man'. BHR, Sept. 1951, 25(3):127–48.

821 Grant, A.C. 'New light on an old view (Combe's phrenology and Robert Owen)'. JHI, April–June 1968, 29(2):293–301.

822 Harrison, J.F.C. *Robert Owen and the Owenites in Britain and America: the quest for the New Moral World*. Routledge, 1969. xi, 392pp.

823 Harvey, R.H. *Robert Owen: social idealist*. Berkeley, University of California, 1949. vii, 269pp.

824 Johnson, O.C. *Robert Owen in the United States*. New York, Humanities Press, 1970. xiv, 86pp.
      Reprints two Owen speeches, before the U.S. Congress (1825) and at Harmony Hall (1826).

825 Marx Memorial Library. 'Robert Owen'. MML, Oct.–Dec. 1958, 8:2–8.

826 Miliband, R. 'The politics of Robert Owen'. JHI, April 1954, 15(2):223–45.

827 Morton, A.L. *The life and ideas of Robert Owen*. Lawrence and Wishart, 1969. 240pp.

828 Murphy, J. 'Robert Owen in Liverpool'. HSLC, 1961, 112:79–103.

829 Oliver, W.H. 'Robert Owen and the English working-class movements'. HT, Nov. 1958, 8(11):787–96.

830 Pike, E.R. 'The master of New Lanark: Robert Owen: man of big business, socialist, co-operator, and educationalist', *Pioneers of social change*, pp.118–36. Barrie and Rockcliff, 1963.

831 Robertson, A. 'Robert Owen'. LM, Nov. 1958, 40(11):521–5.

832 Robertson, A.J. 'Robert Owen and the Campbell debt, 1810–22'. BH, Jan. 1969, 11(1):23–30.

833 Stephen, L. 'Robert Owen'. DNB, 1967–8 reprint, Vol. 14, pp.1338–46.

834 Tawney, R.H. 'Robert Owen', *The radical tradition: twelve essays on politics, education and literature,* pp.32–9. Allen and Unwin, 1964.

T. Paine

835 Cole, M. 'Tom Paine (1737–1809)', *Makers of the Labour movement,* pp.6–22 (*see* no.19). Longmans, 1948.

836 Derry, J.W. 'Tom Paine: an international radical', *The radical tradition: from Tom Paine to Lloyd George,* pp.1–45. Macmillan, 1967.

837 Hobsbawm, E.J. 'Thomas Paine', *Labouring men: studies in the history of Labour,* pp.1–4 (*see* no.1191). Weidenfeld, 1968.

838 Jackson, T.A. 'Thomas Paine and the Rights of Man', *Trials of British freedom: being some studies in the history of the fight for democratic freedom in Britain,* pp.25–36 (*see* no.1193). Lawrence and Wishart, 1945.

F. Pakenham (Lord Longford)

839 Pakenham, F. *Born to believe: an autobiography.* Cape, 1953. 245pp.

840 Pakenham, F. *Five lives.* Hutchinson, 1964. 280pp.

S. Pankhurst

841 Kamm, J. *Rapiers and battleaxes: the women's movement and its aftermath.* Allen and Unwin, 1966. 240pp.

842 Mitchell, D. *The fighting Pankhursts.* Cape, 1967. 352pp.

W. Pare

843 Boase, F. 'William Pare'. MEB, 1965 reprint, Vol. 2, Col. 1334.

844 Hewkins, W.A.S. 'William Pare'. DNB, 1967–8 reprint, Vol. 15, pp.203–4.

J.H. Parry

845 Boase, F. 'John Humffreys Parry'. MEB, 1965 reprint, Vol. 2, Col. 1364.

846 Hamilton, J.A. 'John Humffreys Parry'. DNB, 1967–8 reprint, Vol. 15, p.378.

D.J.F. Parsons

847 A., P. 'D.J.F. Parsons, 1900–1965'. LM, June 1965, 47(6):257.

L. Paul

848 Paul, L. *Angry young man.* Faber, 1951. 302pp.

W. Paul

849 Marx Memorial Library. 'William Paul: a life for socialism'. MML, April–June 1958, 6:2–3.

A. Peacock

850 Peacock, A. *Yours fraternally*. Pendulum, 1945. 126pp.

J.M. Peacock

851 Boase, F. 'John Macleay Peacock'. MEB, 1965 reprint, Vol. 2, Col. 1413.

852 Lewin, W. 'John Macleay Peacock'. DNB, 1967–8 reprint, Vol. 15, pp.587–8.

K. Pearson

853 Semmel, B. 'Karl Pearson: socialist and Darwinist'. BJS, June 1958, 9(2):111–25.

D. Penderyn

854 Webb, H. *Dic Penderyn and the Merthyr rising of 1831*. Swansea, Gwasg Penderyn, 1956. 16pp.

855 Williams, G.A. 'The Merthyr of Dic Penderyn', *Merthyr politics: the making of a working-class tradition*, pp.9–27. Edited by G. Williams. Cardiff, University of Wales Press, 1966.

T. Perronet Thompson

856 Johnson, L.G. *General T. Perronet Thompson 1783–1869: his military, literary and political campaigns*. Allen and Unwin, 1957. 294pp.

F. Pethick-Lawrence

857 Brittain, V. *Pethick-Lawrence: a portrait*. Allen and Unwin, 1963. 232pp.

858 Gooch, G.P. 'Vera Brittain on Pethick-Lawrence'. CNR, Aug. 1963, 204:72–5.
    Review of no.857.

R.K. Philp

859 Boase, F. 'Robert Kemp Philp'. MEB, 1965 reprint, Vol. 2, Col. 1517.

860 Fell-Smith, C. 'Robert Kemp Philp'. DNB, 1967–8 reprint, Vol. 15, pp.1111–12.

B. Pickard

861 MacDonald, J.R. 'Benjamin Pickard'. DNB, 1901–11, 1969 reprint, pp.117–18.

A. Pinkerton

862 Boase, F. 'Allan Pinkerton'. MEB, 1965 reprint, Vol. 2, Col. 1541.

P. Piratin

863 Piratin, P. *Our flag stays red*. Thames Publications, 1948. xii, 91pp.

F. Place

864 Boase, F. 'Francis Place'. MEB, 1965 reprint, Vol. 2, Col. 1552.

865 Cole, M. 'Francis Place (1771–1854)', *Makers of the Labour movement*, pp.40–61 (*see* no.19). Longmans, 1948.

866 Harrison, B. 'Two roads to social reform: Francis Place and the "Drunken Committee" of 1834'. HJ, 1968, 11(2):272–300.

867 Pike, E.R. 'The radical tailor of Charing Cross: Francis Place and the "Diabolical propaganda of Birth Control"', *Pioneers of social change*, pp.74–88. Barrie and Rockcliff, 1963.

868 Thomas, W.E.S. 'Francis Place and working class history'. HJ, 1962, 5(1):61–70.

869 Wallas, G. 'Francis Place'. DNB, 1967–8 reprint, Vol. 15, pp.1276–9.

870 Wallas, G. *The life of Francis Place*. Allen and Unwin, 1951 (first pub. 1898). xiv, 415pp.

H.C. Plunkett

871 Adams, W.G.S. 'Sir Horace Curzon Plunkett'. DNB, 1931–40, 1970 reprint, pp.706–8.

872 Digby, M. *Horace Plunkett: an Anglo-American Irishman*. Oxford, Blackwell, 1949. xvi, 314pp.

F. Podmore

873 Hooper, E.S. 'Frank Podmore'. DNB, 1901–11, 1969 reprint, pp.121–2.

H. Pollitt

874 Communist Party. *Greetings to Harry Pollitt . . . on his sixtieth birthday*. The Party, 1951. 22pp.

875 Communist Party. *Harry Pollitt: a tribute, July 9th 1960*. The Party, 1960. 31pp.
    Speeches at the funeral, July 9th 1960.

876 Dutt, R.P. 'Harry Pollitt Born 22nd November 1890 Died 26 June 1960'. LM, Aug. 1960, 42(8):357–62.

877 Pollitt, H. *Selected speeches and articles*. Vol. 1, *1919–36*. 1953. 180pp. Vol. 2, *1936–39*. 1954. 144pp. Lawrence and Wishart.

878 Pollitt, H. *Serving my time: an apprenticeship to politics*. Lawrence and Wishart, 1961 (first pub. 1940). 292pp.

A.A.W.H. Ponsonby

879 Gore, J. 'Arthur Augustus William Hardy Ponsonby, 1871–1946'. DNB, 1941–50, 1967 reprint, pp. 683–5.

D. Postgate

880 Postgate, D. 'A child in George Lansbury's house'. 1. F, Nov. 1948, 164(983):315–22.

881 Postgate, D. 'A child in George Lansbury's house'. 2. F, Dec. 1948, 164(984):390–4.

G. Potter

882 Boase, F. 'George Potter'. MEB, 1965 reprint, Vol. 2, Cols. 1601–2.

883 Boase, G.C. 'George Potter'. DNB, 1967–8 reprint, Vol. 16, pp.215–16.

884 Coltham, S. 'George Potter, the Junta and The Beehive'. IRSH, 1964, 9(3):391–432.

885 Coltham, S. 'George Potter, the Junta and The Beehive'. IRSH, 1965, 10(1):23–65.

H. Pratt

886 Owen, W.B. 'Hodgson Pratt'. DNB, 1901–11, 1969 reprint, pp.132–3.

M.P. Price

887 Price, M.P. *My three revolutions*. Allen and Unwin, 1969. 310pp.

W. Price

888 Boase, F. 'William Price'. MEB, 1965 reprint, Vol. 2, Cols. 1639–40.

D.N. Pritt

889 Arnot, R.P. 'From right to left'. LM, Feb. 1966, 48(2):89–92.
   Review of no.893, Pt. 1, *From right to left*.

890 Jagan, J. 'D.N. Pritt: defender of civil liberties'. LM, May 1967, 49(5):228–30.
   Review of no.893, Pt. 3, *The defence accuses*.

891 Labour Monthly. 'D.N. Pritt: a tribute from the Editorial Board'. LM, Sept. 1967, 49(9):397–8.

892 Montagu, I. [Review]. LM, June 1966, 48(6):286–7.
   Review of no.893, Pt. 2, *Brasshats and Bureaucrats*.

893 Pritt, D.N. *Autobiography*. Pt. 1, *From right to left*. *1887–1941*. 1961. 319pp.

Pt. 2, *Brasshats and bureaucrats. 1941–1950*. 1966. 320pp. Pt. 3, *The defence accuses. 1950–*. 1966. 228pp. Lawrence and Wishart.

A.A.W. Purcell

894 Middleton, J.S. 'Albert Arthur William Purcell'. DNB, 1931–40, 1970 reprint, pp.722–3.

H. Quelch

895 Lenin, V.I. 'Harry Quelch'. LM, Sept. 1953, 35(9):424–6.

896 Rothstein, A. 'Harry Quelch'. MML, July–Sept. 1963, 27:4–6.

H.R.P. Rathbone

897 Arnot, R.P. 'H.P.R. Rathbone (January 1895–October 1969)'. LM, Nov. 1969, 51(11):514.

P. Redfern

898 Redfern, P. *Journey to understanding*. Allen and Unwin, 1946. 219pp.
   Secularist, Labour Church, Christian Socialist.

G.W. MacA. Reynolds

899 Boase, F. 'George William MacArthur Reynolds'. MEB, 1965 reprint, Vol. 3, Cols. 121–2.

900 MacDonald, J.R. 'George William MacArthur Reynolds'. DNB, 1967–8 reprint, Vol. 16, pp.929–31.

R. Reynolds

901 Reynolds, R. *My life and crimes*. Jarrolds, 1956. 260pp.

B. Roberts

902 Craik, W.W. *Bryn Roberts and the National Union of Public Employees*. Allen and Unwin, 1955. 238pp.
   Pub. to mark his period as General Secretary, 1934–55.

H. Roberts

903 Stamp, W. *'Doctor himself': an unorthodox biography of Harry Roberts 1871–1946*. Hamilton, 1949. xi, 163pp.

W.P. Roberts

904 Boase, F. 'William Prowting Roberts'. MEB, 1965 reprint, Vol. 3, Cols. 202–3.

905 Sutton, C.W. 'William Prowting Roberts'. DNB, 1967–8 reprint, Vol. 16, p.1284.

J. Robinson

906 Peacock, A. (J.) 'Joseph Robinson'. SSLH, Autumn 1962, 5:36–8.

R. Rocker

907 Fishman, W.J. 'Rudolf Rocker: an Anarchist missionary 1873–1958'. HT, Jan. 1966, 16(1):45–52.

908 Rocker, R. *The London years.* Anscome, 1956. 360pp.
    Book ends with author's deportation from England in the Great War.

J. Rogers

909 Boase, F. 'John Rogers'. MEB, 1965 reprint, Vol. 3, Col. 260.

E. Romilly

910 Toynbee, P. *Friends apart: a memoir of Esmond Romilly and Jasper Ridley in the thirties.* MacGibbon and Kee, 1954. 189pp.

A. Rothstein

911 Labour Monthly. 'Tribute to Andrew Rothstein (70th birthday)'. LM, Sept. 1968, 50(9):428.

T. Rothstein

912 Hannaford, N. 'A pioneer Marxist historian'. LM, Oct. 1960, 42(10):478–9.

913 Labour Monthly. 'Theodore Rothstein'. LM, Oct. 1953, 35(10):462.

B. Russell

914 Burnett, H., ed. 'Bertrand Russell: television interview by John Freeman', *Face to face*, pp.6–11. Cape, 1964.

915 Buttle, M., *pseud. The bitches' brew or the plot against Bertrand Russell.* Watts, 1960. vi, 87pp.

916 Dutt, R.P. 'Bertrand Russell 1872–1970'. LM, Mar. 1970, 52(3):97–110.

917 Gottschalk, H. *Bertrand Russell: a life.* Baker, 1965. 128pp.

918 Hardy, G.H. *Bertrand Russell and Trinity.* CUP, 1970. xiii, 61pp.
    Facsimile of pamphlet issued in 1942 for private circulation.

919 Russell, B. *Autobiography.* Vol. 1, 1872–1914. 1967. 230pp. Vol. 2, 1914–1944. 1968. 268pp. Vol. 3, 1944–1967. 1969. 232pp. Allen and Unwin.

920 Wood, A. *Bertrand Russell: the passionate sceptic.* Allen and Unwin, 1957. 249pp.

W. Rust

921 Labour Monthly. 'William Rust 24 April 1903–3 February 1949'. LM, Mar. 1949, 31(3):91.

J.H. Rutherford

922 Boase, F. 'John Hunter Rutherford'. MEB, 1965 reprint, Vol. 3, Col. 356.

J. Sage

923 Sage, J. *The memoirs of Josiah Sage concerning Joseph Arch and the pioneering days of trade unionism among the agricultural workers.* Lawrence and Wishart, 1951. 63pp.

S. Saklatvala

924 Middleton, J.S. 'Shaphurji Saklatvala'. DNB, 1931–40, 1970 reprint, pp.777–8.

925 Sana, P. *Shapurji Saklatvala 1874–1936.* New Delhi, People's Publishing House (P) Ltd., 1970. x, 104pp.

H.S. Salt

926 Winsten, S. *Salt and his circle.* Hutchinson, 1951. 224pp.

A. Salter

927 Brockway, F. *Bermondsey story: the life of Alfred Salter.* Allen and Unwin, 1951. xi, 246pp.

H. Scanlon

928 New Left Review. 'The role of militancy: interview with Hugh Scanlon'. NLR, Nov.–Dec. 1967, 46:3–15.

J. Scholefield

929 Boase, F. 'James Scholefield'. MEB, 1965 reprint, Vol. 3, Col. 439.

B. Selkirk

930 Selkirk, B. *The life of a worker.* Dundee, Dundee Printers, 1967. 47pp.

Sir J. Sexton

931 Middleton, J.S. 'Sir James Sexton'. DNB, 1931–40, 1970 reprint, pp.802–3.

Sir D.J. Shackleton

932 Wilson, H. 'Sir David James Shackleton'. DNB, 1931–40, 1970 reprint, pp.804–5.

G.B. Shaw

933 Arnot, R.P. *Bernard Shaw and William Morris*. William Morris Society, 1957. 26pp.

934 Baylen, J.O. 'George Bernard Shaw and the Socialist League. Some unpublished letters'. IRSH, 1962, 7(3):426–40.

935 Bissell, C.T. 'The novels of George Bernard Shaw'. UTQ, Oct. 1947, 17(1):38–51.
   The socialist content of his five novels.

936 Brome, V. 'Shaw versus Wells', *Six studies in quarrelling*, pp.1–39. Cresset, 1958.

937 Cauldwell, C. 'George Bernard Shaw: a study of the bourgeois superman', *Studies in a dying culture*, pp. 1–19. Bodley Head, 1957 (first pub. 1938).

938 Chappelow, A. *Shaw "The Chucker-Out"*. Allen and Unwin, 1969. xx, 558pp.

939 Cherry, D.R. 'The Fabianism of Shaw'. QQ, Spring 1962, 69(1):83–93.

940 Dalton, H. 'Shaw as economist and politician', *Shaw and society*, pp.250–62 (*see* no.947). Edited by C.E.M. Joad. Odhams, 1953.

941 Dutt, R.P. *George Bernard Shaw: a memoir*. Labour Monthly, 1951. i, 30pp.

942 Ervine, St. John. 'George Bernard Shaw'. DNB, 1941–50, 1967 reprint, pp.773–82.

943 Hobsbawm, E.J. 'Bernard Shaw's socialism'. SAS, Fall 1947, 11(4):305–26.

944 Hulse, J.W. 'Shaw: socialist maverick' and 'Shaw: beyond socialism', *Revolutionaries in London: a study of five unorthodox socialists*, pp.111–37 and 192–228. Oxford, Clarendon Press, 1970.

945 Irvine, W. 'George Bernard Shaw and Karl Marx'. JEH, May 1946, 6(1):53–72.

946 Irvine, W. 'Shaw, war and peace, 1894 to 1919'. FA, Jan. 1947, 25(2):314–27.

947 Joad, C.E.M., ed. *Shaw and society*. Odhams, 1953. 279pp.
   See nos.940, 948, 950, 951, 955, 961, 2457.

948 Joad, C.E.M. 'Shaw the philosopher', *Shaw and society*, pp.233–49 (*see* no.947). Odhams, 1953.

949 Kaye, J.B. *Bernard Shaw and the nineteenth-century tradition*. Norman, University of Oklahoma Press, 1955. xv, 222pp.
   Particularly Chap. VIII: Radical and socialist artists, pp.153–77.

950 Levy, B. 'Shaw the dramatist', *Shaw and society*, pp.263–79 (*see* no.947). Edited by C.E.M. Joad. Odhams, 1953.

951 Martin, K. 'GBS', *Shaw and society*, pp.23–38 *(see* no.947). Edited by C.E.M. Joad. Odhams, 1953.

952 Minney, R.J. *The bogus image of Bernard Shaw*. Frewin, 1969. 223pp.

953 Parker, R.B. 'Bernard Shaw and Sean O'Casey'. QQ, Spring, 1966, 71(1):13–34.

954 Pearson, H. *Bernard Shaw: his life and personality*. Methuen, 1961 (first pub. 1942). 480pp.

955 Ratcliffe, S.K. 'Shaw as a young socialist', *Shaw and society*, pp.54–65 *(see* no.947). Edited by C.E.M. Joad. Odhams, 1953.

956 Robson, W.A. 'Bernard Shaw and the Political Quarterly'. PQ, July–Sept. 1951, 22(3):221–39.

957 Sadleir, M. 'George Bernard Shaw'. TC, Aug. 1946, 140(834):61–6.

958 Smith, J.P. *Unrepentant pilgrim: a study of the development of Bernard Shaw*. Gollancz, 1966. xii, 274pp.

959 Stokes, E.E., Jnr. *Morris and Bernard Shaw*. WMS, Winter 1961, 1(1):13–18.

960 West, A. *'A good man fallen among Fabians'*. Lawrence and Wishart, 1950. vii, 172pp.
  Studies 'the conflict between Shaw's dramatic vision and his Fabianism'.

961 Woolf, L. 'The early Fabians and British socialism', *Shaw and society*, pp.39–53 *(see* no.947). Edited by C.E.M. Joad. Odhams, 1953.

T. Shaw

962 Middleton, J.S. 'Thomas (Tom) Shaw'. DNB, 1931–40, 1970 reprint, pp.808–9.

Lord (H.) Shawcross

963 Burnett, H., ed. 'Lord Shawcross: television interview by John Freeman', *Face to face*, pp.42–3. Cape, 1964.

Lord Shinwell

964 Gallacher, W. 'Bloodless'. LM, Jan. 1956, 38(1):41–4.
  Review of no.965.

965 Shinwell, E. *Conflict without malice*. Odhams, 1955. 252pp.

966 The Word. *The truth about Shinwell*. Glasgow, Strickland Press, 1951. 16pp.

S. Silverman

967 Hughes, E. *Sydney Silverman, rebel in Parliament*. Skilton, 1969. xi, 236pp.

Lord (E.) Simon

968 Beales, H.L. 'Three octogenarians'. PQ, Jan.–Mar. 1961, 32(1):62–70.
E. Simon, R.H. Tawney, L. Woolf.

969 Stocks, M. *Ernest Simon of Manchester*. Manchester, University Press, 1963.
viii, 181pp.

M. Slater

970 Labour Monthly. 'Montagu Slater, 1902–1956'. LM, Feb. 1957, 39(2):64.

R. Smillie

971 Hamilton, M.A. 'Robert Smillie'. DNB, 1931–40, 1970 reprint, pp.813–5.

972 Johnston, T. 'Robert Smillie', *Memories*, pp.236–8 (*see* no.454). Collins,
1952.

H. Smith

973 Middleton, J.S. 'Herbert Smith'. DNB, 1931–40, 1970 reprint, pp.817–8.

J.E. Smith

974 Boase, F. 'James Elimalet Smith'. MEB, 1965 reprint, Vol. 3, Col. 634.

975 Laughton, J.K. 'James Elimalet Smith'. DNB, 1967–8 reprint, Vol. 18,
pp.472–3.

T.D. Smith

976 Smith, T.D. *An autobiography*. Newcastle, Oriel, 1970. 151pp.

Lord Snell

977 Grimsditch, H.B. 'Henry Snell'. DNB, 1941–50, 1967 reprint, pp.806–7.

Viscount Snowden

978 Cross, Colin. *Philip Snowden*. Barrie and Rockcliff, 1966, xii, 356pp.

979 Ensor, R.C.K. 'Philip Snowden'. DNB, 1931–40, 1970 reprint, pp.822–5.

Viscount Southwood

980 Crossman, R.H.S. 'The press Lord of Long Acre', *The charm of politics and
other essays in political criticism*, pp.233–8. Hamilton, 1958.
Review of no.982.

981 Grimsditch, H.B. 'Viscount Southwood'. DNB, 1941–50, 1967 reprint,
pp.233–4.

982 Minney, R.J. *Viscount Southwood*. Odhams, 1954. 384pp.

T. Spence

983 Brunel, C. 'The radical philosopher of Holborn'. MML, July–Sept. 1964, 31:8–10.

S. Spender

984 Maxwell, D.E.S. 'Louis MacNeice and Stephen Spender: sense and sensibility', *Poets of the thirties*, pp.186–201. Routledge, 1959.

985 Spender, S. *World within world; the autobiography of Stephen Spender*. Hamilton, 1951. ix, 349pp.

J.R. Stephens

986 Boase, F. 'Joseph Rayner Stephens'. MEB, 1965 reprint, Vol. 3, Col. 732.

987 Cole, G.D.H. 'Joseph Rayner Stephens', *Chartist portraits*, pp.63–79 (*see* no.1411). Macmillan, 1965 (first pub. 1941).

988 Edwards, M.S. *Joseph Rayner Stephens 1805–1879*. Manchester, Wesley Historical Society (Lancashire and Cheshire Branch), 1968. ii, 20pp.

989 Gordon, A. 'Joseph Rayner Stephens'. DNB, 1967–8 reprint, Vol. 18, pp.1065–6.

990 Ward, J.T. 'Revolutionary Tory: the life of Joseph Rayner Stephens of Ashton-under-Lyne (1805–79)'. LCAS, 1958, 68:93–116.

T.P. Stevens

991 Stevens, Thomas P. *Cassock and surplus: incidents in clerical life mainly in London*. Laurie, 1947. 183pp.
    Hon. Canon of Southwark where he was a Labour Councillor.

W.C. Stevens

992 Labour Monthly. 'Walter Stevens 26 September 1904–24 October 1954'. LM, Dec. 1954, 36(12):564.

R. Stewart

993 Stewart, R. *Breaking the fetters: the memoirs of Bob Stewart*. Lawrence and Wishart, 1967. 200pp.
    Memoirs end at 1931. Final chapter is a series of reminiscences.

M. Stocks

994 Stocks, M. *My commonplace book*. Davies, 1970. ix, 246pp.

J. Strachey

995 Crossman, R.H.S. 'John Strachey and the Left Book Club', *The charm of politics and other essays in political criticism*, pp.139–43. Hamilton, 1958.

996 Galbraith, J.K. 'John Strachey'. EN, Sept. 1963, 21(3):53–4.

J. Sturge

997 Boase, F. 'Joseph Sturge'. MEB, 1965 reprint, Vol. 3, Col. 816.

998 Cole, G.D.H. 'Joseph Sturge', *Chartist portraits*, pp.163–86 (*see* no.1411). Macmillan, 1965 (first pub. 1941).

999 Fell-Smith, C. 'Joseph Sturge'. DNB, 1967–8 reprint, Vol. 19, Cols. 130–1.

E. Summerskill

1000 E. Summerskill. *A woman's world*. Heinemann, 1967. 258pp.

R.H. Tawney

1001 Ashton, T.S. 'Richard Henry Tawney (1880–1962)'. BA, 1962, XLVIII:461–82.

1002 Beales, H.L. 'Three octogenarians'. PQ, Jan.–March 1961, 32(1):62–70. E. Simon, R.H. Tawney, L. Woolf.

1003 Briggs, A. 'R.H. Tawney'. SSLH, Spring 1962, 4:3.

1004 Court, W.H.B. 'R.H. Tawney', *Scarcity and choice in history*, pp.127–40. Arnold, 1970.

1005 Gaitskell, H. 'Postscript: an appreciation' [of R.H. Tawney], *The radical tradition: twelve essays on politics, education and literature*, pp.211–14. Edited by Rita Hinden. Allen and Unwin, 1964.

1006 Jones, A.C., ed. *A portrait by several hands*. Shenval Press, ?1960. 33pp.

1007 Knight, F.H. 'Professor Tawney: essayist and Christian socialist'. JPE, Oct. 1953, 61(5):406–12.

1008 Nelson, W.H. 'R.H. Tawney', *Some modern historians of Britain, essays in honor of R.L. Schuyler*, pp.325–40. Edited by Herman Ausubel, J. Bartlet Brebner and E.M. Hunt. New York, Dryden Press, 1951.

1009 Stone, L. 'R.H. Tawney'. PP, April 1962, 21:73–7.

1010 Toynbee, A. 'The Tawneys', *Acquaintances*, pp.86–94. OUP, 1967.

1011 Winter, J.M. 'R.H. Tawney's early political thought'. PP, May 1970, 47:71–96.

W. Temple (Archbishop of Canterbury)

1012 Davies, D.R. 'William Temple: a critical appreciation'. TC, Nov. 1948, 144(861):293–8.

1013 Iremonger, F.A. 'William Temple'. DNB, 1941–50, 1967 reprint, pp.869–73.

1014 Iremonger, F.A. *William Temple, Archbishop of Canterbury: his life and letters*. OUP, 1948. xvi, 663pp.

J. Thelwall

1015 Secombe, T. 'John Thelwall'. DNB, 1967–8 reprint, Vol. 19, pp.590–3.

J.H. Thomas

1016 Blaxland, G. *J.H. Thomas: a life for unity*. Muller, 1964. 303pp.

1017 Ensor, R.C.K. 'James Henry Thomas'. DNB, 1941–50, 1967 reprint, pp.875–7.

W. Thompson

1018 Lynch, P. 'William Thompson and the socialist tradition', *Leaders and workers*, pp.9–16 (*see* no.18). Edited by J.W. Boyle. Dublin, Mercier Press, 1966.

1019 Pankhurst, R.K.P. *William Thompson (1775–1833), Britain's pioneer socialist, feminist and co-operator*. Watts, 1954. xi, 228pp.

W.H. Thompson

1020 Arnot, R.P. 'W.H. Thompson'. LM, Sept. 1947, 29(9):284.
(*see* no.90).

W.M. Thompson

1021 Owen, W.B. 'William Marcus Thompson'. DNB, 1901–11, 1969 reprint, pp.506–7.

W. Thorne

1022 Cole, G.D.H. 'William (Will) James Thorne'. DNB, 1941–50, 1967 reprint, pp.882–4.

1023 Stafford, A. 'Will Thorne', *A match to fire the Thames*, pp.51–2. Hodder, 1961.

1024 Van Den Bergh, T. 'Will Thorne', *The trade unions—what are they?*, pp.58–74. Pergamon, 1970.

E. Thurtle

1025 Thurtle, E. *Time's winged chariot: memories and comments*. Chaterson, 1945. xii, 190pp.

B. Tillett

1026 Fulford, R. 'Ben Tillett'. CNR, Sept. 1960, 198:473–5.

1027 Light, G. *Ben Tillett, the grand old man of British Labour: a personal tribute*. Blandford, Press, ?1945. 16pp.

1028 Stafford, A. 'Ben Tillett', *A match to fire the Thames*, pp.48–50. Hodder, 1961.

1029 Taylor, J.J. 'Benjamin (Ben) Tillett'. DNB, 1941–50, 1967 reprint, pp.884–6.

1030 Van Den Bergh, T. 'Ben Tillett', *The trade unions—what are they?*, pp.43–57. Pergamon, 1970.

G. Tomlinson

1031 Blackburn, F. *George Tomlinson*. Foreword by C.R. Attlee. Heinemann, 1954. xi, 210pp.

J.H. Tooke

1032 Stephen, L. 'John Horne Tooke'. DNB, 1967–8 reprint, Vol. 19, pp.967–974.

J. Toole

1033 Toole, M. *Our old man: a biographical portrait of Joseph Toole by his daughter.* Dent, 1948. 208pp.
    Toole was Lord Mayor of Manchester 1936–7 and Labour M.P.

D. Torr

1034 Hutt, A. 'Dona Torr'. LM, Mar. 1957, 39(3):132–4.

P. Toynbee

1035 Toynbee, P. 'A voice from the thirties'. TC, Dec. 1960, 168(1006):503–8.

R. Tressell

1036 Ball, F.C. *Tressell of Mugsborough.* Lawrence and Wishart, 1951. 224pp.

1037 Mitchell, J. *Robert Tressell and the ragged trousered philanthropists.* Lawrence and Wishart, 1969. xiv, 200pp.
    First full-length appraisal of the novel.

Sir B. Turner

1038 Middleton, J.S. 'Sir Ben Turner'. DNB, 1941–50, 1967 reprint, pp.891–2.

F. Utley

1039 Utley, F. *Lost illusion.* Allen and Unwin, 1949. ix, 237pp.

J. Vaughan

1040 Grant, B. *The story of Joe Vaughan, first Labour mayor of Bethnal Green.* Communist Party, East London Area Committee, 1954. ii, 27pp.
    Period 1907–27.

H. Vincent

1041 Boase, F. 'Henry Vincent'. MEB, 1965 reprint, Vol. 3, Cols. 1101–2.

1042 Nicholson, A. 'Henry Vincent'. DNB, 1967–8 reprint, Vol. 20, pp.358–9.

T. Wakley

1043 Boase, F. 'Thomas Wakley'. MEB, 1965 reprint, Vol. 3, Col. 1132.

1044 Brook, C. *Thomas Wakley*. Socialist Medical Association, 1962. i, 33pp.

1045 Carlyle, E.I. 'Thomas Wakley'. DNB, 1967–8 reprint, Vol. 20, pp.461–5.

T. Walker

1046 Knight, F. *The strange case of Thomas Walker: ten years in the life of a Manchester radical (1784–94)*. Foreword by G.D.H. Cole. Lawrence and Wishart, 1957. 184pp.

W. Walker

1047 Boyle, J.W. 'William Walker', *Leaders and workers*, pp.57–65 (*see* no.18). Edited by J. W. Boyle. Dublin, Mercier Press, 1966.

G. Wallas

1048 Mack, M.P. 'Graham Wallas's new individualism'. WPQ, March 1958, 11(1):14–32.

1049 Zimmern, A. 'Graham Wallas'. DNB, 1931–40, 1970 reprint, pp.888–9.

S. Walsh

1050 Watkin, A.E. 'Stephen Walsh'. DNB, 1922–30, 1967 reprint, pp.880–1.

J. Ward

1051 Middleton, J.S. 'John Ward'. DNB, 1931–40, 1970 reprint, pp.889–90.

Countess of Warwick

1052 Blunden, M. *The Countess of Warwick*. Cassell, 1967. xiv, 356pp.

1053 Bolitho, H. '(Greville) Frances Evelyn, Countess of Warwick'. DNB, 1931–40, 1970 reprint, pp.365–6.

1054 Lang, T. *My darling Daisy*. Joseph, 1966. 196pp.

J. Watson

1055 Boase, F. 'James Watson'. MEB, 1965 reprint, Vol. 3, Col. 1225.

1056 Secombe, T. 'James Watson'. DNB, 1967–8 reprint, Vol. 20, pp.923–4.

S. Watson

1057 Chaplin, S. 'A tribute to Sam Watson'. NEG, Oct. 1967, 1:13–14.

J. Watts

1058 Boase, F. 'John Watts'. MEB, 1965 reprint, Vol. 3, Col. 1233.

1059 Sutton, C.W. 'John Watts'. DNB, 1967–8 reprint, Vol. 20, pp.982–3.

H.S. Weaver

1060 Nicholson, M. *Dear Miss Weaver: Harriet Shaw Weaver 1876–1961*. Faber, 1970. 509pp.

B. Webb

1061 Cole, M. *Beatrice Webb*. Longmans, 1946. 197pp.

1062 Cole, M. 'Beatrice Webb', *Women of today*, pp.261–87. Nelson, 1946.

1063 Garman, D. 'Beatrice Webb; and the other one'. MDQ, Winter 49–50, 5(1):67–76.

1064 Letwin, S.R. 'Beatrice Webb: science and the apotheosis of politics', *The pursuit of happiness*, pp.319–91. CUP, 1965.
'a reformer who synthesized the intellectual fashion of late Victorian England'.

1065 Muggeridge, K. and R. Adam. *Beatrice Webb; a life, 1858–1943*. Secker and Warburg, 1967. 272pp.

1066 Tawney, R.H. 'Beatrice Webb, 1858–1943', *The attack*, pp.101–28. Allen and Unwin, 1953.

1067 Webb, B. *Beatrice Webb's diaries*. Edited by Margaret Cole. *1912–24*, 1952. xxvi, 272pp. *1924–32*, 1956. xxv, 327pp. Longmans.

1068 Webb, B. *My apprenticeship*. Longmans, 1950 (first pub. 1926). xii, 390pp. To 1892.

1069 Webb, B. *Our partnership*. Edited by Barbara Drake and Margaret Cole. Longmans, 1948. xiii, 544pp.
Covers 1892–1911 and supplements *My apprenticeship*.

S. Webb

1070 Beveridge, Lord. 'Sidney Webb (Lord Passfield) (1859–1947)'. EJ, Sept. 1948, 58(231):428–34.

1071 Cole, M. 'Sidney Webb (1859–1947)', *Makers of the Labour movement*, pp.227–47 (*see* no.19). Longmans, 1948.

1072 Dutt, R.P. 'Sidney Webb, 1859–1947'. LM, Nov. 1947, 29(11):344–6.

1073 Harrison, R. 'The young Webb 1859–92'. SSLH, Autumn 1968, 17:15–18.

1074 Murphy, M.E. 'In memoriam: Sidney Webb 1859–1947'. AJS, Jan. 1948, 53(4):295–6.

1075 Tawney, R.H. 'In memory of Sidney Webb'. E, Nov. 1947, 14(56):245–53.

S. and B. Webb

1076 Cole, M. *Beatrice and Sidney Webb*. Fabian Society, 1955. 47pp.

1077 Cole, M. *The social services and the Webb tradition*. Fabian Society for the Webb Memorial Trust, 1946. 12pp.

1978 Cole, M. 'The Webbs and social theory'. BJS, June 1961. 12(2):93–105.

1079 Cole, M., ed. *The Webbs and their work*. Muller, 1949. xvi, 304pp.

1080 Evans, J.N. 'Beatrice and Sidney Webb', *Great figures in the Labour movement*, pp.62–77. Pergamon, 1966.

1081 Hamilton, M.A. 'Sidney and Beatrice Webb'. DNB, 1941–50, 1967 reprint, pp.935–40.

1082 Laski, H.J. *The Webbs and Soviet communism*. Fabian Society for the Webb Memorial Trust, 1947. 20pp.

1083 MacRae, D.G. 'The Webbs and their work'. PQ, Jan.–March 1948, 19(1):14–23.

1084 Martin, K. 'The Webbs remembered', *Other people's lives*, pp.17–23. Contact Publications, 1948.

1085 Ratcliffe, S.K. 'Beatrice and Sidney Webb'. CNR, Aug. 1948, 174:91–5.

1086 Simey, T.S. 'The contribution of Sidney and Beatrice Webb to sociology'. BJS, June 1961, 12(2):106–23.

1087 Strachey, J. 'The Webbs', *The strangled cry and other unparliamentary papers*, pp.183–9. Bodley Head, 1962.

1088 Tawney, R.H. 'The Webbs and their work', *The attack*, pp.129–46. Allen and Unwin, 1953.

1089 Tawney, R.H. *The Webbs in perspective*. Athlone Press, 1953. 21pp.

1090 Toynbee, A. 'The Webbs', *Acquaintances*, pp.108–28. OUP, 1967.

1091 Warner, M. 'The Webbs, Keynes and the economic problem in the inter-war years'. PS, Feb. 1966, 14(1):81–6.

J.C. Wedgwood

1092 Wedgwood, C.V. 'Josiah Clement Wedgwood'. DNB, 1941–50, 1967 reprint, pp.941–3.

1093 Wedgwood, C.V. *The last of the radicals: Josiah Wedgwood M.P.* Cape, 1951. 252pp.

H.G. Wells

1094 Arnot, R.P. 'Retrospect on H.G. Wells'. MDQ, Summer 1947, 2(3):194–207.

1095 Brome, V. *H.G. Wells: a biography*. Longmans, 1951. ix, 255pp.

1096 Brome, V. 'Shaw versus Wells', *Six studies in quarrelling*, pp.1–39. Cresset, 1958.

1097 Calder, R. 'H.G. Wells'. DNB, 1941–50, 1967 reprint, pp.944–9.

1098 Cauldwell, C. 'H.G. Wells: a study in Utopianism', *Studies in a dying culture*, pp.73–95. Bodley Head, 1957 (first pub. 1938).

1099 Chappelow, A. 'To H.G. Wells—in heaven or hell. A centenary tribute'. CNR, Dec. 1966, 209:305–8.

1100 Cole, M. 'H.G. Wells (1866–1946)', *Makers of the Labour movement*, pp.288–308 (*see* no.19). Longmans, 1948.

1101 Dawson, C. 'Historians reconsidered: 4 H.G. Wells and the Outline of history'. HT, Oct. 1951, 1(10):28–32.

1102 Granada Television. *The worlds of Mr. Wells.* Foreword by Kingsley Martin. Manchester, Granada Television, 1966. 19pp.
    Programme transmitted on centenary of Wells's birth, 21 September 1966.

1103 Hyde, W.J. 'The socialism of H.G. Wells'. JHI, April 1965, 17(2):217–34.

1104 Lodge, D. 'Assessing H.G. Wells'. EN, Jan. 1967, 28(1):54–64.

1105 Shaw, B. 'H.G. Wells on the rest of us [Wells' view of some fellow socialists]', *Pen portraits and reviews*, pp.279–83. Constable, 1949 (first pub. 1931).

1106 Wells, H.G. *Experiment in autobiography: discoveries and conclusions* of a very ordinary brain (since 1866). 2 vols. Gollancz and Cresset, 1966 (first pub. 1934). 840pp.

1107 West, A. 'H.G. Wells'. EN, Feb. 1957, 8(2):52–9.

A. West

1108 West, A. *One man in his time: an autobiography.* Allen and Unwin, 1969. 193pp.

J. West

1109 Boase, F. 'John West'. MEB, 1965 reprint, Vol. 3, Col. 1278.

Bishop B.F. Westcott

1110 Best, G. *Bishop Westcott and the miners.* CUP, 1967. 40pp.

1111 Stanton, V.S. 'Brooke Foss Westcott'. DNB, 1901–11, 1969 reprint, pp.635–41.

1112 Vidler, A.R. 'Westcott's Christian socialism', *F.D. Maurice and company: nineteenth century studies*, pp.259–78. S.C.M., 1966.

C. Westerton

1113 Boase, F. 'Charles Westerton'. MEB, 1965 reprint, Vol. 3, Cols. 1282–3.

J. Wheatley

1114 Johnston, T. 'John Wheatley'. DNB, 1922–30, 1967 reprint, pp.904–5.

A. Wheeler

1115 Pankhurst, R.K.B. 'Anna Wheeler: a pioneer socialist and feminist'. PQ, April–June 1954, 25(2):132–43.

W. Whiteley

1116 Pearce, C. 'An interview with Wilfred Whiteley (1882–)'. SSLH, Spring 1969, 18:14–21.

P.E.T. Widdrington

1117 Reckitt, M.B. *P.E.T. Widdrington: a study in vocation and versatility*. S.P.C.K., 1961. xv, 168pp.

E. Wilkinson

1118 Blythe, R. 'Jarrow', *The age of illusion: England in the twenties and thirties, 1919–40*, pp.179–99. Penguin, 1964 first pub. 1963).

1119 Davies, S. 'The young Ellen Wilkinson'. MLPS, 1964–5, 107:34–9.

1120 Elliott, D.M. 'Ellen Cicely Wilkinson'. DNB, 1941–50, 1967 reprint, pp.955–6.

1121 Lockett, T.A. 'Red Ellen—Ellen Cicely Wilkinson (1891–1947)', *It happened around Manchester. Three lives . . .*, pp.46–61. University of London Press, 1968.

F. Williams

1122 Williams, F. *Nothing so strange: an autobiography*. Cassell, 1970. ix, 354pp.

H. Williams

1123 Williams, D. 'Hugh Williams'. DWB, 1959, pp.1041–2.

J. Williams

1124 Boase, F. 'James Williams'. MEB, 1965 reprint, Vol. 6, Col. 891.

T. Williams

1125 Williams, T. *Digging for victory*. Hutchinson, 1965. 200pp.

Z. Williams

1126 Boase, F. 'Zephaniah Williams'. MEB, 1965 reprint, Vol. 6, Cols. 898–9.

127 Jones, O. 'Zephaniah Williams and the Chartists', *The early days of Sirhowy and Tredegar*, pp.91–109. Tredegar Historical Society, 1970 (first pub. 1969).

128 Williams, D. 'Zephaniah Williams'. DWB, 1959, p.1086.

129 Williams, D. 'Zephaniah Williams'. SSLH, Autumn 1962, 5:43–4.

T. Willis

130 Willis, T. *Whatever happened to Tom Mix: the story of one of my lives*. Cassell, 1970. vii, 197pp.

B. Wilson

131 Boase, F. 'Benjamin Wilson'. MEB, 1965 reprint, Vol. 6, Col. 911.

H. Wilson

132 Ali, T., comp. *The thoughts of Chairman Harold*. Gnome Press, 1967, 47pp.

133 Atkins, A.H. 'Wilson—the undergraduate I remember'. CNR, Dec. 1964, 205:645–7.

134 Blake, B. 'The family background of Harold Wilson', *Studies in British politics: a reader in political sociology*, pp.78–84. Edited by R. Rose, Macmillan, 1969.

135 Booker, C. 'Is Harold Wilson a hypocrite?' (3). TC, Summer 1965, 174(1026):34–5.

136 [A Bow Grouper]. 'Thoughts of a Bow Grouper on Mr. Harold Wilson'. C. April-June 1963, 6(23):10–11.

137 Broad, L. 'Harold Wilson', *The path of power: the rise of the premiership from Rosebery to Wilson*, pp.200–16. Muller, 1965.

138 Brogan, C. *The world of Harold Wilson*. O'Brien, 1959. 24pp.

139 Chater, T. 'Science, socialism and Mr. Wilson'. LM, Sept. 1964, 46(9):414–17.

140 Elletson, D.H. 'The third Labour Prime Minister and the thirty-seventh President', *Chequers and the Prime Ministers*, pp.164–74. Hale, 1970.

141 Foot, M. *Harold Wilson: a pictorial biography*. Pergamon, 1964, 100pp.

142 Foot, P. *The politics of Harold Wilson*. Penguin, 1968. 347pp.

143 Gallacher, W. '"Purpose" and Mr. Wilson'. LM, May 1964, 46(5):227–31. Review of no.1157.

144 Hackett, D. 'Is Harold Wilson a hypocrite?' (2). TC, Summer 1965, 174(1026):33–4.

145 Harris, K. 'Harold Wilson, 1963', *Conversations*, pp.266–86. Hodder, 1967.

146 Howard, A. and R. West. *The making of the Prime Minister*. Cape, 1965. 239pp.
     Labour's 1964 General Election victory.

1147 Irving, C. 'Is Harold Wilson a hypocrite?' (1). TC, Summer 1965, 174(1026):31–3.

1148 Irving, C. 'Wilson, the improved Prime Minister'. TC, Winter 1966, 174(1029):34–7.

1149 Kay, E. *Pragmatic Premier: an intimate portrait of Harold Wilson.* Frewin, 1967. 239pp.

1150 Kay, E., comp. *The wit of Harold Wilson.* Frewin, 1967. 84pp.

1151 Noel, G.E. *Harold Wilson and the "New Britain".* Gollancz, 1964. 199pp.

1152 Noel, G.E. *Harold Wilson and the "New Britain": the making of a modern Prime Minister.* Campion Press, 1964. 143pp.

1153 Shahani, G. *Harold Wilson and the forty thieves.* Shahani, 1968. 109pp.
    Characterises Harold Wilson as the Ali Baba of Britain.

1154 Shrimsley, A. *The first hundred days of Harold Wilson.* Weidenfeld, 1965. xii, 162pp.

1155 Smith, D. *Harold Wilson: a critical biography.* Hale, 1964. 224pp.

1156 Smith, L. *Harold Wilson: the authentic portrait.* Hodder, 1964. 222pp.

1157 Wilson, H. *Purpose in politics: selected speeches (1956–63).* Weidenfeld, 1964. xi, 270pp.

J.H. Wilson

1158 Watkin, A.E. 'Joseph Havelock Wilson'. DNB, 1922–30, 1967 reprint, pp.916–17.

J. Winstone

1159 Morris-Jones, H. 'James Winstone'. DWB, 1965 reprint, p.1088.

L. Woolf

1160 Annan, Lord. 'Leonard Woolf's autobiography'. PQ, Jan.-March 1970, 41(1):35–41.

1161 Beales, H.L. 'Three octogenarians'. PQ, Jan.–March 1961. 32(1):62–70.
    Ernest Simon, R.H. Tawney, L. Woolf.

1162 Woolf, L. *Beginning again: an autobiography of the years 1911–18.* Hogarth, 1964. 260pp.

1163 Woolf, L. *Downhill all the way: an autobiography of the years 1919–39.* Hogarth, 1967. 259pp.

1164 Woolf, L. *The journey not the arrival matters: an autobiography of the years 1939–69.* Hogarth, 1969. 217pp.

B. Wootton

1165 Wootton, B. *In a world I never made: autobiographical reflections.* Allen and Unwin, 1967. 283pp.

W. Wyatt

1166 Wyatt, W. *Into a dangerous world.* Weidenfeld, 1952. 238pp.

B. Wynn

1167 Harrison, R. 'Obituary: Bert Wynn (1901–66)'. SSLH, Spring 1966, 12:47.

1168 Labour Monthly. 'Bert Wynn'. LM, April 1966, 48(4):181.

L. Youle

1169 Harrison, R. and P. Seyd. 'An interview with Len Youle (1890–)'. SSLH, Spring 1970, 20:35–41.

K. Zilliacus

1170 Labour Monthly. 'Konni Zilliacus (1894–1967)'. LM, Aug. 1967, 49(8):367.

1171 Zilliacus, K. *Why I was expelled. Bevinism v. election pledges, socialism and peace.* Collet's, 1949. 72pp.

General histories

1172 Adnitt, F.W. 'The rise of English radicalism (1789–1901)'. CNR, May 1967, 210:258–72.

1173 Anderson, P. 'Socialism and pseudo-empiricism'. NLR, Jan.–Feb. 1966, 35:3–42.
   Reply to no.1218.

1174 Armstrong, G., ed. *London's struggle for socialism, 1848–1948.* Thames, 1948. viii, 56pp.

1175 Barrow, L. *A short history of the British Labour movement.* Sheed and Ward, 1969. vii, 56pp.

1176 Bell, P. 'Eleanor Marx on our history'. MML, July–Sept. 1967, 43:10–16.
   Discusses Eleanor Marx's pamphlet: *The working-class movement in England,* pub. in 1895 by Twentieth Century Press.

1177 Boyle, J. W. 'The sum of things', *Leaders and workers,* pp.87–95 (*see* no.18). Edited by J.W. Boyle. Dublin, Mercier Press, 1966.

1178 Briggs, A. 'The language of "class" in early nineteeth-century England',

Essays in Labour history, pp.43–73 (*see* no.1179). Edited by A. Briggs and J. Saville. Macmillan, 1960.

1179 Briggs, A. and J. Saville, eds. *Essays in Labour history: in memory of G.D.H. Cole, 25 September 1889–14 January 1959*. Macmillan, 1960. vii, 364pp.
      See nos.93, 212, 214, 215, 217, 585, 1178, 2166, 2338, 3114, 3717.

1180 Cole, G.D.H. *British Labour movement—retrospect and prospect*. Fabian Society, 1951. 20pp.
      Ralph Fox Memorial Lecture, Halifax, April 1951.

1181 Cole, G.D.H. *British working-class politics, 1832–1914*. Routledge, 1965 (first pub. 1941). viii, 320pp.
      See also no.1543.

1182 Cole, G.D.H. 'Phases of Labour's development in Great Britain, 1914–58', *Essays in Jewish sociology, Labour and co-operation in memory of Dr. Noah Barou, 1889–1955*, pp.99–124. Edited by H.F. Infield. Yoseloff, 1962.

1183 Cole, G.D.H. *A short history of the British working-class movement, 1789–1947*. Allen and Unwin, 1960. xii, 500pp.
      First pub. in three separate vols., 1925–7; then as one vol. 1932; republished as a complete, revised work, 1948.

1184 Cole, G.D.H. and R. Postgate. *The common people 1746–1946*. Methuen, 1968 (first pub. 1938). x, 754pp.

1185 Collins, H. and C. Abramsky. *Karl Marx and the British Labour movement: years of the First International*. Macmillan, 1965. xxii, 356pp.
      'examines the revival and rise of the Labour movement in England and Europe after its defeat in the 1848 revolution'. (*See* no.1212).

1186 Collins, H. and C. Abramsky. 'Karl Marx and the British Labour movement'. LM, Aug. 1965, 47(8):376–7.
      Reply to no.1212.

1187 Currie, R. and R.M. Hartwell. 'The making of the English working class?'. ECHR, Dec. 1965, 18(3):633–43.
      Review of no.1217.

1188 Fagan, H. *The unsheathed sword: episodes in English history. Part 2, Champions of the workers*. Lawrence and Wishart, 1959. 108pp.
      See nos.377, 588, 818, 1389, 1415, 2825.

1189 Harrison, R. *Before the socialists: studies in Labour and politics 1861 to 1881*. Routledge, 1965. xiii, 369pp. (*see* no.1211).
      'A study of working-class politics during the two decades which separated the last of the Chartists from the first of the modern socialists.'

1190 Hobley, L.F. *Working-class and democratic movements*. Blackie, 1970. x, 102pp.

1191 Hobsbawm, E.J. *Labouring men: studies in the history of labour*. Weidenfeld, 1963 (first pub. 1968). viii, 401pp.
      See nos.436, 837, 1381, 2188, 2190, 2192, 2193, 2390, 2443, 2897–9, 2901.

92 Hodgskin, T. *Labour defended against the claims of capital*. Hammersmith Bookshop, 1964 (first pub. 1825). 110pp.

93 Jackson, T.A. *Trials of British freedom: being some studies in the history of the fight for democratic freedom in Britain*. Lawrence and Wishart, 1945. 192pp.
    See nos.1394, 1420, 2510, 2925, 3560.

94 Maccoby, S. *The English radical tradition, 1764–1914*. Black, 1966. xxiii, 238pp.

95 Maccoby, S. *English radicalism: 1786–1832: from Paine to Cobbett*. Allen and Unwin, 1955. 559pp.

96 Maccoby, S. *English radicalism: 1886–1914*. Allen and Unwin, 1953. 540pp.

97 Maccoby, S. *English radicalism: the end?* Allen and Unwin, 1961. 640pp.
    Covers period 1906–39. Previous vols. covering periods 1832–52 and 1853–86 pub. in 1935 and 1938 respectively.

98 Mahon, J. 'New perspectives for unity in the British Labour movement'. MDQ, Autumn 1953, 8(4):213–24.

99 Marwick, W.H. 'Developments in the Labour movement in Scotland since 1880'. SSLH, Spring 1963, 6:8–10.

200 Marwick, W.H. *Labour in Scotland: a short history of the Scottish working class movement*. Glasgow, Scottish Secretariat, ?1950. 32pp.

201 Marwick, W.H. *A short history of Labour in Scotland*. Edinburgh, Chambers, 1967. vi, 119pp. (*see* no.1265).

202 Miliband, R. 'Socialism and the myth of the golden past'. SR, 1964. 1:92–103.

203 Morton, A.L. *A people's history of England*. Lawrence and Wishart, 1968 (first pub. 1938). 562pp.
    See no.1253.

204 Morton, A.L. and G. Tate. *The British Labour movement, 1770–1920: a history*. Lawrence and Wishart, 1956. 313pp.
    See no.1227.

205 Mowat, C.L. *Britain between the wars 1918–1940*. Methuen, 1968 (first pub. 1955). ix, 698pp.

206 Nairn, T. 'The English working class'. NLR, Mar.–April 1964, 24:43–57.

207 Nairn, T. 'The fateful meridian'. NLR, Mar.–April 1970, 60:3–35.
    Victorian England—framework for the development of the Labour movement.

208 Pelling, H. *America and the British left from Bright to Bevan*. Black, 1956. xi, 174pp.
    Biographical index—48 short biographies of British socialists, radicals, liberals.

209 Postgate, R. *A pocket history of the British working class*. Tillicoultry, National Council of Labour Colleges, 1964 (first pub. 1942). 103pp.

1210 Ridley, F.A. *The revolutionary tradition in England*. National Labour Press, 1948. 316pp.

1211 Rothstein, A. 'British Labour in Marx's day'. LM, Oct. 1965, 47(10):474–8.
Review of no.1189.

1212 Rothstein, A. 'Marx and British Labour, 1863–1872'. LM, June 1965, 47(6):280–4.
Review of no.1185.

1213 Rothstein, A. 'Reply: Karl Marx and the British Labour movement'. LM, Aug. 1965, 47(8):377–9.
See no.1186.

1214 Samuel, R. 'Class and classlessness'. ULR, Spring 1959, 1(6):44–50.

1215 Saville, J., ed. *Democracy and the Labour movement: essays in honour of Dona Torr*. Lawrence and Wishart, 1954. 275pp.
See nos.2168, 2420, 3132.

1216 Stammers, J. *British workers in action, 1800–1945*. Bombay, People's Publishing House, 1945. ii, 89pp.
Written to refute the charge that 'every Briton . . . is a reactionary and an imperialist'.

1217 Thompson, E.P. *The making of the English working class*. Penguin, 1968 (first pub. 1963). 958pp.
See no.1187.

1218 Thompson, E.P. 'The peculiarities of the English'. SR, 1965. 2:311–62.
See no.1173.

Sources for research, study and teaching

1219 Allen, V.L. 'The need for a sociology of Labour'. BJS, Sept. 1959. 10(3):181–92.

1220 Backstrom, P.N. 'The British Labour movement: a challenge to the young historian'. HIST, Aug. 1962, 24(4):415–22.

1221 Briggs, A. 'Open questions of Labour history'. SSLH, Autumn 1960, 1:2–3.

1222 Briggs, A. 'Trade union history and Labour history'. BH, Jan. 1966, 8(1):39–47.

1223 Brunel, C. and P.M. Jackson. 'Notes on tokens as a source of information on the history of the Labour and radical movement'. Part 1. SSLH, Autumn 1966, 13:26–36.

1224 Clarke, J.F. 'The shipwrights (inc. local rules and laws)'. NEG, Oct. 1967, 1:21–40.

225 Clarke, J.F. and D.J. Rowe. 'Local records for Labour history. Tape recordings'. NEG, Oct. 1968. 2:10–12.

226 Cole, G.D.H. *Course on Labour movements*. 5 parts. Oxford, Ruskin College, 1950. 100pp.

227 Communist Party. *Study guide to the British Labour movement*. Communist Party, 1962. 31pp.
    See no.1204. To be used with A.L. Morton and G. Tate: *The British Labour movement, 1770–1920.*

228 Craig, F.W.S., comp. *British General Election manifestos 1918–1966.* Chichester, Political Reference Books, 1970. xii, 303pp.

229 Craig, F.W.S., comp. *British parliamentary election results 1918–1949.* Glasgow, Political Reference Publications, 1969. xviii, 742pp.

230 Craig, F.W.S., comp. *British parliamentary election statistics 1918–1968.* Glasgow, Political Reference Publication, 1968. xiii, 110pp.

231 Dunsmore, M. 'Library sources for Labour history. Bradford Reform Societies, 1835–68, Mss. in Bradford Reference Library'. SSLH, Autumn 1963, 7:36–7.

232 Fox, A. 'Library sources in Labour history. (1) Nuffield College, Oxford'. SSLH, Spring 1961, 2:11–12.

233 Frankenberg, R. 'On the writing of miners' trade union history'. SSLH, Autumn 1962, 5:47–9 (*see* no.1271).

234 Garnett, R.G. 'The records of early co-operation, with particular reference to pre-Rochdale co-operation'. LHN, Nov. 1970, 9(4):163–71.

235 Garside, W.R. 'On writing trade union history—with special reference to the Durham Miners' Association 1919–47'. NEG, Oct. 1967, 1:8–10.

236 Griffin, A.R., ed. 'Documents: Checkweighing arrangements at the Butterley Company's collieries, Derbyshire, 1871–3'. SSLH, Spring 1969, 18:21–7.

237 Griffin, A.R., ed. 'Documents: Contract rules in the Notts. and Derbyshire coalfield'. SSLH, Spring 1968, 16:12–18.

238 Griffin, A.R. 'On the writing of miners' trade union history'. SSLH, Autumn 1962, 5:44–6 (*see* no.1271).

239 Guttsman, W.L. 'Materials on Labour history in British libraries. (6) Sources on the history of the British Labour movement in the British Library of Political and Economic Science'. SSLH, Spring 1964, 8:23–30.

240 Harrison, J.F.C. 'The Philip Snowden Library'. SSLH, Autumn 1960, 1:27.

241 Harrison, J.F.C. 'The Society for the Study of Labour History'. VS, Sept. 1961, 5(1): 68–9.

1242 Hobsbawm, E.J. 'Commitment and working class history: a review of recent Labour movement history'. ULR, Spring 1959, 1(6):71–2.

1243 Hobsbawm, E.J. 'Records of the trade union movement'. AR, Lady Day 1960, 4(23):129–37.

1244 Hobsbawm, E.J. 'Where are British historians going?'. MQ, Jan. 1955, 2(1):14–26.

1245 Hunt, C.J. 'Northern Pennines. Lead mining industry. Sources for Labour history'. NEG, Oct. 1968, 2:13–17.

1246 John Rylands Library. [Rare items of Labour history interest given by Sir George Benson]. SSLH, Spring 1961, 2:13–14.

1247 Large, M. 'Library sources in Labour history. (2) Birmingham Local Collection'. SSLH, Autumn 1961, 3:13–15.

1248 Leventhal, F.M. 'Library sources: George Howell Collection, Bishopsgate Institute, London'. SSLH, Spring 1965, 10:38–40.

1249 Line, M.B. 'Library sources in Labour history. Southampton University'. SSLH, Spring 1962, 4:55.

1250 MacDougall, I. 'The study of Labour history'. SHR, Oct. 1966, 45(140):226–7.

1251 MacKenna, R.O. [Library sources in Labour history]. 'Glasgow University Library'. SSLH, Spring 1963, 6:33.

1252 Marx Memorial Library. Quarterly Bulletin. '40th anniversary of the General Strike: exhibition at Marx House'. MML, July–Sept. 1966, 39:5–9.

1253 May, D. *Study guide to A people's history of England* (*see* no.1203). Lawrence and Wishart, 1948. 62pp.

1254 Millar, J.P.M. 'The Labour College movement. Select list of items'. SSLH, Autumn 1964, 9:40–1.

1255 Musson, A.E. 'Writing trade union history'. LHN, Dec. 1953–Jan. 1954, 1(9):273–7.

1256 Pelling, H. 'Manuscript sources of British Labour history in the United States'. SSLH, Autumn 1962, 5:39–40.

1257 Pollard, S. 'Sources for trade union history'. LHN, Autumn 1959, 4(5):177–81.

1258 Rowe, D.J. 'The Keelmen'. NEG, Oct. 1967, 1:19–20.

1259 Rowe, D.J. 'Local records for Labour history'. NEG, Oct. 1967, 1:15–16.

1260 Saville, J. 'Labour movement historiography'. ULR, Winter 1958, 1(3):73–7.

1261 Saville, J. 'A note on the present position of working-class history'. YB, Sept. 1952, 4(2):125–32.

1262 Saville, J. 'The present position and prospects of Labour history'. NEG, Oct. 1967, 1:4–6.

1263 Saville, J. 'Research facilities and the social historian'. Library Association Record, Sept. 1963, 65(9):320–3.

1264 Sellers, I. 'Library sources of Labour history: City of Liverpool, Picton Reference Library. Record Office'. SSLH, Autumn 1962, 5:42–3.

1265 Simpson, J. 'Scottish Labour historiography: a progress report'. SSLH, Autumn 1968, 17:29–32.
  Review of no.1201.

1266 Society for the Study of Labour History. Bulletin. 'Editorial: The teaching of Labour history, 1: Special papers'. SSLH, Spring 1962, 4:33–43.

1267 Society for the Study of Labour History. Bulletin. 'Editorial: The teaching of Labour history in British universities, 2'. SSLH, Autumn 1962, 5:3–8.

1268 Society for the Study of Labour History. Bulletin. 'Editorial: The teaching of Labour history in adult classes'. SSLH, Spring 1963, 6:3–7.

1269 Society for the Study of Labour History. Bulletin. 'Editorial: A further note on the teaching of Labour history to adults'. SSLH, Autumn 1963, 7:3.

1270 Tsuzuki, C. 'Japanese archives relating to British Labour history (1)'. SSLH, Autumn 1963, 7:29–33.
  G. Toike Collection.

1271 Williams, J.E. 'A reply to A.R. Griffin and R. Frankenberg'. SSLH, Autumn 1962, 5:49–54. (*See* nos.1233, 1238).

Socialism: history and theory

1272 Abel-Smith, B. *Labour's social plans.* Fabian Society, 1966. 20pp.

1273 Albu, A. *Socialism and the study of man.* Fabian Society, 1951. 20pp.

1274 Amis, K. *Lucky Jim's politics.* Conservative Political Centre, 1968. 20pp. Lecture originally entitled 'Confessions of an ex-radical'—refutation of no.1275.

1275 Amis, K. *Socialism and the intellectuals.* Fabian Society, 1957. 13pp. *(see* no.1280).

1276 Anderson, P. and R. Blackburn. *Towards socialism.* Fontana and New Left Review, 1965. 397pp.

1277 Bateson, F.W. *Socialism and farming.* Fabian Society, 1948. 23pp.

1278 Beer, M. *A history of British socialism.* Vol. 1. xxxi, 361pp; Vol. 2. 451pp, bound in one volume. Allen and Unwin, 1948.
First pub. in two volumes in 1919, then as one volume in 1940.

1279 Benn, A.W. 'The new politics: a socialist reconnaissance'. Fabian Society, 1970. 28pp.

1280 Berger, J. 'The new nihilists'. LM, Mar. 1957, 39(3):123–6.
Review of no.1275.

1281 Besant, A. 'Modern socialism', *A selection of the social and political pamphlets of Annie Besant,* 51pp. New York, Kelley, 1970 (first pub. 1886).

1282 Besant, A. 'Radicalism and socialism', *A selection of the social and political pamphlets of Annie Besant,* 20pp. New York, Kelley, 1970 (first pub. 1887).

1283 Besant, A. 'Socialism: for and against', *A selection of the social and political pamphlets of Annie Besant,* 31pp. New York, Kelley, 1970 (first pub. 1887).

1284 Besant, A. 'The socialist movement', *A selection of the social and political pamphlets of Annie Besant,* 24pp. New York, Kelley, 1970 (first pub. 1887).

1285 Bestor, A.E., Jnr. 'The evolution of the socialist vocabulary'. JHI, June 1948, 9(3):259–302.

1286 Bull, T. 'Towards a British socialist policy'. SP, Lent-Hilary 1968, 2:11–14.

1287 Calder-Marshall, A. 'Socialism and the colonies'. F, Feb. 1947, 161(962):89–94.

1288 Cardan, P. *The meaning of socialism.* Solidarity, 1968. 26pp.

84

1289 Clay, E. 'The Labour alternative to socialism'. SP, Michaelmas 1967, 1:5–9.

1290 Clegg, H. 'Guild socialism in the Post Office'. PAD, Summer 1950, 28:129–33.

1291 Coates, K., ed. *A future for British socialism?* Nottingham, Centre for Socialist Education, 1968. 95pp.
Proceedings of a 'Teach in' held at 1967 Labour Party Conference.

1292 Cohn, N. 'The Saint-Simonian extravaganza'. TC, Nov. 1953, 154(921):354–63.

1293 Cole, G.D.H. *The development of socialism during the past fifty years.* Athlone Press, 1952. 32pp.

1294 Cole, G.D.H. *Facts for socialists, including some unwelcome home truths which call for attention.* Fabian Society, 1949 (first pub. 1887). 60pp.

1295 Cole, G.D.H. *A guide to the elements of socialism.* Labour Party, 1958. 40pp.

1296 Cole, G.D.H. *A history of socialist thought.* Vol. 1, *Socialist thought: the forerunners 1789–1850.* 1953. xi, 346pp. Vol. 2, *Socialist thought: Marxism and anarchism 1850–1890.* 1954. xi, 482pp. Vol. 3, Pt. 1, *The Second International 1889–1914.* 1956. xvii, 518pp. Vol. 3, Pt. 2, *The Second International.* 1956. viii, pp.519–1043. Vol. 4, Pt. 1, *Communism and social-democracy 1914–31.* 1958. x, 455pp. Vol. 4, Pt. 2, *Communism and social-democracy.* 1958. viii, pp.457–940. Vol. 5, *Socialism and fascism 1931–39.* 1960. xvi, 351pp. Macmillan.

1297 Cole, G.D.H. *Is this socialism?* New Statesman and Fabian Society, 1954. 32pp.

1298 Cole, G.D.H. 'What is socialism? 1'. PS, Feb. 1953, 1(1):21–33.

1299 Cole, G.D.H. 'What is socialism? 2'. PS, June 1953, 1(2):175–83.

1300 Cole, G.D.H. *World socialism re-stated.* New Statesman, 1956. 48pp.

1301 Cole, H.J.D. *Facts for socialists.* Fabian Society, 1956. 49pp.

1302 Crosland, A. *The future of socialism.* Cape, 1956. 540pp.

1303 Crossman, R.H.S. *Socialism and planning.* Fabian Society, 1967. 24pp.

1304 Crossman, R.H.S. *Socialist values in a changing civilisation.* Fabian Society, 1951. 16pp.

1305 Crossman, R.H.S. 'Towards a philosophy of socialism', *New Fabian essays,* pp.1–32 (*see* no.2437). Edited by R.H.S. Crossman. Turnstile, 1952.

1306 Davis, L. 'British socialism and the perils of success'. PSQ, Dec. 1954, 69(4):502–16.

1307 Deakins, E. *A faith to fight for.* Gollancz, 1964. 173pp.

1308 Demand, V.A. *Religion and the decline of capitalism.* Faber, 1952. 204pp.
Discusses socialism and human nature.

1309 Dewey, D. 'Notes on the analysis of socialism as a vocational problem'. MS, Sept. 1948, 16(3):269–88.

1310 Dewey, D. 'Professor J.A. Schumpeter on socialism, the case of Britain'. JPE, June 1950, 58(3):187–210.

1311 Dobb, M. *Argument on socialism.* Lawrence and Wishart, 1966. 64pp.

1312 Dobb, M. *Socialist planning: some problems.* Lawrence and Wishart, 1970. 69pp.

1313 Dutt, R.P. 'Marxism and Mr. Strachey'. LM, Dec. 1957, 39(12):514–17.

1314 Dutt, R.P. 'What is socialism?'. LM, Jan. 1960, 42(1):1–16.

1315 Dutt, R.P. 'What is socialism?'. LM, Nov. 1966, 48(11):497–509.

1316 Eaton, J. 'A mixed economist'. LM, May 1962, 44(5):233–6.
     Review of no.1334.

1317 Eaton, J. *Socialism in the nuclear age.* Lawrence and Wishart, 1961. 191pp.

1318 Fabian Group, A. *The future of public ownership.* Fabian Society, 1963. 33pp.

1319 Florence, P.S. 'Socialism and sociology today'. PQ, Oct.–Dec. 1948, 19(4):301–12.

1320 Fried, A. and R. Sanders. *A documentary history of socialist thought.* Edinburgh, University Press, 1964. xii, 591pp.

1321 Fryer, P. *The battle for socialism.* Socialist Labour League, 1959. viii, 192pp.

1322 Gaitskell, H. *Recent developments in British socialist thinking.* Co-operative Union, 1956. ii, 42pp.

1323 Gaitskell, H. *Socialism and nationalisation.* Fabian Society, 1956. 36pp.

1324 Glass, S.T. *The responsible society: the ideas of the English Guild Socialists.* Longmans, 1966. vii, 79pp.

1325 Gollan, J. *The case for socialism in the sixties.* Communist Party, 1966. 98pp.

1326 Gray, A. *The socialist tradition: Moses to Lenin.* Longmans, 1963 (first pub. 1948). xx, 523pp.

1327 Hacker, A. 'Original sin vs Utopia in British socialism'. RP, Apr. 1956, 18(2):184–206.

1328 Halévy, E. 'The problem of worker control', *The era of tyrannies: essays on socialism and war,* pp.123–40. Allen Lane, 1967.
     Discusses Guild Socialism.

1329 Hanson, (A.) H. 'Socialism and affluence'. NLR, Sept.–Oct. 1960, 5:10–16.

1330 Huddleston, J. 'Socialism in the sixties'. CNR, July 1967, 211:1–9.

1331 Hughes, H.D. *Towards a classless society.* Fabian Society, 1947. 17pp.

1332 Inchfield, J. 'Poland and Britain: two concepts of socialism'. IA, Jan. 1957, 33(1):2–11.

1333 Jackson, T.A. *Socialism. What? How? Why?* Communist Party, 1945. 72pp.

1334 Jay, D. *Socialism in the new society*. Longmans, 1962. viii, 414pp. (*see* nos.1316, 1346).

1335 Jay, D. *The socialist case*. Faber, 1946 (first pub. 1938). xviii, 298pp.

1336 Johnson, D. McI. *The end of socialism: the reflections of a radical*. Johnson, 1946. iv, 172pp.
        Why an independent radical rejects 'collectivism' (i.e. socialism) and so would not join the Labour Party.

1337 Jones, W.H.M. *Socialism and bureaucracy*. Fabian Society, 1949. 29pp.

1338 Jupp, J. 'Socialist "Rethinking" in Britain and Australia'. AJPH, Aug. 1958, 4(2):193–207.

1339 Klugman, J. 'G.D.H. Cole and unity'. LM, Oct. 56, 38(10):452–5.
        Review of no.1300.

1340 Laidler, H.W. *History of socialism: a comparative study of socialism, communism, trade unionism, co-operation, Utopianism and other systems of reform and reconstruction*. Routledge, 1968 (first pub. 1944). xx, 970pp.

1341 Lang, C. and D. Chapman. *More socialisation—or less?* Fabian Society, 1948. 24pp.

1342 Lauchlan, W. 'Socialist nationalisation'. LM, Oct. 1964, 46(10):447–9.

1343 Letwin, S.R. 'Representation without democracy: the Webbs' contribution'. RP, July 1954, 16(3):352–75.
        Discusses 'A constitution for the Socialist Commonwealth of Great Britain', pub. 1920.

1344 Lewis, J. *Socialism and the individual*. Lawrence and Wishart, 1961. 88pp.

1345 Lindsay, J. 'Discussion: socialist humanism'. NR, Winter 1957–8, 3:94–102.

1346 Longford, F. 'What light may shine? The future of socialism'. DR, Summer 1962, 236(492):168–76.
        Review of nos.258 (*Hightide and after*), and 1334.

1347 Mackenzie, N. *Socialism: a short history*. Hutchinson, 1966 (first pub. 1949). 192pp.

1348 Maris, R. 'Socialist thoughts out of season'. EN, Sept. 1958, 11(3):40–54.

1349 Marx Memorial Library. Quarterly Bulletin. 'Who will lead the struggle for socialism?'. MML, Jan.–March. 1969, 49:5–7.
        Conference held on 8th December 1968.

1350 Mayhew, C. *Socialist economic planning: the overall picture*. Fabian Society, 1946. 23pp.

1351 Mortimer, J. 'No socialism without public ownership'. LM, Sept. 1964, 46(9):399–402.

1352 Morton, A.L. *The English Utopia*. Lawrence and Wishart, 1952. 230pp.

1353 Morton, A.L. *Socialism in Britain*. Lawrence and Wishart, 1963. 80pp.

1354 Pankhurst, R.K.P. 'Saint-Simonism in England (1)'. TC, Dec. 1952, 152(910):499–512.

1355 Pankhurst, R.K.P. 'Saint-Simonism in England (2)'. TC, Jan. 1953, 153(911):47–58.

1356 Parkinson, C.N. *Left luggage: from Marx to Wilson*. Murray, 1967. x, 203pp. 'the rise and decline of the British socialist idea'—believes the British Labour Party has now become the Establishment.

1357 Radice, G. *Democratic socialism: a short survey*. Longmans, 1965. ix, 164pp.

1358 St. John, J. 'Discussion: socialist humanism'. NR, Winter 1957–8, 3:102–4.

1359 Saville, J. 'The background to the revival of socialism in England'. SSLH, Autumn 1965, 11:13–19.

1360 Saville, J. and E.P. Thompson. 'The case for socialism'. R, Sept. 1956, 2:1–7.

1361 Schumacher, E.F. 'In search of socialism'. TC, July 1952, 152(905):33–40. Review of no.2437.

1362 Sedgwick, P. 'Varieties of socialist thought'. PQ, Oct.–Dec. 1969, 40(4):394–410.

1363 Smith, H. 'The economies of socialism reconsidered'. EJ, Sept. 1955, 65(257):411–21.

1364 Socialist Union. *Socialism: a new statement of principles*. Lincolns-Praeger, 1952. 64pp.

1365 Socialist Union. *Twentieth century socialism: the economy of to-morrow*. Penguin, 1956. 152pp.

1366 Tawney, R.H. 'British socialism today', *The radical tradition: twelve essays on politics, education and literature*, pp.168–80. Allen and Unwin, 1964.

1367 Tawney, R.H. 'English politics today: we mean freedom'. RP, Apr. 1946, 8(2):223–39.

1368 Taylor, A.J.P. 'A look back at British socialism 1922–37'. EN, Mar. 1958, 10(3):27–33.

1369 Thompson, E.P. 'Socialist humanism: an epistle to the Philistines'. NR, Summer 1957, 1:105–43.

1370 Titmuss, R.M. *Choice and the 'welfare state'*. Fabian Society, 1967. 16pp.

1371 Townsend, P. *Poverty, socialism and Labour in power*. Fabian Society, 1967. 32pp.

1372 Ulam, A.B. *Philosophical foundations of English socialism*. Harvard, University Press, 1951. x, 173pp.

1373 Walsh, R. *Labour's socialism*. Ilfracombe, Stockwell, 1967. 48pp.

1374 Williams, F. *The triple challenge: the future of socialist Britain*. Heinemann, 1948. viii, 306pp.

1375 Wilson, H. *The relevance of British socialism*. Weidenfeld, 1964. ix, 115pp.

1376 Young, M. *What is a socialised industry?* Fabian Society, 1948. 21pp.

1377 Young, W. and E. *The socialist imagination*. Fabian Society, 1960. 21pp.

Early radicalism

Luddism

378 Berry, J. *The Luddites in Yorkshire*. Clapham, via Lancaster, Dalesman, 1970. 30pp.

379 Communist Party. History Group. 'Luddism in the period 1779–1830'. OH, Summer 1956. 2:25pp.

380 Darvall, F.O. *Popular disturbances and public order in Regency England; being an account of the Luddite and other disorders in England during the years 1811–1817 and of the attitude and activity of the authorities.* OUP, 1969 (first pub. 1934). 363pp.

381 Hobsbawm, E.J. 'The machine breakers', *Labouring men: studies in the history of Labour*, pp.5–22 (*see* no.1191). Weidenfeld, 1968.

382 Nottingham. The University. Manuscripts Department. *Working class unrest in Nottingham 1800–1850.* Nottingham, The University. 1970 (first pub. 1965).
Facsimiles of 7 contemporary documents with 4 explanatory booklets: 1 Introduction, 2 Luddism, 3 Reform, 4 Chartism.

383 Patterson, A.T. 'Luddism, Hampden clubs and trade unions in Leicestershire, 1816–17'. EHR, April 1948, 63(247):170–88.

384 Peel, F. *The risings of the Luddites, Chartists and Plug-Drawers.* New introduction by E.P. Thompson. Cass, 1968 (first pub. 1880). xv, 349pp.

385 Rudé, G. 'Luddism', *The crowd in history: a study of popular disturbances in France and England, 1730–1848*, pp.77–92. New York, Wiley, 1964. ix, 281pp.
See also no.1430.

386 Thomis, M.I. *The Luddites: machine breaking in Regency England.* Newton Abbot, David and Charles, 1970. 196pp.

387 Thomis, M.I. 'The Nottingham Luddites—a subject for mythology', *Old Nottingham*, pp.157–72. Newton Abbot, David and Charles, 1968.

Peterloo

1388 Communist Party, Lancashire and Cheshire District Committee. *Peterloo*. Manchester, The District Committee, 1969. 12pp.

1389 Fagan, H. 'Peterloo and Parliamentary reform 1819', *The unsheathed sword: episodes in English history. Part 2, Champions of the workers*, pp.24–37. Lawrence and Wishart, 1959 (*see* no.1188).

1390 Foster, J. 'Peterloo—the truth'. LM, Feb. 1970, 52(2):74–6.
    Review of no.1404.

1391 Hipkin, J. *The massacre of Peterloo*. Heinemann, 1968. 112pp.

1392 Horton, H., comp. *Peterloo, 1819. A portfolio of reproductions of contemporary documents*. Manchester, Libraries Committee, 1969.
    Explanatory text accompanies the 20 reproductions.

1393 House, H. 'Peterloo', *All in due time: the collected essays and broadcast talks of Humphry House*, pp.46–9 and 50–7. Hart Davis, 1955.

1394 Jackson, T.A. 'Peterloo; and Henry Hunt', *Trials of British freedom: being some studies in the history of the fight for democratic freedom in Britain*, pp.91–8. Lawrence and Wishart, 1945.
    See no.1193.

1395 Langdon-Davies, J., comp. *Peterloo and radical reform*. Jackdaw, 1965.
    Reproductions of contemporary documents and broadsides.

1396 McCord, N. 'Tyneside discontents and Peterloo'. NH, 1967, 2:91–111.

1397 Marlow, J. *The Peterloo massacre*. Rapp and Whiting, 1969. 238pp.

1398 Priestley, J.B. '1819. The Year of Peterloo', *The Prince of Pleasure and his Regency 1811–20*, pp.233–56. Heinemann, 1969.

1399 Read, D. *Peterloo: the 'Massacre' and its background*. Manchester, University Press, 1958. ix, 235pp.
    Attempts to explain why and how the crowds came together in St. Peter's Fields, August 16th 1819.

1400 Read, D. 'The social and economic background to Peterloo'. LCAS, 1954, 64:1–18.

1401 Shercliff, W.H. *150 years on: a short account of Peterloo*. Manchester, the Corporation, 1969. 12pp.

1402 Smith, E. *The story of Peterloo*. Manchester, Lancashire and Cheshire Federation of Trades Councils, 1952. 17pp.

1403 Thompson, E.P. 'God and King and Law'. NR, Winter 1957–8, 3:69–86.
    Review of nos.1399 and 1405.

1404 Walmsley, R. *Peterloo: the case re-opened*. Manchester, University Press, 1969. xx, 585pp.
Re-assesses the evidence and challenges the conventional view of the events at St. Peter's Fields.

1405 White, R.J. 'Peterloo', *Waterloo to Peterloo*, pp.184–200. Penguin, 1968 (first pub. 1957).

Chartism

I GENERAL

1406 Briggs, A. 'Chartism reconsidered'. HSI, 1959, 2:42–59.

1407 Briggs, A. *Chartist studies*. Macmillan, 1959. xi, 423pp.
See nos. 1408, 1409, 1423, 1446, 1453, 1456, 1457, 1461, 1473, 1474, 1487, 1488.

1408 Briggs, A. 'National bearings', *Chartist studies*, pp.288–303 (*see* no.1407). Edited by A. Briggs. Macmillan, 1959.

1409 Brown, L. 'The Chartist and the Anti-Corn Law League', *Chartist studies*, pp.342–71 (*see* no.1407). Edited by A. Briggs. Macmillan, 1959.

1410 Clark, G.K. 'Hunger and politics in 1842'. JMH, Dec. 1953, 25(4):355–74.

1411 Cole, G.D.H. *Chartist portraits*. New introduction by A. Briggs. Macmillan, 1965 (first pub. 1941). xvi, 378pp.
See nos.74, 232, 299, 309, 392, 458, 532, 747, 754, 759, 987, 998.

1412 Dawson, K. and Peter Wall. 'Chartism', *Parliamentary representation*, pp.19–26. OUP, 1968.

1413 Derry, J.W. 'Chartist interlude', *The radical tradition, Tom Paine to Lloyd George*, pp.155–81. Macmillan, 1967.

1414 Edwards, M.L. 'Methodism and the Chartist movement'. LQ, Oct. 1966, 301–10.

1415 Fagan, H. 'Chartism: or the knife and fork question 1838–1848', *The unsheathed sword: episodes in English history. Part 2. Champions of the workers*, pp.52–65. Lawrence and Wishart, 1959 (*see* no.1188).

1416 Gammage, R.G. *History of the Chartist movement, 1837–54*. Cass, 1969 (first pub. 1854). xvi, 465pp.
New introduction by J. Saville, pp.5–66 (not included in general pagination), includes pamphlet 'The social oppression of the working classes, its causes and cure'. This edition is a facsimile of second ed. of 1894.

1417 Gammage, R.G. *History of the Chartist movement, 1837–54*. Merlin, 1969 (first pub. 1854). xvi, 438pp.
This edition is a facsimile of second ed. of 1894.

1418 Glasgow, E. 'The establishment of the Northern Star newspaper'. H, Feb.–Oct. 1954, 39(135–6):54–67.

1419 Hovell, M. *The Chartist movement*. Manchester, University Press, 1966 (first pub. 1918). xxxvii, 327pp.

1420 Jackson, T.A. 'Chartism: the first crisis', pp.118–32; 'Chartism: the second crisis', pp.132–8; 'Chartism: the third crisis', pp.139–51, *Trials of British freedom; being some studies in the history of the fight for democratic freedom in Britain (see* no.1193). Lawrence and Wishart, 1945.

1421 Lovett, W. and J. Collins. *Chartism: a new organisation of the people*. Leicester, University Press, 1969 (first pub. 1840). 124pp.
This ed. contains a new introduction by A. Briggs.

1422 Mather, F.C. *Chartism*. Historical Association, 1966. 32pp.

1423 Mather, F.C. 'The Government and the Chartists', *Chartist studies*, pp.372–405 *(see* no.1407). Edited by A. Briggs. Macmillan, 1959.

1424 Morgan, W.T. 'Chartism and the industrial unrest in South Wales in 1842'. NLW, Summer 1957, 10(1):8–16.

1425 Morris, M. 'Chartism and the British working-class movement'. SAS, Fall 1948, 12(4):400–17.

1426 Prothero, I. and D.J. Rowe. 'Debate and rejoinder: the London Working Men's Association and the "People's Charter"'. PP, Dec. 1967, 38:169–76.
See no.1429.

1427 Reeder, D.A. *The age of the Chartists*. Bath, Brodie, 1963. 85pp.

1428 Rowe, D.J. 'The Chartist Convention and the regions'. ECHR, April 1969, 22(1):58–74.

1429 Rowe, D.J. 'The London Working Men's Association and the "People's Charter"'. PP, April 1967, 36:73–86.
See no.1426.

1430 Rudé, G. 'Chartism', *The crowd in history: a study of popular disturbances in France and England, 1730–1848*, pp.179–91. New York, Wiley, 1964.
See also no.1385.

1431 Saville, J. 'Chartism in the year of revolution (1848)'. MDQ, Winter 1952–3, 8(1):23–33.

1432 Saville, J. 'Some aspects of Chartism in decline'. SSLH, Spring 1970, 20:16–18.

1433 Slosson, P.W. *The decline of the Chartist movement*. Cass, 1967 (first pub. 1916). 216pp.

1434 Tatarinova, K. 'Soviet historians on Chartism'. SSLH, Autumn 1962, 5:27–32.

1435 Thompson, D. 'Chartism as a historical subject'. SSLH, Spring 1970, 20:10–12.

1436 Thompson, D. 'Notes on aspects of Chartist leadership'. SSLH, Autumn 1967, 15:28–33.

1437 Thompson, D. 'The working people organise—trade unions, unstamped press and Chartism', *The British people*, pp.108–19. Heinemann, 1969.

1438 Thorne, C. *Chartism: a short history*. Macmillan, 1966. vi, 58pp.

1439 Ward, J.T. 'Chartism and reaction', *The factory movement 1830–55*, pp.186–210. Macmillan, 1962.

1440 Wilson, A. 'Chartism', *Popular movements c.1830–50*, pp.116–34. Edited by J.T. Ward. Macmillan, 1970.

II LOCAL AND SPECIAL STUDIES

1441 Armytage, W.H.G. 'The Chartist land colonies 1846–8'. AH, April 1958, 32(2):87–96.

1442 Armytage, W.H.G. *Heavens below: Utopian experiments in England 1560–1960*. Routledge, 1968. vii, 458pp.
    Discusses Chartist land colonies.

1443 Armytage, W.H.G. and J. Salt. 'The Sheffield land colony: failure of a "back to the land scheme"'. AH, Oct. 1961, 35(4):202–6.

1444 Barnett, C. *The Monmouthshire Chartists*. Newport, Museum and Art Gallery, 1968. 35pp.

1445 Barnsby, G. 'Chartism in the Black Country 1850–60'. OH, Winter 1965–6, 40:24pp.

1446 Briggs, A. 'The local background of Chartism', *Chartist studies*, pp.1–28 (*see* no.1407). Edited by A. Briggs. Macmillan, 1959.

1447 Cannon, J. *The Chartists in Bristol*. Bristol, Historical Association (Bristol Branch), 1964. 18pp.

1448 Communist Party. History Group. 'Chartism and the trade unions'. OH, Autumn 1963, 31:17pp.

1449 Cowherd, R.G. 'Christian Chartists and complete suffrage', *The politics of English dissent: the religious aspects of liberal and humanitarian reform movements, from 1815 to 1848*. Epworth, 1959.

1450 Dalby, G.R. 'The Chartist movement in Halifax and district'. HAS, Nov. 1956, 93–111.

1451 Edwards, J.K. 'Chartism in Norwich'. YB, Nov. 1967, 19(2):85–100.

1452 Faulkner, H.U. *Chartism and the churches: a study in democracy*. Cass, 1970 (first pub. 1916). 152pp.

1453 Fearn, H. 'Chartism in Suffolk', *Chartist studies*, pp.147–73 (*see* no.1407). Edited by A. Briggs. Macmillan, 1959.

1454 Goodway, D. 'Chartism in London'. SSLH, Spring 1970, 20:13–16.

1455 Hadfield, A.M. *The Chartist Land Company*. Newton Abbot, David and Charles, 1970. 248pp.

1456 Harrison, J.F.C. 'Chartism in Leeds', *Chartist studies*, pp.65–98 (*see* no.1407). Edited by A. Briggs. Macmillan, 1959.

1457 Harrison, J.F.C. 'Chartism in Leicester', *Chartist studies*, pp.99–164 (*see* no.1407). Edited by A. Briggs. Macmillan, 1959.

1458 Kovalev, Y.V. 'An anthology of Chartist literature'. OH, Spring 1960, 17:19pp.
     English introduction to no.1459.

1459 Kovalev, Y.V. *An anthology of Chartist literature*. Moscow, Foreign Languages Publishing House, 1966. 413pp.
     Introduction in Russian.

1460 Kovalev, Y.V. 'The literature of Chartism'. VS, Dec. 1958, 2(2):117–138.

1461 MacAskill, J. 'The Chartist land plan', *Chartist studies*, pp.304–41 (*see* no.1407). Edited by A. Briggs. Macmillan, 1959.

1462 McCalman, S.D. 'Chartism in Aberdeen'. SLH, April 1970, 2:5–24.

1463 Maehl, W.H. 'Chartism in northeastern England'. NEG, Oct. 1969, 3:10–16.

1464 Maehl, W.H. 'Chartist disturbances in northeastern England, 1839'. IRSH, 1963, 8(3):389–414.

1465 Mather, F.C. *Public order in the age of the Chartists*. Manchester, University Press, 1966 (first pub. 1959). ix, 260pp.

1466 Mather, F.C. 'The railways, the electric telegraph and public order during the Chartist period, 1837–48'. H, Feb. 1953, 38(132):40–53.

1467 Neale, R.S. 'Class and ideology in a provincial city, Bath 1800–50'. OH, Summer 1966, 42:25pp.

1468 Nottingham. The University. Manuscripts Department. *Working class unrest in Nottingham 1800–1850*. Nottingham, The University, 1970 (first pub. 1965).
     Facsimiles of 7 contemporary documents with 4 explanatory booklets: 1 Introduction, 2 Luddism, 3 Reform, 4 Chartism.

1469 O'Higgins, R. 'The Irish influence in the Chartist movement'. PP, Nov. 1961, 20:83–96.

1470 Patterson, A.T. *Radical Leicester: a history of Leicester 1780–1850*. Leicester, University College, 1954. x, 405pp.

1471 Peacock, A.J. *Bradford Chartism 1838–1840*. York, St. Anthony's Press, 1969. ii, 53pp.

1472 Prothero, I. 'Chartism in London'. PP, Aug. 1969, 44:76–105.

1473 Pugh, R.B. 'Chartism in Somerset and Wiltshire', *Chartist studies*, pp.174–219 (*see* no.1407). Edited by A. Briggs. Macmillan, 1959.

1474 Read, D. 'Chartism in Manchester', *Chartist studies*, pp.29–64 (*see* no.1407). Edited by A. Briggs. Macmillan, 1959.

1475 Rosenblatt, F.F. *The Chartist movement in its social and economic aspects*. Cass, 1967 (first pub. 1916). 248pp.

1476 Rowe, D.J. 'Chartism and the Spitalfields silk-weavers'. ECHR, Dec. 1967, 20(3):482–93.

1477 Rowe, D.J. 'The failure of London Chartism''. HJ, 1968, 11(3):472–87.

1478 Salt, J. *Chartism in South Yorkshire*. Sheffield, University Institute of Education, 1967. 28pp.

1479 Saville, J. 'The Chartist land plan'. SSLH, Autumn 1961, 3:10–12.

1480 Searby, P. *The Chartists*. Longmans, 1968. vi, 96pp.

1481 Searby, P. *Coventry politics in the age of the Chartists 1836–48*. Coventry, Historical Association, Coventry Branch, 1964. 32pp.

1482 Searby, P. 'Great Dodford and the later history of the Chartist land scheme'. AHR, 1968, 16(1):32–45.

1483 Seth, R. *The Specials: the story of the Special Constabulary in England, Wales and Scotland*. Gollancz. 1961.
    Chartism—pp.53–61.

1484 Soffer, R.N. 'Attitudes and allegiances in the unskilled North 1830–50'. IRSH, 1965, 10(3):429–54.

1485 Tholfsen, T.R. 'The Chartist crisis in Birmingham'. IRSH, 1958, 3(3):461–79.

1486 Thompson, D. 'Chartism in industrial areas'. LHN, Autumn 1956, 3(1):13–19.

1487 Williams, D. 'Chartism in Wales', *Chartist studies*, pp.220–48 (*see* no.1407). Edited by A. Briggs. Macmillan, 1959.

1488 Wilson, A. 'Chartism in Glasgow', *Chartist studies*, pp.249–87 (*see* no.1407). Edited by A. Briggs. Macmillan, 1959.

1489 Wilson, A. *The Chartist movement in Scotland*. Manchester, University Press, 1970. x, 294pp.

1490 Wright, D.G. 'A radical borough: parliamentary politics in Bradford 1832–41'. NH, 1969, 4:132–64.

1491 Wright, L.C. *Scottish Chartism*. Edinburgh, Oliver and Boyd, 1953. vii, 242pp.

1492 Wyncoll, P. *Nottingham Chartism*. Nottingham, Trades Council, 1966. 69pp.

Labour: Party and Government

Labour Party

I GENERAL

1493 Abrams, M. 'Class and politics; another look at the British electorate'. EN, Oct. 1961, 17(4):39–44.

1494 Abrams, M. and R. Rose. *Must Labour lose?* Penguin, 1960. 127pp.

1495 Abrams, P. and A. Little. 'The young activist in British politics'. BJS, Dec. 1965, 16(4):315–33.

1496 Aceland, R. and others. *Keeping left*. New Statesman, 1950. 48pp.
Twelve Labour M.P.s 're-thinking our whole policy in the terms of the principles of socialism'.

1497 Adams, W.S. 'Lloyd George and the Labour movement'. PP, Feb. 1953, 3:55–64.

1498 Aitken, I. 'The structure of the Labour Party', *The left: a symposium*, pp.9–30 (*see* no.2595). Edited by G. Kaufman. Blond, 1966.

1499 Allison, G. 'Industrial battlefront'. LM, Aug. 1948, 30(8):245–7.

1500 Anderson, P. 'Critique of Wilsonism'. NLR, Sept.–Oct. 1964, 27:3–27.

1501 Arnot, R.P. 'Jubilee of the Labour Party'. LM, Mar. 1950, 32(3):97–106.

1502 Arnot, R.P. 'Lenin and the British Labour Party'. LM, Apr. 1970, 52(4):173–7.

1503 Arnot, R.P. 'Stepping backwards'. LM, Nov. 1958, 40(11):481–8.

1504 Attlee, C.R. *The Labour Party in perspective—and twelve years later*. New foreword by Attlee. Introduction by Francis Williams. Gollancz, 1949 (first pub. 1937). 199pp.

1505 B., J. 'Mr. Attlee in danger?'. TC, June 1954, 155(928):483–5.

1506 Baird, J. 'The far-sighted militants'. LM, Sept. 1956, 38(9):399–401.

1507 Balogh, T. 'British party programs: the miracle and the mirage'. FA, April 1955, 33(3):458–72.

1508 Balogh, T. *Planning for progress: a strategy for Labour.* Fabian Society, 1963. 48pp.

1509 Beales, H.L. 'Has Labour come to stay?'. PQ, Jan.–Mar. 1947, 18(1):48–60.

1510 Beales, H.L. 'The Labour Party in its social context'. PQ, Jan.–Mar. 1953, 24(1):90–8.

1511 Bealey, F. 'The Northern Weavers, Independent Labour representation and Clitheroe, 1902'. MS, Jan. 1957, 25(1):26–60.
Election of David Shackleton as L.R.C. member for Clitheroe.

1512 Bealey, F., ed. *The social and political thought of the British Labour Party.* Weidenfeld, 1970. xvi, 233pp.
Selections from Labour Party publications and the views of leading party personalities illustrating the development of the aims and policy of the party.

1513 Bealey, F. and H. Pelling. *Labour and politics, 1900–6: a history of the Labour Representation Committee.* Macmillan, 1958. xi, 313pp.
Sequel to no.1727.

1514 Beer, S.H., ed. 'The Labour Party', *Modern British politics: a study of parties and pressure groups,* pp.103–242. Faber, 1969.

1515 Beer, S.H. 'Pressure groups and parties in Britain'. APSR, Mar. 1956, 50(1):1–23.

1516 Beever, R.C. 'The consequences for Labour and social policy'. PQ, Jan.–Mar. 1963, 34(1):78–87.

1517 Benn, A.W. *The regeneration of Britain.* Gollancz, 1965. 144pp.

1518 Brand, C.F. 'British Labor and Soviet Russia'. SAQ, July 1949, 48(3):327–40.

1519 Brand, C.F. *The British Labour Party: a short history.* OUP, 1965. x, 340pp.

1520 Brand, C.F. 'The British Labour Party and nationalization'. SAQ, Spring 1959, 58(2):153–66.

1521 Brogan, C. *The alternatives.* Joseph, 1964. 96pp.

1522 Brogan, C. *Fifty years on.* Hollis and Carter, 1950. 72pp.

1523 Brogan, C. 'The left-wing circus'. C, Autumn 1958, 2(1):46–9.

1524 Brogan, C. *Socialism conquers Labour.* Hollis and Carter, 1949. 32pp.

1525 Brooks, E. 'Comrades and Alderman'. NR, Autumn 1959, 10:32–8.

1526 Brown, N. 'The meaning of the docks dispute'. LM, Dec. 1945, 27(12):368–72.

1527 Bulmer-Thomas, I. *The growth of the party system.* Vol. 1, 1640–1923. *Entry of the Labour Party: 1900–1906.* x, 344pp. Vol. 2, 1924–1964. *The four Labour governments.* v, 223pp. Baker, 1965.

1528 Bulmer-Thomas, I. *The party system in Great Britain*. Phoenix, 1953, vii, 328pp. Includes progress of the Labour Party until 1931.

1529 Burn, W.L. 'Liberalism, socialism and communism' (1). TC, Apr. 1948, 143(854):181–7.

1530 Burn, W.L. 'Liberalism, socialism and communism' (2). TC, May 1948, 143(855):241–8.

1531 Burns, E. *Right-wing Labour: its theory and practice*. Lawrence and Wishart, 1961. 128pp.

1532 Butler, D. and J. Freeman. 'Labour Party', *British political facts 1900–18*, pp.102–11. Macmillan, 1969.

1533 Butt, R. 'The Labour Party: can the centre be held?'. C, Jan.–Mar. 1967, 10(38):19–21.

1534 Campbell, J.R. 'Labour on the eve'. LM, May 1945, 27(5):143–6.

1535 Campbell, J.R. 'Neither plan nor progress'. LM, Oct. 1958, 40(10):463–6.

1536 Casasola, R.C. 'Labour wants socialism'. LM, Nov. 1954, 36(11):499–506.

1537 Chapman, D. 'What prospects for the Labour Party?'. PQ, July–Sept. 1954, 25(3):205–16.

1538 Clarke, D. 'the organisation of political parties'. PQ, Jan.–Mar. 1950, 21(1):79–90.

1539 Clements, R. 'The life-cycles of the Labour Party'. TC, 4, 1969, 178(1043):22–3.

1540 Cline, C.A. *Recruits to Labour: the British Labour Party 1914–31*. Syracuse, University Press, 1963. ix, 198pp.
Period of Liberal Party decline and rise of Labour. Biographies of 67 of the most prominent Labour recruits.

1541 Cohn, E.J. 'The political parties and legal aid'. MLR, July 1945, 8(23):97–119.

1542 Cole, G.D.H. 'The dream and the business'. PQ, July–Sept. 1949, 20(3):201–210.

1543 Cole, G.D.H. *A history of the Labour Party from 1914*. Routledge, 1969 (first pub. 1948). x, 517pp.
Sequel to no.1181.

1544 Cole, G.D.H. 'The Labour Party: history'. PA, Winter 1951, 5(1):59–70.

1545 Cole, G.D.H. 'The Labour Party and the trade unions'. PQ, Jan.–Mar. 1953, 24(1):18–27.

1546 Cole, G.D.H. *Labour's second term*. Fabian Society, 1949. 17pp.
Comment on the draft programme 'Labour believes in Britain' issued for the 1949 party conference.

1547 Connell, J. *Death on the left: the moral decline of the Labour Party*. Pall Mall, 1958. 71pp.

1548 Coulishaw, T.E. 'Battle of Brighton [i.e. party conference]'. LM, Oct. 1966, 48(10):462–3.

1549 Cowles, V. 'The Labour Party', pp.113–34, 'How socialist are the socialists', pp.135–44, and 'Socialism in the countryside', pp.177–84, *No cause for alarm: a study of trends in England today*. Hamilton, 1949 *(see no.2781).*

1550 Crane, P. 'Labour its own worst enemy'. PQ, July–Sept. 1960, 31(3):374–84.

1551 Crosland, A. *Can Labour win?* Fabian society, 1960. 24pp.

1552 Crosland, A. 'The future of public ownership'. EN, May 1961, 16(5):61–5.

1553 Crossman, R.H.S. 'Britain and the outside world'. PQ, Jan.–Mar. 1953, 24(1):28–38.

1554 Crossman, R.H.S. 'British Labor looks at Europe'. FA, July 1963, 41(4):732–43.

1555 Crossman, R.H.S. *Labour in the affluent society*. Fabian Society, 1960. 24pp.

1556 Crossman, R.H.S. *Socialism and the new despotism*. Fabian Society, 1956. 24pp.

1557 Crossman, R.H.S. 'Thoughts on socialist-communist relations'. LM, Oct. 1956, 38(10):448–51.

1558 Crossman, R.H.S., M. Foot and I. Mikardo. *Keep left: by a group of members of parliament.* New Statesman, 1947. 47pp.
Joint statement by 15 M.P.s.

1559 Cyriax, G. 'Labour and the unions'. PQ, July–Sept. 1960, 31(3):324–32.

1560 Dahl, R.A. 'Workers' control of industry and the British Labour Party'. APSR, Oct. 1947, 41(5):875–900.

1561 Darwin, R. 'Labour and local authorities'. LM, Mar. 1949, 31(3):83–7.

1562 Davies, I. 'The Labour Commonwealth'. NLR, Dec. 1963, 22:75–94.

1563 Davies, S.O. 'Labour and re-armament'. LM, June 1951, 33(6):253–6.

1564 Davies, S.O. 'Labour and war'. LM, Sept. 1950, 32(9):400–4.

1565 Davies, S.O. 'Signposts—or windmills?'. LM, Oct. 1961, 43(10):465–7.

1566 Day, A. 'The economic setting'. PQ, July-Sept. 1960, 31(3):255–71.

1567 Dell, E. 'Labour and local government'. PQ, July-Sept. 1960, 31(3):333–47.

1568 Derrick, P. 'Class and the Labour Party'. TC, Spring 1965, 173(1025):121–5.

1569 Ditz, G.W. 'Utopian symbols in the history of the British Labour Party'. BJS, June 1966, 17(2):145–50.

1570 Dowse, R.E. 'The entry of the Liberals into the Labour Party 1910–20'. YB, Nov. 1961, 13(2):78–87.

1571 Dugdale, J. 'The Labour Party and nationalisation'. PQ, July–Sept. 1957, 28(3):254–9.

1572 Dutt, R.P. 'After Brighton'. LM, Nov. 1957, 39(11):492–8.

1573 Dutt, R.P. 'Battle of Scarborough'. LM, Oct. 1960, 42(10):433–46.

1574 Dutt, R.P. 'Blackpool balance sheet'. LM, Nov. 1956, 38(11):481–92.

1575 Dutt, R.P. '1—Blackpool–Brighton–Moscow, 2—Right or left at Blackpool, 3—Lessons for the left'. LM, Nov. 1961, 43(11):497–508.

1576 Dutt, R.P. 'Choice before Margate'. LM, Oct. 1950, 32(10):433–41.

1577 Dutt, R.P. 'Class politics and the election'. LM, Nov. 1969, 51(11):481–496.

1578 Dutt, R.P. 'The crisis in the Labour Party'. LM, Apr. 1955, 37(4):158–162.

1579 Dutt, R.P. 'Crisis of the Labour Party'. LM, Oct. 1955, 37(10):433–446.

1580 Dutt, R.P. 'Douglas and Margate'. LM, Sept. 1953, 35(9):385–99.

1581 Dutt, R.P. 'From Portsmouth to Brighton'. LM, Oct. 1969, 51(10):433–44.

1582 Dutt, R.P. 'How the Labour Party became what it is'. LM, Oct. 1958, 49(10):433–42.
       Review of nos.1731 and 1984.

1583 Dutt, R.P. 'Labour after Margate'. LM, Nov. 1955, 37(11):481–97.

1584 Dutt, R.P. 'Labour and communism'. LM, Oct. 1970, 52(10):433–43.

1585 Dutt, R.P. 'Labour into battle'. LM, Oct. 1956, 38(10):433–45.

1586 Dutt, R.P. 'Labour, Mr. Bevan and Britain's future'. LM, May 1952, 34(5):193–211.

1587 Dutt, R.P. 'Labour policy battle'. LM, July 1957, 39(7):289–302.

1588 Dutt, R.P. 'Labour's assizes, Trade unions and the economic situation, Labour Party testing time'. LM, Sept. 1958, 40(9):385–97.

1589 Dutt, R.P. 'Last thoughts for Brighton'. LM, Oct. 1957, 39(10):433–45.

1590 Dutt, R. P. 'MacDonaldism'. LM, Oct, 1966, 48(10):486–91 (first pub. Labour Monthly, May 1924).

1591 Dutt, R.P. 'Operation chameleon'. LM, Sept. 1957, 39(9):385–97.

1592 Dutt, R.P. 'The stream and the dam'. LM, Nov. 1954, 36(11):481–98.

1593 Dutt, R.P. 'Think fast! Act fast!'.LM, Lov. 1960, 42(11):481–4.

1594 Dutt, R.P. 'Wake up, Britain!' LM, Dec. 1959, 41(12):513–29.

1595 Dutt, R.P. 'What kind of Labour government?'. LM, Oct. 1963, 45(10):433–8.

596 Dyson, A.E. 'Farewell to the Left', *Right turn: a symposium on the need to end the 'progressive' consensus in British thinking and policy*, pp.146–57. Edited by Dr. Rhodes Boyson. Churchill Press, 1970.

597 Epstein, L.D. *Britain—uneasy ally*. Chicago, University Press, 1954. viii, 279pp.

598 Epstein, L.D. 'British class consciousness and the Labour Party'. JBS, May 1962, 1(2):136–50.

599 Epstein, L.D. 'British Labour left and U.S. foreign policy'. APSR, Dec. 1951, 45(4):974–95.

600 Epstein, L.D. 'British mass parties in comparison with American parties'. PSQ, Mar. 1956, 71(1):97–125.

601 Epstein, L.D. *Political parties in western democracies*. Pall Mall, 1967. ix, 374pp.

602 Epstein, L.D. 'Socialism and the British Labour Party'. PSQ, Dec. 1951, 66(4):556–75.

603 Epstein, L.D. 'Who makes party policy: British Labor, 1960–61'. MJPS, May 1962, 6(2):165–82.

604 Fabian Society. *The road to recovery*. Wingate, 1948. 111pp.
    Contributions by D. Jay, G. Bing, H.J. Laski, I. Mikardo, H. Wilson, R. Crossman.

605 Fabian Society. *What Labour could do*. Routledge, 1945. vii, 104pp.
    Contributions by Lord Latham, J.S. Clarke, J. Griffiths, K. Martin, L. Barnes, R.H. Tawney.

606 Fairlie, H. 'The life of politics; politicians, statesmen and leaders'. EN, Jan. 1967, 28(1):25–38.

607 Fanti, G. 'The resurgence of the Labour Party'. NLR, Mar.–Apr. 1965, 30:27–44.

608 Gaitskell, H. 'The economic aims of the Labour Party'. PQ, Jan.–Mar. 1953, 24(1):5–18.

609 Gallacher, W. 'What a programme!'. LM, June 1949, 31(6):170–7.

610 Gelman, N.I. 'Bevanism: a philosophy for British Labor?'. JP, Nov. 1954, 16(4):645–53.

611 Godfrey, J.L. 'British foreign policy and the Labour Party, 1945–7'. SAQ, April 1948, 47(2):137–51.

612 Goldthorpe, J.H. and D. Lockwood. 'Affluence and the British class structure'. SOCR, July 1963, 11(2):133–63.

613 Gollan, J. 'Dorking socialism'. LM, July 1950, 32(7):305–9.

614 Gollan, J. 'The Labour Party and the election'. LM, May 1955, 37(5):213–19.

1615 Gollan, J. 'Labour's election programme'. LM, Apr. 1949, 31(4):116–119.

1616 Gollan, J. 'The Margate conference'. LM, Nov. 1950, 32(11):511–16.

1617 Graubard, S.R. *British Labour and the Russian Revolution, 1917–24.* OUP, 1956. x, 305pp.

1618 Grimshaw, P. 'The Left must fight'. LM, Feb. 1960, 42(2):76–7.

1619 Guttsman, W.L. 'Labour's leaders and Labour led', *The British political elite,* pp.225–77. MacGibbon and Kee, 1963.

1620 Gwyn, W.B. 'The financing of working-class representatives', *Democracy and the cost of politics in Britain,* pp.147–77. Athlone Press, 1962.

1621 Hall, P., ed. *Labour's new frontiers.* Deutsch, 1964. 180pp.
Ten essays 'to trigger off a continuous process of generation of ideas' for the Labour government.

1622 Hall, S. 'The conference and its consequences'. NLR, Nov.–Dec. 1960, 6:3–7.

1623 Hall, W.G. *The Labour Party.* Collins, 1949. 50pp.

1624 Halsey, A.H. and S. Marks. 'British student politics'. D, Winter 1968, 97(1):116–36.

1625 Hanson, A.H. 'The future of the Labour Party'. PQ, Oct.–Dec. 1970, 41(4):375–86.

1626 Hanson, A.H. 'The Labour Party and House of Commons reform' (1). PA, Autumn 1957, 10(4):454–68,

1627 Hanson, A.H. 'The Labour Party and House of Commons reform' (2). PA, Winter 1957, 11(1):39–56.

1628 Harley, J.H. 'Labour at the crossways'. CNR, July 1946, 170:12–15.

1629 Harley, J.H. 'Labour faces the future'. CNR, July 1945, 168:22–6.

1630 Harley, J.H. 'Labour plans and policies'. CNR, Feb. 1945, 167:88–93.

1631 Harrington, T. 'The dilemma of the non-communist left'. LM, Jan. 1962, 44(1):32–4.

1632 Haseler, S. *The Gaitskellites: revisionism in the British Labour Party, 1951–64.* Macmillan, 1969. xiv, 286pp.
Gaitskell's rise to power, his distinctive style and political leadership.

1633 Hattersley, R. 'New blood', *The left: a symposium,* pp. 141–66 (*see* no.2595). Blond, 1966.

1634 Healey, D. 'Power politics and the Labour Party', *New Fabian essays,* pp.161–79(*see* no.2437). Edited by R.H.S. Crossman. Turnstile, 1952.

1635 Henderson, F. 'British Labour and the Soviet Union'. LM, Apr. 1956, 38(4):158–66.

1636 Hindell, K. and P. Williams. 'Scarborough and Blackpool: an analysis of some votes at the Labour Party Conferences of 1960 and 1961'. PQ, July–Sept. 1962, 33(3):306–20.

1637 Hughes, J. *An economic strategy for Labour*. Fabian Society, 1967. 41pp.

1638 Hunter, L. *The road to Brighton Pier*. Barker, 1959. 224pp.

1639 Hussey, C. 'Moderation at Margate'. TC, Nov. 1953, 154(921):325–9.

1640 Hutber, P. 'Obsessions on the left'. TC, Spring 1964, 172(1021):56–62.

1641 Jenkins, C. 'Retreat: the Labour Party and the public corporations'. ULR, Winter 1958, 1(3):42–60.

642 Jenkins, H. and W. Wolfgang. *Tho' cowards flinch: democracy, power and socialism in the Labour Party*. Future/Victory for Socialism, 1956. 24pp.

643 Jenkins, R. 'British Labor divided'. FA, Apr. 1960, 38(3):487–96.

644 Jenkins, R. *The Labour case*. Penguin, 1959. 151pp.

645 Jenkins, R. *Pursuit of progress: a critical analysis of the achievement and prospect of the Labour Party*. Heinemann, 1953. 186pp.

646 Jones, M. 'The man from the Labour'. NLR, Jan.–Feb. 1960, 1:14–17.

647 Kay, H. 'Equal pay'. LM, Oct. 1969, 51(10):449–50.

648 Kay, H. 'The Labour Party and the unions'. M, Oct. 1966, 36(4):196–203.

649 Kaye, S. 'The road to Wapping steps'. LM, Aug. 1959, 41(8):340–2.

650 Kelley, D. 'Antidote for defeatism'. LM, Nov. 1960, 42(11):500–2.

651 Kiernan, V.G. 'India and the Labour Party'. NLR, Mar.–Apr. 1967, 42(67):44–55.

652 Klugman, J. 'Labour "rethinkers"'. LM, Aug. 1955, 37(8):363–7.

653 Labour Monthly. 'Labour Parties protest against re-arming Germany'. LM, May 1954, 36(5):232–6.

654 Labour Party. *The Labour Party Foundation conference and Annual Conference Reports 1900–05*. Hammersmith Books, 1967 (first pub. 1900–5). 256pp.

655 Labour Party. *Marching on, 1900–50: the golden jubilee of the Labour Party*. The Party, 1950. 15pp.

656 Labour Party. *Proceedings of the Annual Conference 1945–*. The Labour Party, 1945–.

657 Labour Party. *The rise of the Labour Party*. The Party, 1946. 17pp.

658 Lawrence, J. 'A case of expulsion'. LM, Sept. 1958, 40(9):426–7.

659 Lawrence, J. 'What next for the left?'. LM, Nov. 1957, 39(11):514–17.

660 Lawton, C. 'Labour and Europe'. PQ, Jan.–Mar. 1962, 33(1):41–7.

1661 Lejeune, A. *Shadow over Britain: an examination of Labour Party policies and socialist leaders.* Johnson, 1964. 225pp.

1662 Lester, A. 'The Labour Party: a view from within'. C, Jan.–Mar. 1967, 10(38):16–18.

1663 Lewis, R. 'The Labour Party: a Tory looks at the trend of Labour rule'. C, Jan.–Mar. 1967, 10(38):22–3.

1664 Licinius, *pseud. Vote Labour? Why?* Gollancz, 1945. 78pp.

1665 Lim, H. B. 'The Labour Party and the colonies'. LM, Jan. 1958, 40(1):28–31.

1666 Lindsay, I. 'Young socialists: what now?'. LM, June 1961, 43(6):273–5.

1667 Lipson, L. 'Common ground and emerging conflicts between the British parties'. PQ, Apr.–June 1956, 27(2):182–93.

1668 Loewenberg, G. 'The British constitution and the structure of the Labour Party'. APSR, Sept. 1958, 52(3):771–90.

1669 Loewenberg, G. 'The transformation of British Labour Party policy since 1945'. JP, May 1959, 21(2):234–57.

1670 Longden, G. 'Is socialism really dead?'. C, Jan.–Mar. 1968, 11(42):32–4.

1671 Lyman, R.W. 'The British Labour Party: the conflict between socialist ideals and practical politics between the wars'. JBS, Nov. 1965, 5(1):140–52.

1672 McAllister, G. 'Labour Party policy in transition'. F, June 1952, 171(1026):375–81.

1673 McKenzie, R.T. *British political parties: the distribution of power between the Conservative and Labour Parties.* Heinemann, 1964 (first pub. 1953). xv, 694pp.

1674 McKenzie, R.T. 'Power in British political parties'. BJS, June 1955, 6(2):123–32.

1675 McKenzie, R.T. 'The Wilson Report and the future of the Labour Party organization'. PS, Feb. 1956, 4(1):93–7.

1676 McKenzie, R.T. and S.H. Beer. 'Text of their BBC discussion on Professor Beer's book—*Modern British politics'.* PA, Summer 1966, 19(3):373–84.

1677 McKitterick, T.E.M. 'The membership of the Party'. PQ, July–Sept. 1960, 31(3):312–23.

1678 MacRae, D.G. 'The ideological situation in the Labour movement'. PQ, Jan.–Mar. 1953, 24(1):78–89.

1679 Marquand, D. 'Can Labour recover?'. EN, Oct. 1962, 19(4):57–60.

1680 Marquand, D. 'Has Lib-Lab. a future?'. EN, Apr. 1962, 18(4):63–5.

1681 Marquand, D. 'Labour and the European cause'. EN, Oct. 1961, 17(4):58–61.

682 Marquand, D. 'Lucky Jim and the Labour Party'. ULR, Spring 1957, 1(1):57–60.

683 Marquand, D. 'Passion and politics'. EN, Dec. 1961, 17(6):3–6.

684 Marquand, D. 'The politics of deprivation; reconsidering the failure of Utopianism'. EN, Apr. 1969, 32(4):36–44.

685 Martin, K. *Socialism and the welfare state.* Fabian Society, 1952. 20pp.

686 Marwick, A. 'The Labour Party and the welfare state in Britain, 1900–48'. AHR, Dec. 1967, 73(2):380–403.

687 Marwick, A. 'Youth in Britain, 1920–60: detachment and commitment'. JCH, 1970, 5(1):37–51.

688 Massie, A. 'Labour, socialism—and Mr. Morrison'. LM, Dec. 1946, 28(12):374–7.

689 Matthews, G. 'The great discussion'. LM, Mar. 1953, 35–(3):111–16.

690 Matthews, G. 'What does Mr. Gaitskell offer?'. LM, Mar. 1959, 41(3):113–17.

691 Maynard, J. 'Change, not tinkering'. LM, Oct. 1961, 43(10):467–9.

692 Maynard, J. 'Conference impressions'. LM, Nov. 1969, 51(1):498–500.

693 Maynard, J. 'Sidelights at Brighton'. LM, Nov. 1957, 39(11):511–14.

694 Meehan, E.J. *The British left wing and foreign policy: a study of the influence of ideology.* New Brunswick, (N.J.), Rutgers University Press, 1960. xv, 201pp.

695 Mikardo, I. *The Labour case.* Wingate, 1950. 64pp.

696 Mikardo, I. 'Present-day problems of Great Britain's Labour movement', *Essays in Jewish sociology, Labour and co-operation in memory of Dr. Noah Barou 1889–1955*, pp.125–35. Edited by H.F. Infield. Yoseloff, 1962.

697 Mikardo, I. *The second five years: a Labour programme for 1950.* Fabian Society, 1948. 21pp.

698 Miliband, R. 'The sickness of Labourism'. NLR, Jan.–Feb. 1960, 1:5–9.

699 Millar, J.P.M. *The Labour Party: a discussion between two trade unionists.* Tillicoultry, National Council of Labour Colleges, 1965. 16pp.

700 Miller, K.E. *Socialism and foreign policy: theory and practice in Britain to 1931.* Hague, Nijhoff, 1967. viii, 301pp.

701 Milne, R.S. 'Labour and the planning organisation'. PQ, Apr.–June 1952, 23(2):147–54.

702 Mitchell, Joan. 'The political crisis: crisis in the Labour Party: the Government and its critics', *Crisis in Britain,* 1951, pp.167–93. Secker and Warburg, 1963.

1702a Mitchell, Joan. 'The political crisis, the government and its critics', *Crisis in Britain*, 1951, pp.194–229. Secker and Warburg, 1963.

1703 Montagu, I. 'Bogy over Bournemouth'. LM, June 1946, 28(6):167–70.

1704 Mortimer, J. 'The case for public ownership'. LM, Oct. 1963, 45(10):451–4.

1705 Mortimer, J. 'The Labour Party conference and the economy'. LM, Nov. 1967, 49(11):494–7.

1706 Mortimer, J. 'The way ahead'. LM, Dec. 1959, 41(12):531–4.

1707 Mowat, C.L. 'Britain in the twentieth century: some new assessments'. SAQ, Summer 1965, 64(3):254–62.

1708 Murphy, M.E. 'The British Labor Party and domestic reform'. JPE, Dec. 1946, 54(6):522–37.

1709 Murry, J.M. 'Socialism and the Labour Party'. F, Dec. 1949, 166(996): 357–62.

1710 Nairn, T. 'The nature of the Labour Party' (1). NLR, Sept.–Oct. 1964, 27:38–66.

1711 Nairn, T. 'The nature of the Labour Party' (2). NLR, Nov.–Dec. 1964, 28:33–62.

1712 Naylor, J.F. *Labour's international policy: the Labour Party in the 1930's.* Weidenfeld, 1969. viii, 380pp.

1713 Neustadt, R.E. 'Memorandum on the British Labour Party and the MLF'. NLR, Sept.–Oct. 1968, 51:11–21.

1714 Nordlinger, E.A. *The working-class Tories: authority, defence and a stable democracy.* MacGibbon and Kee, 1967. 276pp.

1715 Norman, W. 'Signposts for the 60's'. NLR, Sept.–Oct. 1961, 11:45–9.

1716 Northcott, J. *Why Labour?* Penguin, 1964. 192pp.

1717 Norwood, C. 'Equal pay'. LM, Oct. 1969, 51(10):447–8.

1718 Ostergaard, G.N. 'Labour and the development of the public corporation'. MS, May 1954, 22(2):192–226.

1719 Panza, S., *pseud.* 'The new "socialism": revolution in Transport House'. LM, Sept. 1956, 38(9):359–68.

1720 Parker, J. *Labour marches on.* Penguin, 1947. 220pp. (*see* no.2093).

1721 Parkin, B. 'Socialist-communist relations'. LM, Jan. 1957, 39(1):13–16.

1722 Paterson, P. 'Who selects the elect?'. TC, 4, 1969, 178(1043):5–6.

1723 Pavitt, L. *The health of the nation: the second stage of the N.H.S.* Fabian Society, 1965 (first pub. 1963). 37pp.

1724 Pelling, H. 'The American economy and the foundation of the British Labour Party'. ECHR, Aug. 1955, 8(1):1–17.

725 Pelling, H. 'British Labour and British imperialism', *Popular politics and society in late Victorian Britain*, pp.82–100. Macmillan, 1968.

726 Pelling, H. 'Labour and the downfall of Liberalism', *Popular politics and society in late Victorian Britain*, pp.101–20. Macmillan 1968.

727 Pelling, H. *The origins of the Labour Party 1880–1900*. Oxford, Clarendon Press, 1968. ix, 256pp.
    See no.1513.

728 Pelling, H. *Popular politics and society in late Victorian Britain: essays*. Macmillan, 1968. vii, 188pp.

729 Pelling, H. *A short history of the Labour Party*. Macmillan 1968 (first pub. 1961). vii, 150pp.

730 Phillips, M. *Labour in the sixties*. Labour Party, 1960. 24pp.

731 Poirer, P.P. *The advent of the Labour Party*. Allen and Unwin, 1958. 288pp.
    See no.1582.

732 Political Quarterly. 'Editorial: The future of the Labour Party'. PQ, July–Sept. 1954, 25(3):201–4.

733 Political Quarterly. 'Editorial: Labour's plan for progress'. PQ, Oct.–Dec. 1958, 29(4):317–22.

734 Political Quarterly. 'Editorial: Let us face the future'. PQ, July–Sept. 1960, 31(3):229–40.

735 Political Quarterly. 'Notes and Comments: the Labour Party and the control of industry'. PQ, Oct.–Dec. 1957, 28(4):309–15.

736 Pollitt, H. 'A common policy for Labour'. LM, Jan. 1954, 36(1):22–30.

737 Pollitt, H. 'How Labour can win'. LM, Jan. 1955, 37(1):15–21.

738 Pollitt, H. 'Lessons of the Labour conference'. LM, Jan. 1945, 27(1):22–7.

739 Pollitt, H. 'Outlook after Bournemouth'. LM, July 1946, 28(7):200–5.

740 Pollitt, H. 'A policy for Labour'. LM, Sept. 1952, 34(9):385–95.

741 Potter, A.M. 'British party organisation, 1950'. PSQ, Mar. 1951, 66(1):65–86.

742 Potter, D. *The glittering coffin*. Gollancz, 1960. 159pp.

743 Pritt, D.N. 'General election ahead'. LM, Feb. 1970, 52(2):64–8.

744 Pritt, D.N. 'An inside story'. LM, July 1959, 41(7):307–9.
    Review of *Road to Wigan Pier*.

745 Pritt, D.N. 'Lessons of Blackpool'. LM, July 1949, 31(7):203–7.

746 Pritt, D.N. 'Open letter to a delegate to the Labour Party Conference, 1968'. LM, Oct. 1968, 50(10):458–62.

747 Pritt, D.N. 'The way onward from Margate'. LM, Nov. 1953, 35(11):499–503.

1748 Ramelson, B. 'Forbid the banns: meaning of the compromise on Clause 4'. LM, May 1960, 42(5):206–10.

1749 Rattray, R.F. 'The decline and fall of the Labour Party'. QR, July 1957, 295(613):249–59.

1750 Rawson, D.W. 'The life-span of Labour Parties (Britain, Norway, Sweden, Australia, New Zealand)'. PS, Oct. 1969, 17(3):313–33.

1751 Rees, M. 'The social setting'. PQ, July–Sept. 1960, 31(3):285–99.

1752 Reid, J.H.S. *The origins of the Labour Party*. Minneapolis, University of Minnesota Press, 1955. xiv, 258pp.
    To 1919.

1753 Rex, J. 'The Labour bureaucracy'. NR, Autumn 1958, 6:49–61.

1754 Roberts, E. 'Labour Party and the unions'. LM, Nov. 1969, 51(11):497–8.

1755 Roberts, G.K. *Political parties and pressure groups in Britain*. Weidenfeld, 1970. ix, 203pp.

1756 Robson, W.A. 'Freedom, equality and socialism: a critique of recent Labour Party statements'. PQ, Oct.–Dec. 1956, 27(4):378–91.

1757 Roche, J.P. and S. Sachs. 'The bureaucrat and the enthusiast: an exploration of the leadership of social movements'. WPQ, June 1955, 8(2):248–61.

1758 Rose, R. 'Class and party divisions: Britain as a test case'. SO, 1968, 2:129–62.
    Relationship between working-class people and Labour Party since 1900.

1759 Rose, R. 'Parties, factions and tendencies in Britain'. PS, Feb. 1964, 12(1):33–46.

1760 Rose, R. 'The political ideas of English party activist'. APSR, June 1962, 56(2):360–71.

1761 Rose, R. *Politics in England*. Faber, 1965. 247pp.

1762 Rose, S. 'The Labour Party and German re-armament: a view from Transport House'. PS, June 1946, 14(2):133–44.

1763 Rothman, S. 'The decline and fall of the Labour Party'. SAQ, Spring 1962, 61(2):151–8.

1764 Rothstein, A. 'Historic issues facing Labour'. LM, Aug. 1960, 42(8):337–46.

1765 Rover, C. 'The political parties: The Labour Party', *Women's suffrage and party politics in Britain 1866–1914*, pp.146–77. Routledge, 1967.

1766 Rowland, C. 'Labour publicity'. PQ, July–Sept. 1960, 31(3):348–60.

1767 Rowse, A.L. 'The British Labour Party: prospects and portents'. FA, July 1945, 23(4):658–67.

768 Runciman, W.G. '"Embourgeoisement", self-rated class and party structure'. SOCR, July 1964, 12(2):137–54.

769 Rustin, M. 'Young socialists'. NLR, May–June 1961, 9:51–3.
Young Socialists 1961 conference.

770 Rutan, G.F. 'The Labour Party in Ulster: opposition by cartel'. RP, Oct. 1967, 29(4):526–35.

771 Sampson, R.V. 'The dilemma of British Labor'. FA, April 1952, 30(3):455–65.

772 Samuel, R. 'Dr. Abrams and the end of politics'. NLR, Sept.–Oct. 1960, 5:2–9.

773 Saville, J. 'Labour and income redistribution'. SR, 1965, 2:147–62.

774 Shanks, M. 'Labour philosophy and the current position'. PQ, July–Sept. 1960, 31(3):241–54.

775 Shepherd, Lord. *Labour's early days*. Tillicoultry, National Council of Labour Colleges, 1950. 48pp.

776 Shinwell, E. *The Labour story*. Macdonald, 1963. 222pp.

777 Shonfeld, A. 'A deadlock on the left'. EN, Sept. 1959, 13(3):11–19.

778 Short, R. 'The way ahead'. LM, Feb. 1958, 40(2):70–5.

779 Shub, D. and R. Alexander. *What do you know about British Labor?* N.Y., Rand School Press, 1946. 61pp.
Includes C.R. Attlee's address to U.S. Congress on 13th November 1945: 'What the British Labor Party stands for'.

780 Silverman, S. 'Signpost—to where?'. LM, Sept. 1961, 43(9):416–19.

781 Silverman, S. 'Socialist–communist relations'. LM, Dec. 1956, 38(12):548–50.

782 Sinclair, W.A. *Socialism and the individual: notes on joining the Labour Party*. Hale, 1955. 168pp.
Conservative candidate in 1945 'came to the conclusion that he ought to support the Labour party'. Joined 1951.

783 Sirockin, P. *The story of Labour youth, 1924–60*. Keep Left, 1960. 16pp.

784 Smith, G.R. *The rise of the Labour Party in Great Britain*. Arnold, 1969. 64pp.

785 Spade, S. 'Signposts of the pause'. NLR, Nov.–Dec. 1961, 12:2–8.

786 Stewart, H.L. 'Laying the blame on Labour'. UTQ, July 1946, 15(4):333–45.

787 Stewart, M. and R. Winsbury. *An income policy for Labour*. Fabian Society, 1963. 33pp.

788 Strachey, J. *Labour's task*. Fabian Society, 1951. 24pp.

1789 Strachey, J. 'The object of further socialization'. PQ, Jan.–Mar. 1953, 24(1):68–77.

1790 Tawney, R.H. 'The choice before the Labour Party', *The attack and other papers*, pp.52–70. Allen and Unwin, 1953.

1791 Tawney, R.H. 'Social democracy in Britain', *The radical tradition: twelve essays on politics, education and literature*, pp.138–67. Allen and Unwin, 1964,

1792 Thomas, N.P. 'Scarborough and Blackpool'. CNR, Nov. 1954, 186:273–7.
    Labour and Conservative conferences.

1793 Tomlinson, A. 'Labour Party conference: delegate's report'. LM, Nov. 1966, 48(11):535–6.

1794 Tracey, H., ed. *The British Labour Party: its history, growth, policy and leaders.* Vol. 1, *History.* x, 274pp. Vol. 2, *Policy.* viii, 301pp. Vol. 3, *Present leaders: 48 biographies; Pioneers and founders: 41 biographies.* x, 347pp. Foreword by C.R. Attlee. Introductory—Labour yesterday and today, Morgan Phillips. Caxton, 1948.

1795 Tucker, W.R. *The attitude of the British Labour Party towards European and collective security problems 1920–39.* Geneva, The University, 1950. 270pp.

1796 Verrier, P. 'British defence policy under Labor'. FA, Jan. 1964, 42(2):282–92.

1797 Wainwright, W. 'Labour's nuclear policy'. LM, July 1960, 42(7):301–305.

1798 Walker, P.C.G. 'The Labor Party's defense and foreign policy'. FA, Apr. 1964, 42(3):391–8.

1799 Watkins, K.W. *Britain divided: the effect of the Spanish Civil War on British political opinion.* Nelson, 1963.
    'The British left', pp.141–95, mainly Labour Party.

1800 Webbe, Sir H. 'Scarborough–and after'. QR, Apr. 1961, 299(628):123–34.

1801 Wertheimer, E. 'Portrait of the Labour Party', *Studies in British politics*, pp.36–51. Edited by R. Rose. Macmillan, 1969.
    Extracts from his book of the same title, pub. 1929.

1802 Williams, A.L. 'Modernizing the Labour Party', *A radical future*, pp.188–201. Edited by B. Whitaker. Cape, 1967.

1803 Williams, F. *Fifty years march: the rise of the Labour Party.* Odhams, 1949. 384pp.

1804 Williams, F. 'The Labour Party: philosophy and principles'. PA, Winter 1951, 5(1):70–6.

1805 Williams, F. 'The program of the British Labour Party: an historical survey'. JP, May 1950, 12(2):189–210.

806 Williams, G. 'Organizing a Labour Party conference'. PA, Summer 1955, 8(3):379–84.

807 Williams, S. 'The external setting'. PQ, July–Sept. 1960, 31(3):272–84.

808 Williams, S. 'The Labour Party'. DR, Winter 1962–3, 236(494): 280–92.

809 Willis, R. 'Blackpool and Berlin'. LM, Nov. 1961, 43(11):515–17.

810 Wilmot, E.P. *The Labour Party: a short history*. Macmillan, 1968. 96pp.

811 Wilson, H. *The new Britain: Labour's plan*. Penguin, 1964. 134pp.
    Pre-election speeches, Jan.–April 1964.

812 Windrich, E. *British Labour's foreign policy*. California, Stanford University Press, 1952. x, 268pp.

813 Winkler, H.R. 'British Labor and the origins of the idea of colonial trusteeship, 1914–19'. HIST, Spring 1951, 13(2):154–72.

814 Winkler, H.R. 'The emergence of a Labor foreign policy in Great Britain, 1918–29'. JMH, Sept. 1956, 28(3):247–58.

815 Winterton, E.M. 'From Gaitskell to Wilson'. LM, Mar. 1963, 45(3):107–10.

816 Winterton, E.M. 'Labour Party boomerang'. LM Sept. 1954, 36(9):405–12.

817 Wollheim, R. 'Old ideas and new men: some reflections on the debate between the Left and Right in Great Britain'. EN, Oct. 1956, 7(4):3–11.

818 Woolf, L. *Foreign policy: the Labour Party's dilemma*. Fabian Society, 1947. 34pp.

819 Wootton, B. 'The Labour Party and social services'. PQ, Jan.–Mar. 1953, 24(1):55–67.

820 Wright, R.W. 'Sedatives and socialism'. LM, Apr. 1960, 42(4):169–70.

821 Yates, I. 'Power in the Labour Party'. PQ, July–Sept. 1960, 31(3):300–11.

822 Young, M. *The chipped white cups of Dover*—a discussion of the possibility of a new progressive party. Unit 2, 1960. 20pp.
    Critical of Labour Party but believes it could still be the new progressive party.

823 Young, M. 'The leadership, the rank and file, and Mr. Bevan'. PQ, Jan.–Mar. 1953, 24(1):99–107.

II LOCAL STUDIES

824 Allen, A.J. 'Voting recollections and intentions in Reading: an opinion poll experiment'. PA, Spring 1967, 20(2):170–7.

825 Awbery, S. *Labour's early struggles in Swansea*. Swansea, Swansea Printers, 1949. iv, 128pp.

1826 Barker, B. *Labour in London: a study in municipal achievement.* Routledge, 1946. x, 232pp.

1827 Bealey, F., J. Blondel and W.P. McCann. *Constituency politics: a study of Newcastle-under-Lyme.* Faber, 1965. 440pp.
The Labour Party since 1918, pp.77–105.

1828 Berry, D. *The sociology of grass roots politics: a study of party membership.* Macmillan, 1970. 155pp.
Contains a special study of Walton, Liverpool.

1829 Birch, A.H. 'The Labour Party', *Small-town politics: a study of political life in Glossop*, pp.60–75, 80–94, OUP, 1959.

1830 Blondel, J. 'The Conservative Association and the Labour Party in Reading'. PS, June 1958, 6(2):101–19.

1831 Brennan, T., E.W. Cooney and H. Pollins. 'Party politics and local government in western South Wales'. PQ, Jan.–Mar. 1954, 25(1):76–83.

1832 Campbell, P.W. and A.H. Birch. 'Politics in the north-west'. MS, Sept. 1950, 18(3):217–43.

1833 Clarke, P.R. 'British politics and Blackburn politics, 1900–40'. HJ, 1969, 12(2):302–7.

1834 Cox, D. 'The Labour Party in Leicester: a study in branch development'. IRSH, 1961, 6(2):197–211.

1835 Donnison, D.V. and D.E.G. Plowman. 'The functions of local Labour parties: experiments in research methods'. PS, June 1954, 2(2):154–67.

1836 Goldthorpe, J.N., D. Lockwood, F. Bechhofer and J. Platt. *The affluent worker: political attitudes and behaviour.* CUP, 1968. vii, 95pp.
Analysis of party and political affiliations in Luton.

1837 Hanham, H.J. 'The local organisation of the British Labour Party'. WPQ, June 1956, 9(2):376–88.

1838 Holborn and St. Pancras Labour Parties—expelled members. *St. Pancras story: an appeal to Labour Party conference delegates, 1958.* John Lawrence, 1958. 20pp.

1839 Janosik, E.G. *Constituency Labour Parties in Britain.* Pall Mall, 1968. viii, 222pp. (*see* no.1845).

1840 Jones, G.W. 'The Labour group' and 'Pressures and controversies—the Labour initiative and the Conservative response', *Borough politics: a study of the Wolverhampton Town Council, 1888–1964*, pp.163–86 and 304–24. Macmillan, 1964.

1841 Mowat, J. and A. Power. *Our struggle for socialism!! A short history of the Barrow-in-Furness Labour Party.* Barrow-in-Furness, Atkinson, 1949.
33pp.—unnumbered.

1842 Parry, C. *The radical tradition in Welsh politics: a study of Liberal and Labour politics in Gwynedd 1900–20.* Hull, University Publications, 1970. ix, 89pp.

1843 Plowman, D.E.G. 'Allegiance to political parties: a study of three parties in one area [Glossop]'. PS, Oct. 1955, 3(3):222–34.

1844 Robson, W.A. 'Labour and local government'. PQ, Jan.–Mar. 1953, 24(1):39–55.

1845 Seyd, P. 'Constituency Labour Parties in Britain'. SSLH, Spring 1969, 18:67–8.
   Review of no.1839.

1846 Stacey, M. *Tradition and change: a study of Banbury*. OUP, 1960. xiv, 231pp.

1847 Thompson, P. 'Liberals, radicals and labour in London, 1880–1900'. PP, Apr. 1964, 27:73–101.

1848 Thompson, P. *Socialists, Liberals and Labour: the struggle for London, 1885–1914*. Routledge, 1967. viii, 376pp.
   Emergence and role of Labour Party, Fabian Society, I.L.P. and S.D.F.

III THE PARLIAMENTARY LABOUR PARTY

849 Alderman, R.K. 'The conscience clause of the Parliamentary Labour Party'. PA, Spring 1966, 19(2):224–32.

850 Alderman, R.K. 'Discipline in the Parliamentary Labour Party 1945–51'. PA, Summer 1965, 18(3):293–305.

851 Alderman, R.K. 'Parliamentary party discipline in opposition: the Parliamentary Labour Party 1951–64'. PA, Spring 1968, 21(2):124–36.

852 Alexander, K.J.W. and A. Hobbs. 'What influence M.Ps?', *Studies in British politics; a reader in political sociology*, pp.153–64. Edited by R. Rose. Macmillan, 1969.

853 Bealey, F. 'The electoral arrangement between the Labour Representation Committee and the Liberal Party'. JMH, Dec. 1956, 28(4):353–73.

854 Bealey, F. 'Negotiations between the Liberal Party and the Labour Representation Committee before the General Election of 1906'. IHR, Nov. 1956, 29(80):261–74.

855 Bogdanor, V. 'The Labour Party in opposition, 1951–64', *The age of affluence*, pp.78–116. Edited by V. Bogdanor and R. Skidelsky. Macmillan, 1970.

856 Brookes, P. *Women at Westminster: an account of women in the British Parliament 1918–1966*. Davies, 1967. xv, 287pp.

857 Buck, P.W. *Amateurs and professionals in British politics 1918–59*. Chicago, University Press, 1963. xii, 143pp.

858 Buck, P.W. 'First time winners in the British House of Commons since 1918'. APSR, Sept. 1964, 58(3):662–7.

859 Bunker, C., comp. *Who's who in Parliament*. St. Botolph, 1947. 176pp.

1860 Burns, J. MacG. 'The Parliamentary Labour Party in Great Britain'. APSR, Dec. 1950, 44(4):855–71.

1861 Christoph, J.B. 'The study of voting behaviour [i.e. in the Labour Party] in the British House of Commons'. WPQ, June 1958, 11(2):301–18.

1862 Conservative Research Department. *What they have said: a dictionary of political quotations.* The Department, 1950. 142pp.
Over 100 M.P.s quoted.

1863 Cross-Bencher, *pseud. The profetariat* [*sic*] *of Westminster*, Sunday Express, 1949. 47pp.
Financial holdings of 25 M.P.s.

1864 Dowse, R.E. 'The Parliamentary Labour Party in opposition'. PA, Autumn 1960, 13(4):520–9.

1865 Epstein, L.D. 'British M.P.s and their local parties: the Suez crisis'. APSR, June 1960, 54(2):374–90.

1866 Epstein, L.D. 'Cohesion of British parliamentary parties'. APSR, June 1956, 50(2):360–77.

1867 Epstein, L.D. 'New M.P.s and the politics of the PLP'. PS, June 1962, 10(2):121–9.

1868 Godfrey, J.L. 'Labor in opposition'. VQR, Spring 1953, 29(2):257–71.

1869 Grainger, J.H. 'Labour's lost leaders', *Character and style in English politics*, pp.178–213. CUP, 1969.
Discusses briefly all the prominent Labour leaders, particularly Ramsay Macdonald.

1870 Hornby, R. 'Parties in Parliament 1959–63. 1 The Labour Party'. PQ, July–Sept. 1963, 34(3):240–8.

1871 Houghton, D. 'The Labour back-bencher'. PQ, Oct.–Dec. 1969, 40(4):454–63.

1872 Hughes, E. 'The revolt in Parliament'. LM, Mar. 1968, 50(3):111–12.

1873 Jackson, R.J. *Rebels and whips: an analysis of dissension, discipline and cohesion in British political parties.* Macmillan, 1968. xii, 346pp.

1874 Jenkins, R. 'From Keir Hardie to Harold Wilson: Labour leadership from 1906–64', *Essays and speeches*, pp.73–8. Gollancz, 1967.

1875 McKenzie, R.T. 'Policy decision in opposition: a rejoinder'. PS, June 1957, 5(2):176–82.

1876 McKitterick, T.E.M. 'The selection of parliamentary candidates. 2 The Labour Party'. PQ, July–Sept. 1959, 30(3):219–23.

1877 Miliband, R. *Parliamentary socialism: a study in the politics of Labour.* Merlin, 1964. 356pp.

1878 Miliband, R. 'Party democracy and parliamentary government'. PS, June 1958, 6(2):170–4.

1879 Muller, W.D. 'Trade union sponsored members of Parliament in the defence dispute of 1960–61'. PA, Summer 1970, 23(3):258–76.

1880 Newens, S. 'Member of Parliament'. NLR, Sept.–Oct. 1968, 51:88–94.

1881 O'Leary, C. 'The Wedgwood Benn case and the doctrine of wilful perversity'. PS, Feb. 1965, 13(1):65–78.

882 Powell, J.E. 'Morality in politics 1951–59: Labour in opposition'. PQ, Oct.–Dec. 1959, 30(4):336–43.

883 Punnett, R.M. 'The Labour shadow cabinet 1955–64'. PA, Winter 1964, 18(1):61–70.

884 Ranney, A. 'Inter-constituency movement of British parliamentary candidates, 1951–9'. APSR, Mar. 1964, 58(1)36–45.

885 Richards, P.G. *Honourable members: a study of the British backbencher*. Faber, 1964. 294pp.

886 Rodgers, W.T. and B. Donoghue. *The people into Parliament: an illustrated history of the Labour Party*. Thames and Hudson, 1966. 192pp.

887 Rose, S. 'Policy decision in opposition'. PS, June 1956, 4(2):128–38.

888 Strauss, G.R. 'The influence of the back-bencher. 1. The Labour view'. PQ, July–Sept. 1965, 36(3):277–85.

889 Tapper, C. 'A case of privilege'. NLR, Nov.–Dec. 1961, 12:39–43.
    The Wedgwood Benn case.

890 White, M. 'Choosing Labour's men'. C, Summer 1961, 4(16):14–15.

891 Winterton, E.M. 'Dreamers in Westminster'. LM, Feb. 1961, 43(2):89–92.

IV ELECTIONS

892 Abrams, M. 'The Labour vote in the General Election'. PPA, Jan. 1946, 1(1):7–26.

893 Alexander, A. 'People, polls and parties: the British General Election of 1970'. QQ, Autumn 1970, 77(3):356–67.

894 Berrington, H.B. 'The General Election of 1964 [with discussion]'. RSS, 1965, 128(1):17–66.

895 Birch, A.H. and P.[W.] Campbell. 'Voting behaviour in a Lancashire constituency'. BJS, Sept. 1950, 1(3):197–208.

896 Bonnar, R. 'Why Labour lost the election'. LM, Aug. 1970, 52(8):372–5.

897 Bowman, D. 'Trade unionists and the General Election'. LM, June 1970, 52(6):256–62.

898 Brand, C.F. 'The British General Election of 1950'. SAQ, Oct. 1951, 50(4):478–98.

1899 Brand, C.F. 'The British General Election of 1951'. SAQ, Jan. 1953, 52(1):29–53.

1900 Brand, C.F. 'The British General Election of 1955'. SAQ, July 1956, 55(3):289–312.

1901 Brand, C.F. 'The British General Election of 1959'. SAQ, Oct. 1960, 59(4):521–42.

1902 Brand, C.F. 'The British General Election of 1964'. SAQ, Summer 1965, 64(3):332–50.

1903 Brand, C.F. 'The British General Election of 1966'. SAQ, Winter 1967, 66(1):131–47.

1904 Bromhead, P. 'The General Election of 1966'. PA, Summer 1966, 19(3):332–45.

1905 Burn, W.L. 'The General Election [of 1945] in retrospect'. TC, July 1947, 142(843):17–25.

1906 Butler, D.E. *The British General Election of 1951*. Macmillan, 1952. viii, 289pp.

1907 Butler, D.E. *The British General Election of 1955*. Macmillan, 1955. viii, 236pp.

1908 Butler, D.E. 'Trends in British by-elections'. JP, May 1949, 11(2):396–407.

1909 Butler, D.E. and A. King. *The British General Election of 1964*. Macmillan, 1965. ix, 401pp.

1910 Butler, D.E. and A. King. *The British General Election of 1966*. Macmillan, 1966. xi, 338pp.

1911 Butler, D.E. and R. Rose. *The British General Election of 1959*. Cass, 1970 (first pub. 1960). viii, 293pp.

1912 Campbell, J.R. 'When will they ever learn?'. LM, June 1967, 49(6):259–63.

1913 Campbell, P.W., D. Donnison and A. Potter. 'Voting behaviour in Droylsden in October 1951'. MS, Jan. 1952, 20(1):57–65.

1914 Cook, C.P. 'Wales and the General Election of 1923'. WH, Dec. 1969, 4(4):387–95.

1915 Douglas, M.F. 'A note on recent British general elections'. SAS, Winter 1961, 25(1):54–8.
     The three Labour defeats of 1951, 1955 and 1959.

1916 Dutt, R.P. 'After the election'. LM, Nov. 1959, 41(11):465–79.

1917 Dutt, R.P. 'Britain moves left'. LM, Aug. 1945, 27(8):225–30.

1918 Dutt, R.P. 'Election choice'. LM, Feb. 1950, 32(2):49–59.

1919 Epstein, L.D. 'The nuclear deterrent and the British election of 1964'. JBS, May 1966, 5(2):139–63.

920 Fagan, H. 'The election: a factual survey'. LM, Apr. 1950, 32(4):177–80.

921 Fitzsimmons, M.A. 'The British elections [Oct. 1951]'. RP, Jan. 1952, 14(1):102–20.

922 Fox, K.O. 'Labour and Merthyr's khaki election of 1900'. WH, 1965, 2(4):351–66.

923 Fox, K.O. 'The Merthyr election of 1906'. NLW, Winter 1962, 14(2):237–41.

924 Gallacher, W. 'Lessons of the election'. LM, Dec. 1951, 33(12):562–5.

925 Garth, C. *The party that runs away: a floating voter sums up the socialists.* Hutchinson, 1945. 60pp.
Reflections on the 1945 election.

926 George W. 'Social conditions and the Labour vote in the county boroughs of England and Wales'. BJS, Sept. 1951, 2(3):255–9.

927 Gradwell, J. 'Election impressions'. LM, Dec. 1969, 51(12):561–3.
Swindon by-election.

928 Grundy, J. 'Non-voting in an urban district'. MS, Jan. 1950, 18(1):83–99.

929 Harrison, L.A. and F.E. Crossland. 'The British Labour Party in the General Elections, 1906–45'. JP, May 1950, 12(2):383–404.

930 Hindess, B. 'Local elections and the Labour vote in Liverpool'. SO, 1967, 1:187–95.

931 Holt, R.T. and J.E. Turner. *Political parties in action: the battle of Barons Court.* Collier-Macmillan, 1968. xii, 311pp.
Detailed study of the 1964 election in this constituency.

932 Jenkin, T.P. 'The British General Election of 1950'. WPQ, June 1950, 3(2):179–89.

933 Jenkin, T.P. 'The British General Election of 1951'. WPQ, Mar. 1952, 5(1):51–65.

934 Jenkins, P. 'Electoral post-mortem'. EN, Aug. 1970, 35(2):12–17.

935 Laing, L.H. 'Fifty British by-elections'. CJEPS, May 1950, 16(2):222–7.

936 McCallum, R.B. and A. Readman. *The British General Election of 1945.* Cass, 1964 (first pub. 1947). xv, 311pp.

937 McKenzie, R.T. 'Between two elections (1)'. EN, Jan. 1966, 26(1):11–21.

938 McKenzie, R.T. 'Between two elections [2?]'. EN, Feb. 1966, 26(2):21–9.

939 Mander, Sir G. 'The General Election'. CNR, Sept. 1945, 168:135–9.

940 Maynard, J. 'Why we lost: and what now?'. LM, Dec. 1959, 41(12):538–40.

941 Middleton, P.A. 'Housing and the local elections'. LM, Mar. 1970, 52(3):122–5.

942 Montagu, I. 'The election campaign'. LM, Aug. 1945, 27(8):231–3.

1943 Morgan, W. 'The British General Election of 1945'. SAQ, July 1946, 45(3):297–312.

1944 Nicholas, H.G. *The British General Election of 1950*. Cass, 1968 (first pub. 1951). x, 353pp.

1945 Nicholas, H.G. 'The British General Election of 1951'. APSR, June 1952, 46(2):398–405.

1946 Noel, G.E. *The new Britain and Harold Wilson: interim report, 1966 General Election*. Campion Press, 1966. viii, 103pp.

1947 Pattee, R. 'The election victory of the Labour Party and Latin America'. M, Sept./Oct. 1945, 181(947):324–30.

1948 Pelling, H. 'Two by-elections: Jarrow and Colne Valley 1907', *Popular politics and society in Victorian England*, pp.130–46. Macmillan, 1968.

1949 Pethick-Lawrence, F.W. 'Election issues'. CNR, July 1945, 168:2–4.

1950 Pethick-Lawrence, F.W. 'The General Election'. CNR, Feb. 1950, 177:65–7.

1951 Pethick-Lawrence, F.W. 'The General Election. After the battle'. CNR, Apr. 1950, 177:193–5.

1952 Pethick-Lawrence, F.W. 'The General Election'. CNR, Dec. 1951, 180:321–2.

1953 Pethick-Lawrence, F.W. 'The General Election'. CNR, July 1955, 188:2–3.

1954 Pollitt, H. 'The Tory victory and Labour's future'. MQ, July 1955, 2(3):130–40.

1955 Pritt, D.N. 'A Labour independent looks at the election'. LM, Apr. 1950, 32(4):174–6.

1956 Reeves, J. 'The Labour triumph of 1945'. LM, Sept. 1945, 27(9):268–9.

1957 Richards, P.G. 'The Labour victory'. PQ, Oct.–Dec. 1945, 16(4):350–356.

1958 Richards, P.G. 'The political temper'. PQ, Jan.–Mar. 1945, 16(1):57–66.

1959 Robson, W.A. 'Post-war municipal elections in Great Britain'. APSR, Apr. 1947, 41(2):294–306.

1960 Rose, R., ed. *The polls and the 1970 election*. Glasgow, University of Strathclyde, 1970. ii, 67pp.

1961 Saville, J. 'A note on West Fife'. NR, Autumn 1959, 10:9–13.
Lawrence Daly and the 1959 election.

1962 Scammon, R.M. 'British by-elections, 1950'. APSR, June 1951, 45(2):474–8.

1963 Scammon, R.M. 'British by-elections, 1952'. APSR, June 1953, 47(2):533–6.

1964 The Times. *The Times House of Commons 1945; with full results of the polling and biographies of members and unsuccessful candidates and a complete analysis, statistical tables, and a map of the General Election, 1945.* The Times, 1945. vi, 170pp.

1965 The Times. *The Times House of Commons 1950* [as for 1945 but entries now include photographs of all members]. The Times, 1950. 320pp.

1966 The Times. *The Times House of Commons 1951* [as for 1950]. The Times, 1951. 256pp.

1967 The Times. *The Times House of Commons 1955* [as for 1950]. The Times, 1955. 284pp.

1968 The Times. *The Times House of Commons 1959* [as for 1950]. The Times, 1959. 272pp.

1969 The Times. *The Times House of Commons 1964* [as for 1950]. The Times, 1964. 304pp.

1970 The Times. *The Times House of Commons 1966* [as for 1950]. The Times, 1966. 319pp.

1971 The Times. *The Times House of Commons 1970* [as for 1950]. The Times, 1970. 304pp.

972 Topsell, J. 'The Brighouse defeat'. NLR, May-June 1960, 3:55–8.
      1960 by-election.

Labour Governments

I GENERAL

973 Bonnor, J. 'The four Labour cabinets'. SOCR, July 1958, 6(1):37–48.

974 Bulmer-Thomas, I. *The growth of the party system.* Vol. 2, 1924–1964. Baker, 1965. v, 323pp.
      The four Labour governments.

975 Gordon, M.R. *Conflict and consensus in Labour's foreign policy, 1914–1965.* Stanford, University Press, 1969. xiii, 333pp.
      Examines and contrasts socialist foreign policy with traditional British foreign policy.

976 Lovell, C.R. 'Antecedents of British Labour government policies'. HIST, Spring 1951, 13(2):173–88.

II 1924

1977 Chester, L., S. Fay and H. Young. *The Zinoviev letter*. Heinemann, 1967. xix, 219pp.

1978 Greaves, H.R.G. 'Complacency or challenge'. PQ, Jan.–Mar. 1961, 32(1):53–61.
Discusses no.1983.

1979 Lyman, R.W. *The first Labour government 1924*. Chapman and Hall, 1957. x, 302pp.

1980 Newark, F.H. 'The Campbell case and the first Labour government'. Northern Ireland Legal Quarterly, Mar. 1969, 20(1):19–42.

1981 Pelling, H. 'Governing without power'. PQ, Jan.–Mar. 1961, 32(1):45–52.
Discusses no.1983.

1982 Warth, R.D. 'The mystery of the Zinoviev letter'. SAQ, Oct. 1950, 49(4):441–53.

1983 Webb, S. 'The first Labour government. PQ, Jan.–Mar. 1961, 32(1):6–44.
Includes historical note with Cabinet ministers' biographical details. *See* nos.1978, 1981.

III 1929–31

1984 Bassett, R. *Nineteen thirty-one: political crisis*. Macmillan, 1958. xvi, 464pp. *See* nos.552, 554 and 1582.

1985 Carlton, D. *MacDonald versus Henderson: the foreign policy of the second Labour government*. Macmillan, 1970. 239pp.

1986 Denman, Sir R. *Political sketches*. Carlisle, Thurman, 1948. 123pp.
Pro-MacDonald backbencher's view of 1931 crisis.

1987 Dowse, R.E. 'A comment on "The second Labour government—some Soviet views".' SSLH, Spring 1964, 8:16–17.
Discusses no.1992.

1988 Dowse, R.E. 'The left wing opposition during the first two Labour governments' (1). PA, Winter 1961, 14(1):80–93.

1989 Dowse, R.E. 'The left wing opposition during the first two Labour governments' (2). PA, Spring 1962, 14(2):229–43.

1990 Gregory, R.G. *Sidney Webb and East Africa: Labour's experiment with the doctrine of native paramountcy*. Berkeley, University of California Press, 1962. xii, 183pp.

1991 Lammers, D.N. 'The second Labour government and the restoration of relations with Soviet Russia (1929)'. IHR, May 1964, 37(95):60–72.

1992 Loone, E. 'The second Labour government: some Soviet views'. SSLH, Spring 1963, 6:19–25 (*see* no.1987).

1993 Pollard, S. 'The great disillusion'. SSLH, Spring 1968, 16:33–42.
     Review of no.1994.

1994 Skidelsky, R. *Politicians and the slump: the Labour government of 1929–31.*
     Penguin, 1970 (first pub. 1967). 477pp. (*see* no.1993).

IV 1945–51

1995 Attlee, C.R. *Purpose and reality (selected speeches).* Hutchinson, 1947. x,
     212pp.
     May 1945–November 1946.

1996 Balmer, T. 'Poignard of truth to Mr. Bevan'. LM, Jan. 1950, 32(1):17–22.

1997 Black, M.M. 'Aspects of national economic planning under the Labour
     government'. JP, May 1950, 12(2):260–81.

1998 Blackburn, R. 'Bevin and his critics'. FA, Jan. 1947, 25(2):239–49.

1999 Boyd-Carpenter, J. 'Labour in power'. F, May 1946, 159(953):328–33.

2000 Brady, R.A. *Crisis in Britain: plans and achievements of the Labour government.*
     CUP, 1950. xiii, 730pp.

2001 Brogan, C. *Our new masters.* Hollis and Carter, 1947. viii, 223pp.

2002 Brogan, C. *Patriots . . . my foot!.* Hollis and Carter, 1949. 86pp.

2003 Brogan, C. *They are always wrong.* Conservative Political Centre, 1949.
     36pp.

2004 Bruce, D. 'A review of socialist financial policy, 1945–9'. PQ, Oct.–Dec.
     1949, 20(4):301–16.

2005 Campbell, J.R. 'Cripps and the alternative'. LM, Nov. 1947,
     29(11):337–41.

2006 Campbell, J.R. 'The "plan" of British socialism'. LM, Feb. 1949,
     31(2):42–7.

2007 Chase, E.P. 'England under the Labour government'. JP, Aug. 1946,
     8(3):278–91.

2008 Cole, G.D.H. *On Labour's foreign policy.* New Statesman, 1946. 48pp.

2009 Cole, G.D.H. 'Why England went socialist'. VQR, Autumn 1947,
     23(4):509–20.

2010 Cole, M. *The General Election. 1945 and after.* Fabian Publications, 1945.
     29pp.

2011 Common Wealth. *Labour's first year 1945–6.* Common Wealth Publi-
     cations Committee, 1946. 24pp.

2012 Conservative Research Department. *Six years of socialist government.* The
     Department, 1951. 222pp.

2013 Coombes, B.L. 'One year of nationalization'. F, Jan. 1948, 163(973):46–52.

2014 Crossman, R.H.S. and K. Younger. *Socialist foreign policy*. Fabian Society, 1951. 28pp.
   Crossman, pp.3–15; Younger, pp.16–28.

2015 Crouch, W.W. 'Local government under the British Labour government'. JP, May 1950, 12(2):232–59.

2016 Davies, E. 'Some aspects of Labour foreign policy'. PQ, Apr.–June 1952, 23(2):122–33.

2017 De Jouvenal, B. *Problems of socialist England*. Batchworth, 1949. xviii, 221pp.
   'a snapshot of the English scene in September–October 1946'.

2018 Dobb, M. 'The economic situation and Labour policy'. LM, Oct. 1945, 27(10):299–304.

2019 Dutt, R.P. 'The awakening of the mass movement'. LM, July 1949, 31(7):193–202.

2020 Dutt, R.P. 'The betrayal of Britain'. LM, Jan. 1949, 31(1):1–10.

2021 Dutt, R.P. 'The class fight in Britain'. LM, Oct. 1948, 30(10):289–97.

2022 Dutt, R.P. 'Election warnings'. LM, June 1949, 31(6):161–9.

2023 Dutt, R.P. 'How to save Britain'. LM, Sept. 1949, 31(9):257–69.

2024 Dutt, R.P. 'Labour's choice'. LM, May 1947, 29(5):131–41.

2025 Dutt, R.P. 'Lessons of Scarborough'. LM, July 1948, 30(7):193–200.

2026 Dutt, R.P. 'The unjust society'. LM, Oct. 1951, 33(10):451–66.

2027 Dutt, R.P. 'What progress for Labour?'. LM, June 1951, 33(6):241–52.

2028 Edwards, N. *Is this the road?*. Wrexham, Hughes, 1955. 21pp.

2029 Ewer, W.N. 'The Labour government's record in foreign policy'. PQ, Apr.–June 1949, 20(2):112–22.

2030 Finer, H. 'The reform of British central government'. JP, May 1950, 12(2):211–31.

2031 Fitzsimmons, M.A. 'British Labor in search of a socialist foreign policy'. RP, Apr. 1950, 12(2):197–214.

2032 Fitzsimmons, M.A. *The foreign policy of the British Labor government 1945–51*. Notre Dame, California, University of Notre Dame Press, 1953. viii, 182pp.

2033 Foot, M. and D. Bruce. *Who are the patriots?*. Gollancz, 1949. 125pp.

2034 Gallacher, W. 'The election—then and now'. LM, Feb. 1950, 32(2):60–5.

2035 Gallacher, W. 'May Day and youth'. LM, May 1951, 33(5):204–12.

2036 Gallacher, W. 'Next year's election'. LM, Nov. 1949, 31(11):334–9.

2037 Gallacher, W. 'The third Labour government'. LM, Aug. 1963, 45(8):375–9.
    Review of no.2070.

2038 Gallacher, W. 'A year of Labour government'. LM, Aug. 1946, 28(8):235–9.

2039 Gore-Brown, P. 'The foreign policy of the Labour government'. JP, May 1950, 12(2):371–82.

2040 Hall, J.E.D. *Labour's first year.* Penguin, 1947. viii, 213pp.

2041 Harley, J.H. 'Labour in the saddle'. CNR, Nov. 1945, 168:261–6.

2042 Harrison, E. 'British Labour takes stock'. QQ, Summer 1948, 55(2):128–39.

2043 Hirst, F.W. 'A budget of triumph and lamentation'. CNR, May 1947, 171:262–7.

2044 Hirst, F.W. 'The budget, the debt and the deficit'. CNR, May 1946, 169:262–8.

2045 Hirst, F.W. 'Dr. Dalton's crisis budget and his resignation'. CNR, Dec. 1947, 172:324–9.

2046 Hirst, F.W. 'Sir Stafford Cripps' first budget'. CNR, May 1948, 173:263–8.

2047 Hitchener, D.G. 'The Labour government and the House of Commons'. WPQ, Sept. 1952, 5(3):417–44.

2048 Hitchener, D.G. 'The Labour government and the House of Lords'. WPQ, Dec. 1948, 1(4):428–38.

2049 Hodgson, G. 'The steel debates: the Tory recovery', *Age of austerity, 1945–51*, pp.306–29 (*see* no.2084). Edited by M. Sissons and P. French. Penguin, 1964 (first pub. 1963).

2050 Hollis, C. *The rise and fall of the ex-socialist government.* Hollis and Carter, 1947. 131pp.

2051 Howard, A. '"We are the masters now". The General election of 5 July 1945', *Age of austerity, 1945–51*, pp.15–34 (*see* no.2084). Edited by M. Sissons and P. French. Penguin, 1964 (first pub. 1963).

2052 Jones, A.C. 'British colonial policy wth particular reference to Africa'. IA, April 1951, 27(2):176–83.

2053 Jones, A.C. 'The Labour Party and colonial policy 1945–51', *New Fabian colonial essays*, pp.19–37. Edited by A.C. Jones. Hogarth, 1959.

2054 Lakeman, E. *When Labour falls.* Joseph, 1947. 146pp.
    Liberal view of 1945 government.

2055 L'Etang, H. 'The Labour ministers wilt under the strain 1949–51', *The pathology of leadership*, pp.136–45. Heinemann, 1969.

2056 Lewis, B. and R.H.B. Condie. 'The British social security programme'. JP, May 1950, 12(2):323–47.

2057 Licinius, *pseud. The big 2½*. St. Botolph Pub. Co., 1947. 99pp.

2058 Lindsay, Lord. 'Britain's new Labour government'. VQR, Spring 1946, 22(2):255–67.

2059 Lindsay, Lord. 'The philosophy of the British Labour government', *Ideological differences and world order: studies in the philosophy and science of the world's cultures*, pp.250–68. New Haven, Yale University Press, 1949.

2060 Mackenzie, N. *The new towns: the success of social planning*. Fabian Society, 1955. 29pp.

2061 McKitterick, T.E.M. 'Arms, the budget and the Labour Party'. TC, June 1951, 149(892):475–82.

2062 McRae, D.G. 'Domestic record of the Labour government'. PQ, Jan.–Mar. 1949, 20(1):1–11.

2063 Martin, J. 'The Labour Party and foreign policy'. CNR, Jan. 1946, 169:7–10.

2064 Matthews, G. 'Attlee's axe'. LM, Dec. 1949, 31(12):369–73.

2065 Matthews, H. and N. *The Britain we saw: a family symposium*. Gollancz, 1950. 317pp.
    American journalists' view of life in Labour Britain.

2066 Mayhew, C. 'British foreign policy since 1945'. IA, Oct. 1950, 26(4):477–86.

2067 Morrison, H. *The peaceful revolution*. Allen and Unwin, 1949. viii, 148pp.
    Speeches 1945–8.

2068 Munro, D., ed. *Socialism the British way: an assessment of the nature and significance of the socialist experiment carried out in Great Britain by the Labour government of 1945*. Essential Books, 1948. viii, 345pp.
    Eleven separate contributions.

2069 [A Political Correspondent]. 'Lesson for Labour'. TC, Dec. 1951, 150(898):466–71.

2070 Pritt, D.N. *The Labour government 1945–51*. Lawrence and Wishart, 1963. 467pp.

2071 Quaestor, *pseud*. 'The Labour government and Labour's future'. LM, Mar. 1951, 33(3):117–27.

2072 Roberts, W. 'The Parliamentary session'. CNR, Sept. 1947, 172:129–133.

2073 Roberts, W. 'The Parliamentary session'. CNR, Sept. 1948, 174:138–142.

2074 Roberts, W. 'The year in Parliament'. CNR, Sept. 1949, 176:129–32.

2075 Rogow, A.A. *The Labour government and British industry, 1945–51*. Oxford, Blackwell, 1955. xv, 196pp.

2076 Rogow, A.A. 'Relations between the Labour government and industry'. JP, Feb. 1954, 16(1):3–23.

2077 Ross, J.F.S. 'The new House of Commons'. PPA, Mar. 1947, 2(1):26–43.

2078 Rowan, D. 'Banking and credit under the Labour government: 1945–49'. JP, May 1950, 12(2):290–322.

2079 Rust, W. 'Reshuffle to the right'. LM, Nov. 1947, 29(11):341–3.

2080 Sagittarius, *pseud. Let cowards flinch*. Turnstile, 1947. 39pp.
Satire on the early days of Attlee government. Cartoons by Vicky.

2081 Sahm, U. 'Britain and Europe 1950'. IA, Jan. 1967, 43(1):12–24.
See no.2099.

2082 Schaffer, G. *Labour rules*. Muse Arts, 1945. 48pp.

2083 Schwartz, R.P. 'Labour's economic policy'. F, Sept. 1946, 160(957): 157–64.

2084 Sissons, M. and P. French. *Age of austerity, 1945–51*. Penguin, 1964 (first pub. 1963). 361pp.
See nos.117, 254, 2049, 2051.

2085 Solidarity. *Labour government vs. the dockers 1945–51*. Solidarity, 1966. iv, 13pp.

2086 Steed, W. 'Dearth of leadership'. CNR, Oct. 1947, 172:193–8.

2087 Strachey, J. 'Tasks and achievement of British Labour', *New Fabian* Essays, pp.181–215 (*see* no.2437). Edited by R.H.S. Crossman. Turnstile, 1952.

2088 Talus, *pseud. Your alternative government*. Eyre and Spottiswoode, 1945, 80pp.
Written to demonstrate the 'unsuitability' of Labour to rule Britain.

2089 Thompson, L. *Portrait of England: news from somewhere*. Gollancz, 1952. 254pp.

2090 Voigt, F.A. 'Mr. Bevin and the balance of power'. TC, Mar. 1948, 143(853):135–6.

2091 Voigt, F.A. 'Twenty-one "rebels" and a letter'. TC, Jan. 1947, 141(839):1–9.

2092 Walker, G. 'The genesis of the British economic plan; 1945 to 1950'. JP, May 1950, 12(2):282–9.

2093 Walker-Smith, D. 'Contemporary socialism'. F, Feb. 1948, 163(974): 166–20.
Review of no.1720.

2094 Watkins, E. *The cautious revolution*. Secker and Warburg, 1951. 247pp.

2095 Webb, B. *The house divided*. Hutchinson, 1945. 96pp.
Written in an attempt to prevent the 1945 Labour victory.

2096 Wilson, H. *Post-war economic policies in Britain*. Fabian Society, 1957. 21pp.

2097 Wootton, B. 'Record of the Labour government in the social services'. PQ, Apr.–June 1949, 20(2):101–12.

2098 Yates, V. *One man at Westminster*. Ultraprint, 1949. 34pp.
     Work of Labour government seen by a backbench M.P.

2099 Younger, K. 'Britain and Europe, 1950'. A comment. IA, Jan. 1967, 43(1):24–8.
     See no.2081.

2100 Zilliacus, K. 'Mr. Bevin and British foreign policy'. LM, Mar. 1946, 28(3):71–4.

2101 Zink, H. 'The role of the government in Britain'. WPQ, Dec. 1948, 1(4):413–25.

IV 1964–70

2102 Abel-Smith, B. *Labour's social plans*. Fabian Society, 1966. 20pp.

2103 Albu, A. 'Lessons of the Labour government. (1) Economic policies and methods'. PQ, Apr.–June 1970, 41(2):141–6.

2104 Ball, J. 'Wilson's law—and all that'. LM, Sept. 1967, 49(9):403–5.

2105 Bray, J. 'Lessons of the Labour government. (3) Tools for the seventies'. PQ, Apr.–June 1970, 41(2):151–5.

2106 Bunyan, N. 'The failure of Labour's economic policies'. SP, Michaelmas 1967, 1:9–12.

2107 Burgess, T., ed. *Matters of principle: Labour's last chance*. Penguin, 1968. 128pp.
     Seven contributors discuss what has gone wrong with the government.

2108 Clay, E. 'The Labour alternative to socialism'. SP, Michaelmas, 1967, 1:5–9.

2109 Crick, B. 'The future of the Labour government'. PQ, Oct.–Dec. 1967, 38(4):375–88.

2110 Davidson, A. 'Why Labour lost'. CNR, Aug. 1970, 217:63–4.

2111 Davies, E. 'Labour's transport policy'. PQ, Oct.–Dec. 1967, 38(4):421–34.

2112 Davis, W. *Three years hard labour: the road to devaluation*. Deutsch, 1968. 224pp.

2113 Demos, *pseud. The go-ahead year: Labour in power*. Leicester, Book Distributors, 1966. 160pp.

2114 Derrick, P. 'The haunting of Brother Brown'. TC, Summer 1965, 174(1026):40–7.

2115 Derrick, P. 'In place of socialism'. CNR, Mar. 1969, 214:137–42.

2116 Donnelly, D. *Gadarene '68: the crimes, follies and misfortunes of the Wilson government*. Kimber, 1968. 192pp.
Reprints text of his letter of resignation from the Labour Party.

2117 Dutt, R.P. 'After Washington'. LM, Jan. 1965, 47(1):1–15.

2118 Dutt, R.P. 'Economic storm-signals'. LM, Aug. 1965, 47(8):337–48.

2119 Dutt, R.P. 'The fight for Labour's future'. LM, May 1969, 51(5):193–204.

2120 Dutt, R.P. 'Into battle'. LM, Sept. 1966, 48(9):401–14.

2121 Dutt, R.P. 'Labour's Gethsemane'. LM, Mar. 1968, 50(3):97–110.

2122 Dutt, R.P. 'Why "plan" a slump?'. LM, Oct. 1966, 48(10):449–60.

2123 Eaton, J. 'Labour and the technological revolution'. LM, Jan. 1965, 47(1):33–43.

2124 Fletcher, R. 'Where did it all go wrong?'. EN, Nov. 1969, 33(5):8–16.

2125 Foot, P. 'Reformism or revolution?'. SP, Michaelmas 1967, 1:3–5.

2126 Hannington, W. 'The fight against unemployment today'. LM, Dec. 1966, 48(12):560–5.

2127 Harrison, R. 'Labour government: then and now'. PQ, Jan.–Mar. 1970, 41(1):67–82.

2128 Howie, W. [Private manifesto]. TC, 4, 1969, 178(1043):16–18.

2129 Jenkins, P. *The battle of Downing Street*. Knight, 1970, xiv, 171pp.
Dispute between the government and unions over *In place of strife*.

2130 Lambton, Viscount. *Harold Wilson and his friends*. O'Brien, 1964. 27pp.

2131 Lapping, B. *The Labour government 1964–70*. Penguin, 1970. 219pp.

2132 Lower, A. 'Great Britain today'. QQ, Summer 1968, 75(2):208–21.

2133 Marquand, D. 'From the other side'. C, Dec. 1970, 14(52):28–9.

2134 Miliband, R. 'The Labour government and beyond'. SR, 1966, 3:11–26.

2135 Mortimer, J.E. 'Labour's income policy and the trade union movement'. LM, Oct. 1966, 48(10):464–7.

2136 Nairn, T. 'Labour imperialism'. NLR, July-Aug. 1965, 32:3–15.

2137 Norwood, C. 'How to fight back'. LM, Feb. 1969, 51(2):61–3.

2138 Paynter, W. 'Future of the coal mining industry'. LM, Sept. 1967, 49(9):412–17.

2139 Prentice, R. 'Lessons of the Labour government. (2) Not socialist enough'. PQ, Apr.–June 1970, 41(2):146–51.

2140 Pritt, D.N. 'Problems of the new Labour government'. LM, Nov. 1964, 46(11):495–8.

2141 Pryke, R. 'Labour and the City'. NLR, Sept.–Oct. 1966, 39:3–15.
     See no.2150.

2142 Punnett, R.M. 'Labour and the Lords'. CNR, May 1965, 206–254–6.

2143 Quaestor, *pseud*. 'Challenge to the left'. LM, Aug. 1966, 48(8):353–62.

2144 Rathbone, H. 'The roots of the crisis'. LM, Jan. 1965, 47(1):16–22.

2145 Roosa, R.V. 'Where is Britain heading?'. FA, Apr. 1968, 46(3):503–18.

2146 Rose, S. 'Labour's Pax Britannica'. PQ, Apr.–June 1965, 36(2):131–41.

2147 Rothstein, A. 'A time for choice—and action'. LM, July 1965, 47(7):289–97.

2148 Saville, J. 'Labourism and the Labour government'. SR, 1967, 4:43–71.

2149 Summerscales, R. 'Labour and inflation'. CNR, Nov. 1970, 217:289–93.

2150 Tarbuck, K. 'On Richard Pryke's *Labour and the City*'. NLR, Nov.–Dec. 1966, 40:94–6.
     See no.2141.

2151 Townsend, P. *Poverty, socialism and Labour in power*. Fabian Society, 1967. 32pp.

2152 Tuckett, A. 'How they held down wages'. LM, July 1965, 47(7):302–7.

2153 Wakeford, G. *The great Labour mirage: an indictment of socialism in Britain*. Hale, 1969. 240pp.
     Analyses Attlee and Wilson governments 'which brought Britain to the brink of economic disaster'.

2154 Walker, P.G. 'On being a Cabinet Minister'. EN, Apr. 1956, 6(4):17–24.

2155 Watkins, A. 'Labour in power', *The left: a symposium*, pp.167–80 (*see* no.2595). Edited by G. Kaufman. Blond, 1966.

2156 Webbe, Sir H. 'The hundred days'. QR, Apr. 1965, 303(644):121–32.

2157 Woddis, J. 'Mr. Wilson and Mr. Brown versus the United Nations'. LM, Mar. 1967, 49(3):116–23.

2158 Woolf, D. 'Wages and the Labour government'. LM, Dec. 1969, 51(12):543–6.

Labour movement

Local and special studies

2159 Adams, W.S. 'British reactions to the 1905 Russian revolution'. MQ, July 1955, 2(3):173–86.

2160 Allen, V.L. 'The need for a sociology of Labour'. BJS, Sept. 1959, 10(3):181–92.

2161 Arnot, R.P. *The impact of the Russian revolution in Britain*. Lawrence and Wishart, 1967. 191pp.
Hands off Russia, Jolly George, etc.

2162 Barnsby, G. *The Dudley working class movement 1750–1832*. Dudley, Public Libraries, 1966. 21 leaves.

2163 Barnsby, G. *The Dudley working class movement 1832–1860*. Dudley, Public Libraries, 1967. iv, 48pp.

2164 Brock, P. 'Polish democrats and English radicals, 1832–62: a chapter in the history of Anglo–Polish relations'. JMH, June 1953, 25(2):139–56.

2165 Brown, A.F.J. 'Working-class movements in the countryside, 1790–1850'. LHN, Winter 1956–7, 3(2):49–54.

2166 Collins, H. 'The English branches of the First International', *Essays in Labour history*, pp.242–75 (*see* no.1179). Edited by A. Briggs and J. Saville. Macmillan, 1960.

2167 Collins, H. 'The International and the British Labour movement'. SSLH, Autumn 1964, 9:24–39.

2168 Collins, H. 'The London Corresponding Society', *Democracy and the Labour movement*, pp.103–34 (*see* no.1215). Edited by J. Saville. Lawrence and Wishart, 1954.

2169 Communist Party. *London landmarks: a guide with maps to places where Marx, Engels and Lenin lived and worked*. The Party, 1963 (first pub. 1960). 12pp.

2170 Communist Party. Lancashire District Committee. *Lancashire 1848–1948*. The Party, Lancashire District Committee, 1948. 29pp.

2171 Cowden, M.H. 'Early Marxist views on British Labor, 1837–1917'. WPQ, Mar. 1963, 16(1):34–52.

2172 Cowherd, R.G. *The humanitarians and the Ten Hour movement in England.* Boston, Harvard Graduate School of Business Studies, 1956. v, 27pp.

2173 Cox, I. *The fight for socialism in Wales, 1848–1948.* Cardiff, Communist Party, Welsh Committee, 1948. 24pp.

2174 Cunningham, H. 'Jingoism and the working classes 1877–8'. SSLH, Autumn 1969, 19:6–9.

2175 Foster, J. 'How Oldham's working-class leaders managed to avoid reformism 1812–47'. SSLH, Spring 1968, 16:6–10.

2176 Greenleaf, R. 'British Labor against American slavery'. SAS, Winter 1953, 17(1):42–58.

2177 Hampton, W. 'Working-class angels'. SSLH, Spring 1969, 18:54–64.

2178 Handforth, P. 'Manchester radical politics, 1789–94'. LCAS, 1956, 66:87–106.

2179 Hanham, H.J. 'Liberal organisations for working men, 1860–1914'. SSLH, Autumn 1963, 7:5–9.

2180 Harrison, R. 'British Labor and American slavery'. SAS, Fall 1961, 25(4):291–319.

2181 Harrison, R. 'British Labour and the confederacy'. IRSH, 1957, 2(1):78–105.

2182 Harrison, R. 'The British Labour movement and the International in 1864'. SR, 1964, 1:293–308.

2183 Harrison, R. 'The British working class and the General Election of 1868' (1). IRSH, 1960, 5(3):424–55.

2184 Harrison, R. 'The British working class and the General Election of 1868' (2). IRSH, 1961, 6(1):74–109.

2185 Harrison, R. '"The free inheritance of us all": Beesly's speech in St. James's Hall, London, March 26, 1863'. SAS, Fall 1963, 27(4):465–73.

2186 Harrison, R. 'The 10th April of Spencer Walpole: the problem of revolution in relation to reform, 1865–1867'. IRSH, 1962, 7(3):351–99.
Working-class political agitation twenty years after Chartism.

2187 Hinton, J. 'The Labour aristocracy'. NLR, July-Aug. 1965, 32:72–7.

2188 Hobsbawm, E.J. 'Economic fluctuations and some social movements since 1800', *Labouring men*, pp.126–57 (*see* no.1191). Weidenfeld, 1968.

2189 Hobsbawm, E.J. 'Friendly societies'. LHN, Spring 1957, 3(3):95–101.

2190 Hobsbawm, E.J. 'The Labour aristocracy in nineteenth century Britain', *Labouring men*, pp.272–315 (*see* no.1191). Weidenfeld, 1968.

2191 Hobsbawm, E.J. 'The Labour sects', *Primitive rebels*, pp.126–49. Manchester, University Press, 1959.

2192 Hobsbawm, E.J. 'Labour traditions', *Labouring men*, pp.371–85 (*see* no.1191). Weidenfeld, 1968.

2193 Hobsbawm, E.J. 'Trends in the British Labour movement since 1850', *Labouring men*, pp.316–43 (*see* no.1191). Weidenfeld, 1968.

2194 Jackson, T.A. 'Irish immigrants and English Labour'. SSLH, Spring 1966, 12:5–9.

2195 Kellas, J.G. 'Highland migration to Glasgow and the origin of the Scottish Labour movement'. SSLH, Spring 1966, 12:9–12.

2196 Kendall, W. 'Russian emigration and British Marxist socialism'. IRSH, 1963, 8(3):351–78.

2197 McCready, H.W. 'Britain's Labour lobby, 1867–75'. CJEPS, May 1956, 22(2):141–60.

2198 MacFarlane, L.J. 'Hands off Russia: British Labour and the Russo-Polish war, 1920', PP, Dec. 1967, 38:126–52.

2199 Mackay, D.I., D.J.C. Forsyth and D.M. Kelly. 'The discussion of public works programmes, 1917–1935: some remarks on the Labour movement's contribution'. IRSH, 1966, 11(1):8–17.

2200 McKenzie, R.T. 'Conservatism and the British working class'. SSLH, Autumn 1963, 7:10–14.

2201 Main, J.M. 'Working-class politics in Manchester from Peterloo to the Reform Bill, 1819–32'. HS, May 1955, 6(24):447–58.

2202 Marwick, A. 'Working-class attitudes to the First World War'. SSLH, Autumn 1966, 13:9–12.

2203 Marx Memorial Library. Quarterly Bulletin. 'The fight for the franchise'. MML, Oct.–Dec. 1966, 40:9–14.

2204 Meynell, H. 'The Stockholm conference of 1917'. IRSH, 1960, 5(1):1–25.

2205 Meynell, H. 'The Stockholm conference of 1917'. IRSH, 1960 5(2):202–25.

2206 Pankhurst, R.K.P. 'Fourierism in Britain'. IRSH, 1956, 1(3):398–432.

2207 Pelling, H. 'The British working-class's attitude to the extension of state powers 1885–1914'. SSLH, Autumn 1966, 13:17–18.

2208 Pelling, H. 'The concept of the Labour aristocracy', *Popular politics and society in late Victorian Britain: essays*, pp.37–61. Macmillan, 1968.

2209 Poale Zion Labour Zionist movement. *100 years of the Jewish Labour movement in Britain*. Poale Zion Labour Zionist movement, ?1967. 16pp.

2210 Pollard, S. 'Aspects of the Labour movement in Sheffield 1880–1939'. SSLH, Spring 1963, 6:11–12.

2211 Poulantzas, N. 'Marxist political theory in Great Britain'. NLR, May–June 1967, 43:57–74.

2212 Reaney, G. *The class struggles in 19th century Oxfordshire: the social and communal background to the Otmoor disturbances of 1830 to 1835.* Oxford, Ruskin College, History Workshop, 1970. 72pp.

2213 Reichenbach, B. 'Why has Marxism failed in England?'. CNR, Dec. 1948, 174:343–8.

2214 Renshaw, P. 'The First International'. HT, Dec. 1964, 14(12):863–9.

2215 Roderick, A.J., ed. G.A. Williams, 'The emergence of a working-class movement', pp.140–6; T.I. Jeffreys–Jones, 'The rise of Labour', pp.201–8, *Wales through the ages.* Vol. 2, *Modern Wales.* Llandybie, Davies, 1960.

2216 Rose, M.E. 'The Anti-Poor Law movement in the North of England'. NH, 1966, 1:70–91.

2217 Rowe, D.J. 'Class and political radicalism in London, 1831–2'. HJ, 1970, 13(1):31–47.

2218 Rowe, D.J. 'The decline of the Tyneside Keelmen in the nineteenth century'. NH, 1969, 4:111–31.

2219 Rowe, D.J. *London's radicalism 1830–43: a selection from the papers of Francis Place.* London Record Society, 1970. xxviii, 266pp.

2220 Saville, J. 'Henry George and the British Labour movement'. SAS, Fall 1960, 24(4):321–33.

2221 Silberner, E. 'British socialism and the Jews'. HJU, Apr. 1952, 14(1):27–52.

2222 Tholfsen, T.R. 'The origins of the Birmingham caucus'. HJ, 1959, 2(2):161–84.

2223 Tholfsen, T.R. 'The transition to democracy in Victorian England'. IRSH, 1961, 6(2):226–48.

2224 Tyrell, T. 'Class consciousness in early Victorian Britain: Samuel Smiles, Leeds politics and the self-help creed'. JBS, May 1970, 9(2):102–25.

2225 Viner, G. *The road leads on . . . a story of 21 years' work of the Welsh Regional Council of Labour 1937–1958.* The Council, ?1958. 16pp.

2226 Ward, J.T. 'The factory movement in Lancashire, 1830–55'. LCAS, 1968, 75/6:186–210.

2227 Williams, Glanmor, ed. *Merthyr politics: the making of a working-class tradition.* Cardiff, University of Wales Press, 1966. 109pp.

2228 Williams, G.A. 'The making of radical Merthyr, 1800–36'. WH, 1961, 1(2):161–92.

2229 Yearley, C.K., Jnr. *Britons in American Labor: a history of the influence of the United Kingdom immigrants on American Labor, 1820–1914.* Baltimore, Johns Hopkins Press, 1957. 332pp.

The Arts

2230 Aveling, E. and E. Marx Aveling. *Shelley's socialism: two lectures.* Manchester, Preger, 1947 (first pub. 1888). vii(ii), 26pp.

2231 Beeching, J. 'The uncensoring of "The ragged trousered philanthropists"'. MQ, Oct. 1955, 2(4):217–30.

2232 Berger, J. 'Art and Labour'. NR, Autumn 1958, 6:74–8.

2233 Berger, J. 'Problems of socialist art'. LM, Mar. 1961, 43(3):135–43.

2234 Berger, J. 'Problems of socialist art (2)'. LM, Apr. 1961, 43(4):178–86.

2235 Bold, A., ed. *The Penguin book of socialist verse.* Penguin, 1970. 550pp.

2236 Bond, R. 'Art is no luxury'. LM, Jan. 1961, 43(1):35–8.

2237 Bond, R. 'A breakthrough to Resolution 42'. TUA, Summer 1961, 3:61–8.

2238 Bush, A. 'A declaration of intent (Why and how I compose)'. LM, Dec. 1970, 52(12):554–5.

2239 Centre 42. *Centre 42: first stage in a cultural revolution.* Centre 42, 1961. 18pp.

2240 Centre 42. *Supplement to the brochure.* Centre 42, 1962. 4pp.

2241 Communist Party. National Cultural Committee. *Essays on socialist realism and the British cultural tradition.* Arena, ?1953. 86pp.

2242 Craig, D. 'The new poetry of socialism'. NLR, Winter 1962, 17:73–84.

2243 Crick, B. 'Socialist literature in the 1950's'. PQ, July-Sept. 1960, 31(3):361–73.

2244 Deller, R. 'Centre 42'. NLR, Sept.–Oct. 1961, 11:60–1.

2245 Douglass, S. 'Socialist drama with the stops out'. LM, June 1967, 49(6):282–4.

2246 Douglass, S. 'Talking to Kathleen Tressell'. LM, June 1968, 50(6):261–5.

2247 Findlater, R. *The future of the theatre.* Fabian Society, 1959. 28pp.

2248 Findlater, R. 'Plays and politics (Arnold Wesker's trilogy)'. TC, Sept. 1960, 168(1003):235–42.

2249 Giannetti, L.D. 'Left-ward and West-ward Ho! the working-class movement and the arts in England'. WHR, Spring 1966, 20(2):113–23.

2250 Gould, T. 'Vintage 42'. TC, Winter 1966, 174(1028):46–9.

2251 Hogarth, P. 'The artist and the working-class movement'. LM, July 1953, 35(7):310–18.

2252 Jones, L. 'The General Strike and the workers' theatre', *Essays in honour of William Gallacher*, pp.153–8 (*see* no.326). Edited by P.M. Kemp-Ashraf and J. Mitchell. Berlin, Humboldt–Universität, 1966.

2253 Landis, H. 'A declaration of intent'. LM, Apr. 1967, 49(4):181–2.

2254 Landis, H. '"Which way unity Theatre?"'. LM, May 1967, 49(5):236–8.

2255 Lloyd, A.L. *Come all ye bold miners: ballads and songs of the coalfields.* Lawrence and Wishart, 1952. 144pp.

2256 Mander, J. 'Arnold Wesker's Roots', *The writer and commitment*, pp.192–211. Secker and Warburg, 1961.

2257 Marx Memorial Library. Quarterly Bulletin. "Merrie England". MML, Oct.–Dec. 1963, 28:3–4.

2258 Mayhew, C. *Commercial television—what is to be done?* Fabian Society, 1959. 24pp.

2259 Miller, J. 'Songs of the Labour movement'. OH, Summer 1963, 30:21pp.

2260 Milner, I. 'An estimation of Lewis Grassic Gibbon's "A Scots Quair"'. MQ, Oct. 1954, 1(4):207–18.

2261 Mitchell, A. 'A declaration of intent'. LM, Mar. 1967, 49(3):132–4.

2262 Mitchell, S. 'Romanticism and socialism'. NLR, Mar.–Apr. 1963, 19:56–68.

2263 Morton, A.L. *The arts and the people.* Lawrence and Wishart, ?1960. 27pp.

2264 O'Casey, S. 'Two letters to Ken Coates'. SR, 1965, 2:237–40.

2265 Priestley, J.B. *The arts under socialism.* Turnstile Press, 1947. 32pp.

2266 Smith, H. 'Towards a socialist literature in Britain', *Essays in honour of William Gallacher*, pp.248–53 (*see* no.326). Edited by P.M. Kemp-Ashraf and J. Mitchell. Berlin, Humboldt-Universität, 1966.

2267 Stross, B. 'Parliament and patronage'. NR, Autumn 1958, 6:66–73.

2268 Sutton, P. 'Films and the Labour movement'. LM, Oct. 1950, 32(10):469–73.

2269 Thomson, G. *Marxism and poetry.* Lawrence and Wishart, 1947. 65pp.

2270 Thomson, G. 'Our cultural heritage', *Britain's cultural heritage*, pp.13–19. Arena, 1952.

2271 Wesker, A. 'Art is not enough'. TC, Feb. 1961, 169(1008):190–4.

2272 Wesker, A. 'The secret reins—"Centre 42"'. EN, Mar. 1962, 18(3):3–4.

2273 Wollheim, R. *Socialism and culture.* Fabian Society, 1961. 48pp.

Education

2274 Barker, R. 'The Labour Party and the education for socialism'. IRSH, 1969, 14(1):22–53.

2275 Bayliss, F.J. 'The future of trade union education'. AE, Autumn 1959, 32(2):109–15.

2276 Bell, P. 'The working men's clubs'. MML, Oct.–Dec. 1965, 36:7–12.

2277 Chester, T.E. 'Education for trade union members—some approaches and suggestions'. AE, Summer 1952, 25(1):20–9.

2278 Cole, G.D.H. 'What workers' education means'. F, June 1952, 171(1026):390–8.

2279 Collins, J.M. 'The Labour Party and the public schools: a conflict of principles'. BJES, Oct. 1969, 17(3):301–11.

2280 Communist Party. History Group. 'The struggle for educational opportunity'. OH, Autumn 1956, 3:27pp.

2281 Corfield, A.J. *Epoch in workers' education: a history of the Workers' Educational Trade Union Committee.* Workers' Educational Association, 1969. 272pp.

2282 Craik, W.W. *The Central Labour College 1909–29: a chapter in the history of adult working-class education.* Lawrence and Wishart, 1964. 192pp.

2283 Cuthbert, T. 'The struggle for comprehensive education'. LM, Mar. 1965, 47(3):132–4.

2284 Dean, D.W. 'Difficulties of a Labour educational policy: the failure of the Trevelyan Bill, 1929–31'. BJES, Oct. 1969, 17(3):286–300.

2285 Elvin, L. 'Ruskin College, 1899–1949'. AE, June 1949, 21(4):189–93.

2286 Garman, D. 'Trade union education'. LM, Sept. 1948, 30(9):275–80.

2287 Harrison, J.F.C. '"The steam engine of the New Moral World". Owenism and education, 1817–29'. JBS, May 1967, 6(2):76–98.

2288 Harrison, J.F.C. 'Working class culture: the Owenite contribution'. SSLH, Autumn 1964, 9:7–9.

2289 Hopkins, P.G.H. 'Labour education in Britain'. AE, May 1965, 38(1):15–20.

2290 Hughes, H.D. *A socialist education policy.* Fabian Society, 1955. 29pp.

2291 Ibbotson, P. 'Labour's educational policy'. NR, Autumn 1958, 6:92–104.

2292 Industrial Research and Information Services Ltd. *Trade union education.* I.R.I.S., 1970. 17pp.

2293 Jefferson, C. 'Worker education in England and France, 1800–1914'. CSSH, Apr. 1964, 6(3):345–66.

2294 Judges, A.V. 'The educational influences of the Webbs'. BJES, Nov. 1961, 10(1):33–48.

2295 Lewis, J. 'The Left Book Club'. MML, Apr.–June 1967, 42:9–10.

2296 Lewis, J. *The Left Book Club: an historical record*. Gollancz, 1970. 163pp.

2297 McCann, W.P. 'Trade unionists, artisans and the 1870 Education Act'. BJES, June 1970, 18(2):134–50.

2298 MacLean, J. *A plea for a Labour college in Scotland*. John MacLean Society, 1970. 25pp.
    First delivered 1916.

2299 Marshall, R.L. 'The Co-operative College: a note on its experience as a long term residential college'. AE, Mar. 1948, 20(3):129–33.

2300 Martindall, R. 'Trade union education: the end of a chapter'. LM, Oct. 1964, 46(10):474–5.
    The closing of the National Council of Labour Colleges.

2301 Marx Memorial Library. Quarterly Bulletin. 'Socialist education and propaganda in Britain before 1917'. MML, Jan.–Mar. 1968, 45:5–9.

2302 Matthews, J.H. 'Trade union education today and tomorrow'. AE, Autumn 1953, 26(2):95–100.

2303 Millar, J.P.M. 'Forty years of independent working-class education'. AE, June 1949, 21(4):210–15.

2304 Nicholson, F. 'Politics and students'. LM, Oct. 1966, 48(10):481–4.

2305 Parkinson, C.N. 'The Left Book Club', *Left luggage: from Marx to Wilson*, pp.183–7. Murray, 1967.

2306 Parkinson, M. *The Labour Party and the organisation of secondary education 1918–65*. Routledge, 1970. viii, 139pp.

2307 Pearce, B. 'Labour notes and queries. The establishment of Marx House—a comment'. SSLH, Spring 1968, 16:20–2.

2308 Pickstock, F.V. 'Teaching trade unionists'. AE, July 1963, 36(2):54–60.

2309 Political Quarterly. 'Notes and comments: Labour and secondary education'. PQ, Oct.–Dec. 1951, 22(4):317–22.

2310 Raybould, S.G. 'The W.E.A. and workers' education'. F, July 1953, 174(1039):15–20.

2311 Rickman, H.P. 'What need for workers' education?'. F, Mar. 1953, 173(1035):170–4.

2312 Rothstein, A. *A house on Clerkenwell Green*. Lawrence and Wishart, 1966. 80pp.
    An account of the Marx Memorial Library and a history of the building.

2313 Rothstein, A. 'The origins of Marx House'. MML, July–Sept. 1965, 35:6–11.

2314 Ruskin College. *The story of Ruskin College*. Oxford, The College, 1955. 25pp.

2315 Samuels, S. 'The Left Book Club'. JCH, 1966, 1(2):65–86.

2316 Shanley, J.R. 'Marxism and trade union education'. MML, July–Sept. 1970, 55:17–19.

2317 Shanley, J.R. 'Trade union education: an end or a beginning?'. LM, Nov. 1964, 46(11):515–17.

2318 Silver, H. *The concept of popular education: a study of ideas and social movements in the nineteenth century*. MacGibbon and Kee, 1965. 284pp.

2319 Silver, H. *Robert Owen on education: selections edited with an introduction and notes*. CUP, 1969. vii, 240pp.

2320 Simon, B. 'Education: Owen, Mill, Arnold and the Woodard Schools'. VS, June 1970, 13(4):403–7.

2321 Simon, B. *Education and the Labour movement 1870–1920*. Lawrence and Wishart, 1965. 387pp.

2322 Simon, B. 'Labour's education policy'. LM, Sept. 1958, 40(9):418–21.

2323 Simon, B. *Studies in the history of education, 1780–1870*. Lawrence and Wishart, 1960. 375pp.

2324 Smith, W.O.L. 'The Labour Party's policy for education'. PQ, Oct.–Dec. 1958, 29(4):338–47.

2325 Thayer, G. 'Collet's Bookshop', *The British political fringe: a profile*, pp.113–18. Blond, 1965.

2326 Thomas, K. 'No. 49, Tottenham Street'. MML, Oct.–Dec. 1970, 56:14–19.
      'Communist Club'.

2327 Thompson, J. *Next steps in education*. Fabian Society, 1949. 23pp.

2328 The Times. 'Historic radical centre threatened [i.e. Marx House]'. MML, Jan.–Mar. 1965, 33:4–6.
      Reprinted from The Times, 20 Oct. 1964.

2329 Williams, J.E. 'An experiment in trade union education'. AE, Autumn 1954, 27(2):113–24.

The Press

2330 Benenson, P. *A free press.* Fabian Society, 1961. 36pp.

2331 Briginshaw, R.W. 'The press jungle'. LM, Dec. 1960, 42(12):543–5.

2332 Brotherstone, T. 'The suppression of "The Forward"'. SLH, May 1969, 1:5–23.

2333 Cairo, J. 'The weeklies: New Statesman'. C, Apr.–June 1970, 13(51):22–3.

2334 Cockburn, C. 'The Morning Star'. NLR, July–Aug. 1966, 38:23–34.

2335 Cockburn, C. '"The Week" today'. TC, Apr. 1956, 159(950):326–31.

2336 Cockburn, P. *The years of The Week.* Macdonald, 1968. 287pp.

2337 Cole, H. *Socialism and the press.* Fabian Publications/Gollancz, 1952. 56pp.

2338 Coltham, S. 'The Bee-Hive newspaper: its origin and early struggles', *Essays in Labour history*, pp.174–204 (*see* no.1179). Edited by A. Briggs and J. Saville. Macmillan, 1960.

2339 Coltham, S. 'The British working class press in 1867'. SSLH, Autumn 1967, 15:4–6.

2340 Coltham, S. 'English working class newspapers in 1867'. VS, Dec. 1969, 13(2):159–80.

2341 Daily Herald. *The story of ten thousand issues of the "Daily Herald" 1911–48.* Odhams, 1948. 20pp.
    Celebration souvenir programme, January 25th 1911–March 22nd 1948, of a concert held at Royal Albert Hall, 21st March 1948. Contains a short history of the Daily Herald.

2342 *Democratic Review.* Vol. 1, June 1849–May 1850. viii, 476pp. Vol. 2, June–Sept. 1850. iv, 156pp. Edited by G. Julian Harney. Merlin, 1968 (first pub. 1849–50).

2343 Dutt, R.P. *The rise and fall of the Daily Herald.* Labour Monthly and Daily Worker, 1964. 17pp.

2344 Dutt, R.P. 'Three decades'. LM, July 1951, 33(7):289–300.
    Labour Monthly.

2345 Fienburgh, W. *1930–55. 25 momentous years: a 25th anniversary in the history of the Daily Herald.* Oldhams, 1955. 208pp.

2346 Hollis, P. *The pauper press: a study in working-class radicalism of the 1830's.* OUP, 1970. xvii, 348pp.

2347 Hutt, A. 'Press problems of the Labour movement'.LM, Mar. 1966, 48(3):127–30.

2348 Hyams, E. *The New Statesman: the history of the first fifty years 1913–63.* Longmans, 1963. xiv, 326pp.

2349 Jackson, F. *18 Years of struggle: the history of the New Builders Leader*. New Builders Leader, 1953. 24pp.

2350 Jackson, F. '"Justice" and the S.D.F.'. MML, Jan.–Mar. 1964, 29:7–8.

2351 Jackson, F. 'On the advent of "Justice"'. MML, Jan.–Mar. 1966, 37:6–9.

2352 Jackson, F. 'The socialist press at Marx House'. MML, Jan.–Mar. 1962, 21:4–7.

2353 Jackson, F. 'The Twentieth Century Press'. MML, July-Sept. 1959, 11:4–6.

2354 Martin, K. *Critic's London Diary: from the New Statesman 1931–56*. Secker and Warburg, 1960. xiii, 312pp.

2355 Martin, W. *The New Age under Orage: chapters in English cultural history*. Manchester, University Press, 1967, xiv, 303pp.

2356 Moonman, E., ed. *The press: a case for commitment*. Fabian Society, 1969. 37pp.

2357 Muratore, G. 'Marxist journals in the Europe of to-day'. SAS, Winter 1947, 11(1):69–75.
  Includes Modern Quarterly and Labour Monthly.

2358 *Notes to the People*. Vol. 1, [iv], ix, pp.1–512. Vol. 2, [iv], v, pp.513–1032. Edited by Ernest Jones. Merlin, 1967 (first pub. weekly, May 1851–May 1852).

2359 'Ormal', *pseud*. 'The rôle of socialist journalism'. LM, Jan. 1962, 44(1):43–5.

2360 Pollitt, H. '30 years of the Labour Monthly'. LM, July 1951, 33(7):311–315.

2361 *The Poor Man's Guardian*. Vol. 1, July 9, 1831–June 16, 1832 (introduction by Patricia Hollis, vii–xxxix). xlv, 432pp. Vol. 2, June 23, 1832–Dec. 29, 1832. [iv], pp.433–664. Jan. 5, 1833–Sept. 7, 1883, pp.1–292. Vol. 3, Sept. 14, 1833–Feb. 1, 1834. [iv], pp.293–460. Feb. 8, 1834–Dec. 27, 1834. pp.1–376. Vol. 4, Jan. 3, 1835–Dec. 26, 1835. [iv], 377–800. Merlin, 1969 (first pub. in London 1831–5 and edited by Henry Hetherington).

2362 *The Red Republican and the Friend of the People*. Vol. 1, *The Red Republican*, June 22–Nov. 30, 1850. [iv] xv [ii], pp.1–20. Vol. 2, *The Friend of the People*, Dec. 14, 1850–July 26, 1851. [vi], pp.1–8, 1–282. Introduction by John Saville. Merlin, 1966 (first pub. 1850–51 and edited by G. Julian Harney).

2363 Rust, W. *The story of the Daily Worker*. Edited and completed by Allen Hutt. People's Press Printing Society, 1949. 128pp.

2364 Thompson, E.P. *The struggle for a free press*. People's Press Printing Society, 1952. 23pp.

2365 Tuckett, A. 'Amongst those present'. LM, Aug. 1966, 48(8):385–6.
  Labour Monthly 45th birthday.

2366 Tuckett, A. 'Behind the times: The Times on the Labour press'. LM, Dec. 1955, 37(12):565–7.

2367 Waller, I. 'The left-wing press', *The left: a symposium*, pp.75–95 (*see* no.2595). Blond, 1966.

2368 Wiener, J. *A descriptive finding list of unstamped British periodicals, 1830–6.* Bibliographical Society, 1970. xiii, 74pp.

2369 Wiener, J. *The war of the unstamped: the movement to repeal the British newspaper tax, 1830–6.* Ithaca, Cornell University Press, 1969. xviii, 310pp.

Religion

2370 Armytage, W.H.G. 'John Minter Morgan's schemes, 1841–1855'. IRSH, 1958, 3(1):26–42.

2371 Backstrom, P.N., Jnr. 'The practical side of Christian socialism in Victorian England'. VS, June 1963, 6(4):305–24.

2372 Barnes, R. 'The late Canon Donaldson and the Leicester unemployed march of 1905: a note on the inter-relation of religion and politics in a Midland town'. SSLH, Autumn 1962, 5:16–17.

2373 Beales, H.L. 'The British Labour movement and religion during the first half of the nineteenth century'. SSLH, Autumn 1962, 5:10–12.

2374 Christensen, T. *Origin and history of Christian socialism, 1848–54.* Universitetsforlaget I, Aarhus, 1962. 369pp.
   Supplements no.2412 and reviews many aspects of the movement 'in a new light'.

2375 Connolly, J. *Labour, nationality and religion.* Dublin, New Books, 1954. 62pp.

2376 Davies, Rev. D.R. *Communism and God.* Ampersand, 1954. 31pp.

2377 Edwards, M.L. 'The Church and the rise of socialism'. LQ, July 1951, 201–8.

2378 Evans, S.G. *Christian socialism: a study outline and bibliography.* Christian Socialist Movement, 1962. 31pp.

2379 Evans, S.G. *Christians and communists.* S.S.C.M., 1949. 16pp.

2380 Evans, S.G. *The social life of the Christian church.* Hodder, 1965. 296pp.

2381 Foinette, T.J. 'Christianity and communism: an assessment of the issue'. LQ, Jan. 1949, 38–42.

2382 Gallacher, W. *Catholics and communism.* Communist Party, 1948. 16pp.

383 Greaves, C.D. 'Paisleyism and "progress"'. LM, Sept. 1966, 48(9):435–439.

384 Greenslade, S.L. *The church and the social order*. S.C.M. Press, 1948. 128pp. Discusses Christian socialism.

385 Griffin, A.R. 'Methodism and trade unionism in the Nottingham-shire–Derbyshire coalfield, 1844–90'. WES, Feb. 1969, 37:2–9.

386 Griffin, A.R. 'Primitive Methodism and the mining unions'. WES, Oct. 1969, 37:91–2.

387 Grisewood, H. 'The Christian socialists'. QR, Oct. 1950, 288(586):526–535.

388 Groser, Rev. J. *Does socialism need religion?* Fabian Society, 1951. 20pp.

389 Groves, R. *The Catholic crusade 1918–36*. Archive One, 1970. 24pp.

390 Hobsbawm, E.J. 'Methodism and the threat of revolution in Great Britain', *Labouring men*, pp.23–33 (*see* no.1191). Weidenfeld, 1968.

391 Horn, P.R. 'Methodism and agricultural trade unionism in Oxfordshire: the 1870's'. WES, Oct. 1969, 37:67–71.

392 Inglis, K.S. *Churches and the working classes in Victorian England*. Routledge, 1963. viii, 350pp.

393 Inglis, K.S. 'Churches and working classes in nineteenth century England'. HS, Nov. 1957, 8(29):44–53.

394 Inglis, K.S. 'English nonconformity and social reform, 1880–1900'. PP, Apr. 1958, 13:73–88.

395 Inglis, K.S. 'The Labour church movement'. IRSH, 1958, 3(3):445–60.

396 Jones, P. d'A. *The Christian socialist revival, 1877–1914, religion, class and social conscience in late Victorian England*. New Jersey, Princeton University Press, 1968. xiii, 504pp. (*see* no.2432).

397 Kay, H. 'The Pope's Mater et Magistra'. TUA, Summer 1962, 5:18–30.

398 Larkin, E. 'Socialism and Catholicism in Ireland'. CH, Dec. 1964, 33(4):462–83.

399 Lewis, G.K. 'The ideas of the Christian socialists of 1848'. WPQ, Sept. 1951, 4(3):397–429.

400 MacLaren, A.A. 'Presbyterianism and the working class in a mid-nineteenth century city [Aberdeen]'. SSLH, Spring 1967, 14:12–13.

401 Mayor, S. *The churches and the Labour movement*. Independent Press, 1967. ii, 414pp.

402 Mayor, S. 'Some Congregational relations with the Labour movement'. CHS, Aug. 1956, 18(1):23–35.

403 Moore, R. 'Methodism and the working classes'. NEG, Oct. 1969, 3:7–9.

2404 Morris, G.M. 'Primitive Methodism and the miners' unions'. WES, June 1969, 37:58.

2405 Morris, W.D. *The Christian origins of social revolt*. Allen and Unwin, 1949. 239pp.

2406 Oliver, J.K. *The church and social order: social thought in the Church of England, 1918–39*. Mowbray, 1968. ix, 228pp.

2407 Osment, R.M. *Heavenwards from communism*. Inter-Varsity Fellowship, 1963 (first pub. 1955). 32pp.

2408 Pearce, B. 'Trotskyism on religion and the British Labour movement'. SSLH, Autumn 1962, 5:14–16.

2409 Pelling, H. 'Religion and the nineteenth-century British working class'. PP, Apr. 1964, 27:128–33.

2410 Pelling, H. and K.S. Inglis. 'Discussion on "The Labour church movement"'. IRSH, 1959, 4(1):111–13.

2411 Pierson, S. 'John Trevor and the Labour church movement in England, 1891–1900'. CH, Dec. 1960, 29(4):463–78.

2412 Raven, C.E. *Christian socialism 1848–54*. Cass, 1968 (first pub. 1920). xii, 396pp. (*see* no.2374).

2413 Reckitt, M.B. *Maurice to Temple: a century of the social movement in the Church of England*. Faber, 1947. 245pp.

2414 Reid, F. 'Socialist sunday schools in Britain, 1892–1939'. IRSH, 1966, 11(1):18–47.

2415 Rhymes, Rev. D.A. *The theory of communism*. Ampersand, 1954. 31pp.

2416 Ridley, F.A. *Socialism and religion*. Engels Society, 1948. 20pp.

2417 Robertson, A. *Socialism and religion: an essay*. Lawrence and Wishart, 1960. 62pp.

2418 Roth, H. 'The Labour churches and New Zealand'. IRSH, 1959, 4(3):361–6.

2419 Rowe, J. 'Faith on the shop floor'. TUA, Spring 1961, 2:17–22.

2420 Saville, J. 'The Christian socialists of 1848', *Democracy and the Labour movement*', pp.135–59 (*see* no.1215). Edited by J. Saville. Lawrence and Wishart, 1954.

2421 Sellers, I. 'Unitarians and the Labour church movement'. UHS, 1959, 12(1):1–6.

2422 Thompson, P. 'Religion and politics in London, 1880–1910'. SSLH, Autumn 1962, 5:12–13.

2423 Thomson, G. *An essay on religion*. Lawrence and Wishart, 1949. 32pp.

2424 Treble, J.H. 'The attitude of the Roman Catholic church towards trade unionism in the north 1833–42'. NH, 1970, 5:93–113.

425 Wearmouth, R.F. *Methodism and the common people of the eighteenth century.* Epworth, 1945. 276pp.

426 Wearmouth, R.F. *Methodism and the struggle of the working classes 1850–1900.* Leicester, Backus, 1954. xv, 269pp.

427 Wearmouth, R.F. *Methodism and the trade unions.* Epworth, 1959. 78pp.

428 Wearmouth, R.F. *Methodism and the working-class movements of England 1800–50.* Epworth, 1947. xi, 242pp.

429 Wearmouth, R.F. *Some working-class movements of the nineteenth century.* Epworth, 1948. xi, 338pp.

430 Wearmouth, R.F. *The social and political influence of Methodism in the twentieth century.* Epworth, 1957. xiii, 265pp.

431 Wicker, B. *First the political kingdom: a personal appraisal of the Catholic left in Britain.* Sheed and Ward, 1967. xv, 143pp.

432 Wickham, The Rt. Rev. E.R. Review of P. d'A. Jones, *The Christian socialist revival, 1877–1914 (see* no.2396). SSLH, Autumn 1968, 17:35–7.

Other organizations

Fabian Society

2433 Arnold, G.L. 'Notes on Fabianism'. TC, June 1956, 159(952):536–48.

2434 Briggs, A., ed. *Fabian essays*. Allen and Unwin, 1962. 322pp.
Contains: new introduction by A. Briggs, pp.11–29; Preface to the 1931
reprint by G.B. Shaw, pp.257–67; Introduction to the 1920 reprint by S.
Webb, pp.268–81; Preface to the 1908 reprint by G. B. Shaw, pp.282–92;
1889 Preface, pp.293–4; Sixty years of Fabianism: a postscript by G.B.
Shaw, pp.294–315.

2435 Cole, G.D.H. *The Fabian Society, past and present*. Fabian Publications,
1952. 17pp.

2436 Cole, M. *The story of Fabian socialism*. Heinemann, 1963. xv, 366pp.
Apart from Pease (*see* no.2453) 'there has not been a straight history of
the oldest socialist society in the world'.

2437 Crossman, R.H.S., ed. *New Fabian essays*. Turnstile, 1952. xv, 215pp.
See nos.1305, 1361, 1634, 2087, 2441 and 3008.

2438 *Fabian essays*. Jubilee edition. Allen and Unwin, 1948. xliii, 246pp.
Contains: Preface to 1980 reprint, pp.xxix–xxxviii by Bernard Shaw;
Introduction to 1920 reprint, pp.xv–xxvii by Sidney Webb; Preface to
1931 reprint, pp.v–xiv by Bernard Shaw and a new Postscript by
Bernard Shaw—Sixty years of Fabianism, pp.207–31.

2439 Fox, P.W and H.S. Gordon. 'The early Fabians—economists and reformers'. CJEPS, Aug. 1951, 17(3):307–19.

2440 Fremantle, A. *This little band of prophets: the story of the gentle Fabians*. Allen
and Unwin, 1960. 256pp.

2441 Gollan, J. 'The new Fabians'. LM, Aug. 1952, 34(8):337–46.
Review of no.2437.

2442 Gundy, H.P. 'The Fabians'. QQ, Summer 1950, 57(2):174–81.

2443 Hobsbawm, E.J. 'The Fabians reconsidered', *Labouring men: studies in the
history of Labour*, pp.250–71 (*see* no.1191). Weidenfeld, 1968.

2444 Hobsbawm, E.J. 'The lesser Fabians'. OH, Winter 1962, 28:14pp.

2445 Irvine, W. 'Shaw, the Fabians and the Utilitarians'. JHI, April 1947, 8(2):218–31.

2446 Lapping, B. and G. Radice. *More power to the people: Young Fabian essays on democracy in Britain*. Longmans, 1968. 196pp.

2447 Lewis, G.K. 'Fabian socialism: some aspects of theory and practice'. JP, Aug. 1952, 14(3):442–70.

2448 McBriar, A.M. *Fabian socialism and English politics 1884–1918*. CUP, 1966. x, 388pp.
     Lists Fabian tracts pub. 1884–1920.

2449 McCarran, Sister M.M.P. *Fabianism in the political life of Britain, 1919–31*. Washington D.C., Catholic University of America Press, 1952. xii, 612pp.
     'Fabianism represents the predominating type of socialism in England.'

2450 Mack, M.P. 'The Fabians and Utilitarianism'. JHI, Jan. 1955, 16(1):76–88.

2451 Milburn, J.F. 'The Fabian Society and the British Labour Party'. WPQ, June 1958, 11(2):319–39.

2452 Murphy, M.E. 'The role of the Fabian Society in British affairs'. SEJ, July 1947, 14(1):14–23.

2453 Pease, E.R. *The history of the Fabian Society*. Introduction by Margaret Cole. Cass, 1963 (first pub. 1918). 306pp.
     This edition taken from the 1925 (slightly revised) edition.

2454 Ricci, D.M. 'Fabian socialism: a theory of rent as exploitation'. JBS, Nov. 1969, 9(1):105–21.

2455 Robson, W.A. 'Fabian socialism'. BJS, Mar. 1962, 13(1):70–2.

2456 Thompson, P. *Socialists, Liberals and Labour: the struggle for London, 1885–1914*. Routledge, 1967. viii, 376pp.

2457 Woolf, L. 'The early Fabians and British socialism', *Shaw and society*, pp.39–53 (*see* no.947). Edited by C.E.M. Joad. Odhams, 1953.

Independent Labour Party

458 Dowse, R.E. 'The Independent Labour Party and foreign politics 1918–23'. IRSH, 1962, 7(1):33–46.

459 Dowse, R.E. *Left in the centre: the Independent Labour Party 1893–1940*. Longmans, 1966. xi, 213pp.

460 Duffy, A.E.P. 'Differing politics and personal rivalries in the origins of the Independent Labour Party'. VS, Sept. 1962, 6(1):43–65.

2461 Marwick, A. 'The Independent Labour Party in the nineteen twenties'. IHR, May 1962, 35(91):62–74.

2462 Middlemas, R.K. *The Clydesiders: a left-wing struggle for parliamentary power.* Hutchinson, 1965. 307pp.

2463 Parry, C. 'The Independent Labour Party and Gwynedd politics 1900–20'. WH, June 1968, 4(1):47–66.

2464 Pelling, H. 'The story of the I.L.P.', *Popular politics and society in late Victorian Britain: essays*, pp.121–9. Macmillan, 1968.

2465 Thayer, G. '(The outside left) I.L.P.', *The British political fringe: a profile*, pp.146–8. Blond, 1965.

2465a Thompson, P. *Socialist, Liberals and Labour: 1885–1914.* Routledge, 1967. viii, 376pp.

The Communist Party

2466 Arnot, R.P. 'The first thirty years'. LM, Aug. 1950, 32(8):371–8.

2467 Arnot, R.P. 'Twenty-fifth anniversary of the Communist Party'. LM, Aug. 1945, 27(8):236–8.

2468 Bailey, J. *The Zig Zag 'Left': an exposure of communist tactics.* Co-operative Union, 1948. 24pp.

2469 Black, R. *Stalinism in Britain.* New Park Publications, 1970. 440pp.
    Reply to no.2651.

2470 Bramley, E. 'Affiliation'. LM, Jan. 1946, 28(1):17–23.

2471 Common Cause. *Communists, their supporters and spurious peace movements.* Common Cause Bulletin No. 109, Spring 1964. 53pp.

2472 Communist Party. *The communist answer to the challenge of our time.* Thames, 1947. viii, 85pp.
    Six lectures.

2473 Communist Party. *Communist Unity Convention. London, July 31st and August 1st, 1920. Official Report.* The Party, 1968. iv, 72pp.
    Facsimile of original publication of 1920.

2474 Communist Party. *1920–1950: episodes from the Communist Party's thirty years of struggle.* The Party, [1950]. 16pp.
    Souvenir booklet.

2475 Communist Party. *1920–1950: on the thirtieth anniversary of the Communist Party.* The Party, 1950. 32pp.

2476 Communist Party. *Speeches and documents of the sixth (Manchester) conference of the Communist Party of Great Britain, May 17, 18 and 19, 1924*. The Party, 1970. 79pp.

Facsimile of original publication of 1924.

2477 Communist Party. History Group. 'The class struggle in local affairs'. OH, Spring 1965, 1:29pp.

2478 Communist Party: History group. 'Labour–Communist relations 1920–39'. OH, Spring 1957, 5:37pp.

2479 Crane, P. 'The English communist mind'. M, Mar. 1960, 23(3):170–2. Review of no.2562.

2480 Crawley, A. *The hidden face of British communism*. Sunday Times, 1962. 16pp.

2481 Crawley, A. 'A red under every bed?'. EN, July 1963, 21(1):50–5.

2482 Darke, R. *The communist technique in Britain*. Collins, 1953. 160pp.

2483 Dutt, R.P. 'Communism and the left'. LM, Apr. 1959, 41(4):145–56.

2484 Dutt, R.P. 'The Communist Party'. PA, Winter 1951, 5(1):89–93.

2485 Dutt, R.P. 'Honour to whom honour: some reflections on Communist Party history'. LM, May 1959, 41(5):193–204.

2486 Dutt, R.P. 'The party of victory'. LM, Apr. 1954, 36(4):145–61.

2487 Feather, V. *How do the communists work?* Batchworth, 1953. 66pp.

2488 Fryer, P. *Hungary and the Communist Party: an appeal against expulsion*. The author, 1957. 48pp.

2489 Gallacher, W. *The case for communism*. Penguin, 1949. 208pp.

2490 Glicksberg, C. 'Converts from communism'. QQ, Summer 1951, 58(2):175–88. Review of *The God that failed. See* no.2548.

2491 Gollan, J. 'After the Communist Congress'. LM, May 1956, 38(5):222–6.

2492 Gollan, J. 'Fiftieth anniversary of the Communist Party'. LM, Aug. 1970, 52(8):357–9.

2493 Gollan, J. 'How to fight the Tory offensive'. LM, Mar. 1956, 38(3):111–15.

2494 Gollan, J. 'A significant congress'. LM, May 1959, 41(5):205–12.

2495 Gollan, J. *30 years of struggle: the record of the British Communist Party*. The Party, 1950. 25pp.

2496 Goodwin, D. and P. Fryer. *The Newsletter conference and the Communist Party*. Newsletter, 1958. 31pp. Statements by Goodwin with replies by Fryer.

2497 Grainger, G.W. 'Oligarchy in the British Communist Party'. BJS, June 1958, 9(2):143–58.

2498 Hanson, A.H. 'On not being a communist: two polemics': 'An open letter to Edward Thompson', pp.261–73; 'How wild is my wilderness?', pp.273–82, *Planning and the politicians and other essays*. Routledge, 1969.

2499 Harley, J.H. 'Communism and the trade unions'. CNR, Dec. 1946, 170:335–9.

2500 Hartley, A. 'You and your victims: a letter to an ex-communist'. TC, April 1957, 161(962):331–4.

2501 Hilton, R. *Communism and liberty*. Lawrence and Wishart, 1950. 32pp.

2502 Hinton, J. [The Communist Party]. SSLH, Autumn 1969, 19:42–9.
    Review of no.2514.

2503 Hobsbawm, E.J. 'The British Communist Party'. PQ, Jan.–Mar. 1954, 25(1):30–43.

2504 Holland, B. 'Smash the bans [i.e. on Communist Party]'. LM, Mar. 1960, 42(3):116–17.

2505 Horner, J. 'Unity then and now'. LM, Mar. 1946, 28(3):75–8.

2506 Hyde, D. *The answer to communism*. Paternoster, 1949. 79pp.
    Ex-communist analyses the appeal of communism and gives his answer.

2507 Industrial Research and Information Services Ltd. *The British road to Stalinism*. I.R.I.S., 1958. x, 65pp.

2508 Industrial Research and Information Services Ltd. *The Communist Party today*. I.R.I.S., 1966. 28pp.

2509 Industrial Research and Information Services Ltd. *The communist solar system: a survey of communist front organisations*. Hollis and Carter (for I.R.I.S.), 1957. 85pp.

2510 Jackson, T.A. 'The communists—the twelve of 1925', *Trials of British freedom: being some studies in the history of the fight for democratic freedom in Britain*, pp.173–83 (*see* no.1193). Lawrence and Wishart, 1945.

2511 Johnstone, M. 'The Communist Party in the 1920's'. NLR, Jan.–Feb. 1967, 41:47–63.

2512 Jones, M. 'Why Britain needs the communists'. TC, Spring 1963, 191(1017):50–60.

2513 Just, W.C. 'With British communists to Russia'. TC, July 1957, 162(965):16–27.

2514 Kendall, W. *The revolutionary movement in Britain 1900–21: the origins of British communism*. Weidenfeld, 1969. xii, 453pp.
    Includes short biographies of many leading personalities. (*See* nos.2502, 2544).

2515 Kendall, W. 'Russian emigration and British Marxist socialism'. IRSH, 1963, 8(3):351–78.

2516 Kerrigan, P. 'The Easter conferences'. LM, May 1961, 43(5):210–14.

517 Kerrigan, P. 'What we fight for'. LM, Sept. 1946, 28(9):261–5.

518 Kettle, A. *Communism and the intellectuals*. Lawrence and Wishart, 196–? 31pp.

519 Klugman, J. 'Communists and socialists'. MQ, July 1956, 3(3):147–57.

520 Klugman, J. *History of the Communist Party of Great Britain*. Vol. 1, *Formation and early years, 1919–24*. 1968. 381pp. Vol. 2, *1925–7: The General Strike*. 1969. 373pp. Lawrence and Wishart.

521 Lane, H. 'Why I joined' [i.e. the Communist Party]. LM, Jan. 1959, 41(1):37–8.

522 Laski, H.J. *The secret battalion: an examination of the communist attitude towards the Labour Party*. Labour Party, 1946. 32pp.

523 [A legal correspondent]. 'The Kinross election petition (Hugh MacDiarmid v. Alec Douglas-Home)'. LM, Feb. 1965, 47(2):65–8.

524 Livingston, W.S. 'Minor parties and university M.P.s, 1945–55'. WPQ, Dec. 1959, 12(4):1017–37.

525 Lockyer, R. *What is a communist?* Batchworth, 1954. 38pp.

526 McCreery, M. *Destroy the old to build the new! A comment on state, revolution and the C.P.G.B.* Committee to defeat Revisionism for Communist Unity, 1963. 13pp.

527 McCreery, M. *The patriots*. Committee to defeat Revisionism for Communist Unity, ?1964. 31pp.
    Criticises the Communist Party for being 'fig-leaf Marxists'.

528 MacFarlane, L.J. *The British Communist Party: its origin and development until 1929*. MacGibbon and Kee, 1966. 338pp. (*see* no.2543).

529 MacFarlane, L.J. 'The Communist Party in the twenties'. SSLH, Spring 1967, 14:4–6.

530 Mauger, S. 'Communist Party congress'. NLR, Jan.–Feb. 1966, 35:100–1.

531 Mitchell, D. 'Ghost of a chance: British revolutionaries in 1919'. HT, Nov. 1970, 20(11):753–61.

532 Murphy, J.T. 'Forty years hard—for what?'. NR, Winter 1958–9, 7:119–24.
    Review of no.2536.

533 Newton, K. *The sociology of British communism*. Lane, 1969. x, 214pp.

534 Pearce, B. (Redman, J., *pseud*.). *The Communist Party and the Labour left 1925–9*. Hull, Reasoner Publications, 1957. 31pp.

535 Pearce, B. *Early history of the Communist Party of Great Britain*. Socialist Labour League, 1966. 62pp.

536 Pelling, H. *The British Communist Party: a historical profile*. Black, 1958. viii, 204pp. (*see* no.2532).

537 Pelling, H. 'The early history of the Communist Party of Great Britain, 1920–9'. RHS, 1958, 5(8):41–57.

2538 [A political correspondent]. 'The British Communist Party'. TC, May 1952, 151(903):395–400.

2539 Pollitt, H. *Communism and Labour: a call for united action*. Communist Party, 1949. 48pp.

2540 Pollitt, H. 'The Communist Party and the election'. LM, July 1945, 27(7):197–201.

2541 Pollitt, H. 'The Communist Party congress'. LM, Jan. 1946, 28(1):12–17.

2542 Richardson, T. 'An election pen-picture'. LM, June 1958, 40(6):286–8.

2543 Rothstein, A. 'The British Communist Party'. LM, July 1966, 48(7):350–1. Review of no.2528.

2544 Rothstein, A. 'Review of W. Kendall "Revolutionary movement in Britain 1900–21: the origins of British communism"'. LM, Dec. 1969, 51(12):563–6.
     See no.2514.

2545 Saville, J. 'A further note on British communist history'. NR, Spring 1959, 8:99–101.

2546 Saville, J. 'On party history: an open letter to Comrade R. Page Arnot'. R, Nov. 1956, 3:23–7.

2547 [A special correspondent]. 'On leaving the Communist Party'. TC, Feb. 1954, 155(924):130–45.

2548 Spender, S. *The God that failed*, pp.231–72. Edited by R.H.S. Crossman. Hamilton, 1950 (*see* no.2490).

2549 Stewart, R. 'Forty splendid years'. LM, Sept. 1960, 42(9):414–17.

2550 Taylor, H.A. *Communism in Great Britain: a short history of the British Communist Party*. Conservative Political Centre, 1951. ii, 37pp.

2551 Thompson, E.P. 'Through the smoke of Budapest'. R, Nov. 1956, 3:1–7 (Supplement).

2552 Warren, W. 'The programme of the C.P.G.B.—a critique'. NLR, Sept.–Oct. 1970, 63:27–41.

2553 White, J.B. *The red network*. The author, 1953. 38pp.
     Soviet influence in Britain.

2554 Williams, D. *Communism—the greater danger*. Common Cause Bulletin no.117, Spring 1967. 32pp.

2555 Williams, D. *The communist challenge* (Part 1). Common Cause Bulletin no.126, Spring 1970. 32pp.

2556 Williams, D. *The communist challenge* (Part 2). Common Cause Bulletin no.127, Summer 1970. 30pp.

2557 Williams, D. *Communist propaganda techniques*. Common Cause Bulletin no.116, Winter 1966/67. 33pp.

2558 Williams, D. *The 1968 Communist World Youth Festival*. Common Cause Bulletin no.121, Winter 1968/69. 41pp.

2559 Williams, D. *The turnabout mechanics of communism and their fronts*. Common Cause Bulletin no.118, Autumn 1967. 37pp.

2560 Williams, D. and others. *Communism and youth*. Common Cause Bulletin no.111, Winter 1964/65. 57pp.

2561 Williams, D. and others. *Communism versus social democracy*. Common Cause Bulletin no.110, October 1964. 49pp.

2562 Wood, N. *Communism and British intellectuals*. Gollancz, 1959. 256pp.
See no.2479.

2563 Wood, N. 'The empirical proletarians: a note on British communism'. PSQ, June 1959, 74(2):256–72.

2564 Wyatt, W. *The peril in our midst*. Phoenix House, 1956. 70pp.

2565 Zilliacus, K. 'Open letter to Gallacher and Piratin'. LM, May 1946, 28(5):140–4.

Other bodies

2566 British Socialist Party. *The first Annual Conference of the British Socialist Party held . . . May 25th, May 26th and May 27th 1912*. Communist Party, ?1969. 72pp.
Facsimile of original publication of 1912 issued by the British Socialist Party.

2567 British Socialist Party. *Official Report of the Socialist Unity Conference . . . held . . . September 30th and October 1st 1911*. Communist Party, 1969. ii, 32pp.
Facsimile of the original publication of 1911 issued by the British Socialist Party.

2568 Communist Party. History Group. 'Some dilemmas for Marxists 1900–14'. OH, Christmas 1956, 4:31pp.

2569 Hanack, H. 'The Union of Democratic Control during the First World War'. IHR, Nov. 1963, 36(94):168–80.

2570 Irish Communist Organisation. *The Connolly Association*. Irish Communist Organisation, ?1967. 32pp.

2571 Pearce, B. 'The last years of the University Socialist Federation'. SSLH, Spring 1962, 4:45–6.

2572 Rothstein, A. 'The Hackney and Kingsland Branch of the S.D.F. (1903–6)'. OH, Autumn 1960, 19:19pp.

2573 Stenning, H.J. '1906 and all that'. WMS, Summer 1970, 2(4):31–3. Reminiscences of the S.D.F.

2574 Student Labour Federation. *This is the S.L.F.* The Federation, 1946. 17pp.

2575 Thayer, G. 'The outside left [S.P.G.B.]', *The British political fringe: a profile*, pp.148–50. Blond, 1965.

2576 Thompson, E.P. 'The North of England Socialist Federation'. SSLH, Spring 1963, 6:30–1.

2576a Thompson, P. *Socialists, Liberals and Labour: the struggle for London, 1885–1914.* Routledge, 1967. viii, 476pp.

2577 Tsuzuki, C. 'The "Impossibilist revolt" in Britain: the origins of the S.L.P. and the S.P.G.B.'. IRSH, 1956, 1(3):377–97.

2578 Wilkins, M.S. 'The non-socialist origins of England's first important socialist organization (SDF)'. IRSH, 1959, 4(2):199–207.

The Left

I GENERAL

2579 Abrams, M. '"The future of the left"; new roots of working-class conservatism'. EN, May 1960, 14(5):57–9.

2580 Anderson, P. 'The left in the fifties'. NLR, Jan.–Feb. 1965, 29:3–18.

2581 Arnold, G.L. 'Socialism in perspective (The left road for Britain?—2)'. TC, May 1950, 147(879):302–10.

2582 Bell, D. '"The future of the left"'. EN, May 1960, 14(5):59–61.

2583 Crosland, A. 'The future of the left'. EN, Mar. 1960, 14(3):3–12.

2584 Crosland, A. 'On the left again: some last words on the Labour controversy'. EN, Oct. 1960, 15(4):3–12.

2585 Crossman, R.H.S. 'The spectre of revisionism: a reply to Crosland'. EN, April 1960, 14(4):24–8.

2586 Derrick, P. 'A new role for the left?'. TC, Winter 1966, 174(1029):37–9.

2587 Dutt, R.P. 'Future of the left'. LM, Nov. 1965, 47(11):481–94.

2588 Dutt, R.P. 'The left and communism'. LM, Jan. 1966, 48(1):1–15.

2589 Fairlie, H. 'Labour loyalty and the left'. EN, Dec. 1960, 15(6):59–62.

2590 Foot, M. '"The future of the left"'. EN, July 1960, 15(1):69–71.

2591 Foster, J.R. 'Because we are the challengers'. LM, July 1968, 50(7):317–19.

2592 Hollis, C. 'A future for socialists (The left road for Britain?—3)'. TC, May 1950, 147(879):311–18.

2593 Hope, F. 'The intellectual left'. EN, Oct. 1966, 27(4):60–8.

2594 Hope, F. 'The intellectual left', *The left: a symposium*, pp.97–114 (*see* no.2595). Edited by G. Kaufman. Blond, 1966.

2595 Kaufman, G., ed. *The left: a symposium*. Blond, 1969. 182pp.
     See nos.1498, 1633, 2155, 2367, 2594, 2648, 2780, 3708.

2596 Mackenzie, N., ed. *Conviction*. MacGibbon and Kee, 1958. 237pp.
     Twelve young writers discuss their socialist beliefs.

2597 Magee, B. *The new radicalism*. Secker and Warburg, 1962. 238pp.

2598 Minogue, K.R. 'The British left: innocent part of the guilty whole'. TC, April 1960, 167(998):291–6.

2599 Pentz, M.J. 'Breaking the stalemate'. LM, Sept. 1968, 50(9):423–5.

2600 Rattray, R.F. 'An indictment of leftism'. QR, Jan. 1952, 290(591):45–55.

2601 Rendle, P. 'For a united socialist front'. LM, July 1968, 50(7):319–22.

2602 Siepman, E.O. 'How many? What for? (The left road for Britain?—1)'. TC, May 1950, 147(879):293–301.

2603 Sigal, C. 'To fly a kite: an open letter to the British comrades of the New Left, Victory for Socialism, Tribune etc.'. NLR, Jan.–Feb. 1960, 1:22–5.

2604 Taylor, A.J.P. 'Confusion on the left', *The Baldwin age*, pp.66–79. Edited by J. Raymond. Eyre and Spottiswoode, 1960.

2605 Williams, D.C. 'An American view (The left road for Britain?—4)'. TC, June 1950, 147(880):388–96.

II THE NEW LEFT

2606 Barnes, H. 'The new left, the consensus and the intelligentsia'. PS, Feb. 1968, 16(1):105–8.

2607 Birnbaum, N., ed. *Out of apathy*. Stevens, 1960. xii, 308pp.
     Eight essays by writers of the new left diagnosing contemporary society.

2608 Coates, K. 'Britain: prospects for the seventies (iii)'. SR, 1970, 7:195–201.

2609 Ellis, C.H. *The new left in Britain*. Common Cause, 1968. 16pp.

2610 Encel, S. 'Forward from Marxism'. NLR, July–Aug. 1960, 4:9–11.

2611 Hall, S., R. Williams and E.P. Thompson, eds. *1967 new left May Day manifesto*. May Day Manifesto Committee, 1967. ii, 46pp.
     See also no.2645. Produced for a group of socialist workers, writers and teachers.

2612 Harris, N. 'Britain: prospects for the seventies (ii)'. SR, 1970, 7:179–193.

2613 Hart, J. 'Comment [on Revolution (*see* no.2637)]'. NLR, Sept.–Oct. 1960, 5:58–9.

2614 Heffer, E. 'Comment [on Revolution (*see* no.2637)]'. NLR, Sept.–Oct. 1960, 5:60.

2615 Hilton, R. 'Discussion [on Socialism and the intellectuals (*see* no.2639)]'. ULR, Summer 1957, 1(2):19–20.

2616 Ivasheva, V. 'Revisionism of Marxism in Britain'. NR, Winter 1958–9, 8:143–8.
    Tr. from *October*, no.8, 1958.

2617 Johnston, M. 'Britain: prospects for the seventies (i)'. SR, 1970, 7:165–177.

2618 Jones, M. 'Discussion [on Socialism and the intellectuals (*see* no.2639)]'. ULR, Summer 1957, 1(2):15–17.

2619 Keenan, J. 'Comment [on Revolution (*see* no.2637)]'. NLR, Sept.–Oct. 1960, 5:59–60.

2620 Lessing, D. 'What should we do about "The Reasoner"'. R, Sept. 1956, 2:11–13.

2621 Marris, P. 'Apathy: a case to answer [on Socialism and the intellectuals (*see* no.2639)]'. NLR, July–Aug. 1960, 4:5–8.

2622 Meek, R. 'What should we do about "The Reasoner"'. R, Sept. 1956, 2:8–10.

2623 Miliband, R. 'What does the left want?'. SR, Sept. 2:184–94.

2624 Miliband, R. and J. Saville. 'Labour policy and the Labour left'. SR, 1965, 1:149–56.

2625 Pritt, D.N. 'Future of the left'. LM, May 1968, 50(8):206–10.

2626 Rothman, S. 'British Labour's "new left"'. PSQ, Sept. 1961, 76(3):393–401.

2627 Samuels, S. 'The English left intelligentsia in the 1930's'. SSLH, Spring 1967, 14:8–9.

2628 Saville, J. 'Apathy into politics'. NLR, July–Aug. 1960, 4:8–9.

2629 Saville, J. 'Britain: prospects for the seventies'. SR, 1970, 7:203–15.

2630 Saville, J. and E.P. Thompson. 'Statement by the editors [of The Reasoner]'. R, Nov. 1956, 3:37–44.

2631 Saville, J. and E.P. Thompson. 'Why we are publishing [i.e. The Reasoner]'. R, July 1956, 1:1–3.

2632 Silver, H. 'Discussion [on Socialism and the intellectuals (*see* no.2639)]'. ULR, Summer 1957, 1(2):17–18.

2633 Taylor, C. 'Changes of quality'. NLR, July–Aug. 1960, 4:3–5.

2634 Taylor, C. 'Discussion [on Socialism and the intellectuals (*see* no.2639)]'. ULR, Summer 1957, 1(2):18–19.

2635 Thompson, E.P. 'Commitment to politics'. ULR, Spring 1959, 1(6):50–5.

2636 Thompson, E.P. 'The new left'. NR, Summer 1959, 9:1–17.

2637 Thompson, E.P. 'Revolution'. NLR, Mar.–June 1960, 3:3–9 (*see* nos. 2613, 2614, 2619).

2638 Thompson, E.P. 'Revolution again! or shut your ears and run'. NLR, Nov.–Dec. 1960, 6:18–31.

2639 Thompson, E.P. 'Socialism and the intellectuals'. ULR, Spring 1957, 1(1):31–6 (*see* nos.2615, 2618, 2621, 2632, 2634).

2640 Thompson, E.P. [Reply]. ULR, Summer 1957, 1(2):20–2.

2641 Vane, H. 'The new left'. C, Summer 1959, 2(8):39–42.

2642 Walker, P.(C.)G. 'The future of the left'. EN, July 1960, 15(1):71–2.

2643 Williams, D. *The new left—its anatomy and student facets*. Common Cause Bulletin no.123, Summer 1969. 30pp.

2644 Williams, R. 'The British left'. NLR, Mar.–Apr. 1965, 30:18–26.

2645 Williams, R., ed. May Day manifesto 1968. Penguin, 1968. 190pp.
    See also no.2611.

III ULTRA AND FRINGE LEFT

2646 Common Cause. *The political and industrial unholy alliance—Part Two*. Common Cause Bulletin no.120, Summer–Autumn 1968. 29pp.
    Largely devoted to the International Socialists.

2647 Evans, A.H. *Against the enemy!* Committee to defeat Revisionism for Communist Unity, 1963. 13pp.

2648 Gardner, L. 'The fringe left', *The left: a symposium*, pp.115–40 (*see* no.2595).
    Edited by G. Kaufman. Blond, 1966.

2649 Industrial Research and Information Services Ltd. *The British 'left'*. I.R.I.S., 1970. 19pp.
    Brief survey of many organizations.

2650 Plant, J. and N. *Why we have resigned from the Socialist Labour Party of Great Britain*. Cambridge, the authors, 1969. 24pp.

2651 Reid, B. *Ultra-leftism in Britain*. Communist Party, 1969. 58pp.
    See no.2469. Criticism of Trotskyist and Maoist groups.

2652 Thayer, G. 'The outside left (The Anarchists)', *The British political fringe: a profile*, pp.150–3. Blond, 1956.

2653 Thayer, G. 'The outside left (McCreery and committee to defeat revisionism for communist unity)', *The British political fringe: a profile*, pp.119–26. Blond, 1965.

2654 Thayer, G. 'The outside left (Syndicalists)', *The British political fringe: a profile*, pp.153–5. Blond, 1965.

2655 Thayer, G. [Trotskyism], *The British political fringe: a profile*, pp.126–46. Blond, 1965.

2656 Welton, H. 'Complete subversion', *'We will bury you': studies in left-wing subversion today*, pp.102–15. Edited by B. Crozier. Stacey, 1970.

2657 Williams, D. 'Subversion in industry', *'We will bury you': studies in left-wing subversion today*, pp.116–41. Edited by B. Crozier. Stacey, 1970.

2658 Williams, D. and others. *Trotskyism and its supporters in Britain, Part 1.* Common Cause Bulletin no.112, Summer 1965. 57pp.

2659 Williams, D. and others. *Trotskyism and its supporters in Britain, Part 2.* Common Cause Bulletin no.113, Winter 1965–1966. 49pp.

2660 Woodcock, G. *Anarchism: a history of libertarian ideas and movements.* Penguin, 1970.
    Includes Great Britain, pp.414–28.

Trade Unionism

Trade Unions

I GENERAL

2661 Abrahams, G. *Trade unions and the law*. Cassell, 1968. xx, 254pp.

2662 Acton Society Trust. *The future of the unions*. The Society, 1951. 31pp.

2663 Alderson, S. 'Labour and redundancy—workers' golden handshake'. CNR, Jan. 1962. 1962, 201:7–11.

2664 Alexander, K.(J.W.) and J. Hughes. *Trade unions in opposition*. Fabian Society, 1961. 37pp.

2665 Alexander, K.J.W. 'Economic research by the trade unions'. YB, Feb. 1954, 6(1):85–90.

2666 Alexander, K.J.W. 'Membership participation in a printing trade union'. SOCR, Dec. 1954, 2(2):161–8.

2667 Allen, V.L. 'Abstract of "A methodological criticism of the Webbs as trade union historians"'. SSLH, Spring 1962, 4:4–6.

2668 Allen, V.L. 'The ethics of trade union leaders'. BJS, Dec. 1956, 7(4):314–36.

2669 Allen, V.L. *Militant trade unionism: a re-analysis of industrial action in an inflationary situation*. Merlin, 1966. 175pp.

2670 Allen, V.L. *Power in trade unions: a study of their organization in Great Britain*. Longmans, 1954. xi, 323pp.

2671 Allen, V.L. 'Some economic aspects of compulsory trade unionism'. OEP, Feb. 1954, 6(1):69–81.

2672 Allen, V.L. 'The trade unions (Powers within the state—4)'. TC, Oct. 1957, 162(968):361–70.

2673 Allen, V.L. *Trade unions and the government*. Longmans, 1960. xii, 326pp.

2674 Allen, V.L. 'Trade unions in contemporary capitalism'. SR, 1964, 1:157–74.

2675 Allen, V.L. and S. Williams. 'The growth of trade unionism in banking, 1914–27'. MS, Sept. 1960, 28(3):299–318.

2676 Alsop, G. 'Force out the facts on pit closures'. LM, Apr. 1959, 41(4):164–6.

2677 Amalgamated Engineering Union. *Trade unions and the contemporary scene.* The Union, 1965. 111pp.
Statement submitted to the Royal Commission on Trade Unions and Employers' Associations.

2678 Ambrose, L. 'Some problems in engineering'. LM, July 1957, 39(7):303–6.

2679 Arnot, R.P. 'Barbara and the blasted Heath'. LM, May 1970, 52(5):218–23.
Barbara Castle and the Industrial Relations Bill.

2680 Arnot, R.P. 'Donovan on trade union law'. LM, Sept. 1968, 50(9):399–403.
Assessment of the Donovan Commission.

2681 Arnot, R.P. 'An earlier attack on trade unions'. LM, Sept. 1970, 52(9):406–9.

2682 Arnot, R.P. 'Shop stewards, beware'. LM, Nov. 1970, 52(11):495–8.

2683 Arnot, R.P. 'Trade unions—the next round'. LM, Aug. 1969, 51(8):351–4.

2684 Arnot, R.P. 'Union law: a practical step'. LM, July 1964, 46(7):300–2.

2685 Bain, G.S. *The growth of white-collar unionism.* Oxford, Clarendon Press, 1970. xvi, 233pp.

2686 Bain, G.S. 'The growth of white-collar unionism in Great Britain'. BJIR, Nov. 1966, 4(3):304–35.

2687 Ball, J. 'The message is—fight!'. LM, Aug. 1968, 50(8):375–7.

2688 Ball, J. 'Power and the unions'. LM, Apr. 1968, 50(4):162–5.

2689 Ball, J. 'Trade unions: strategy for unity'. LM, May 1969, 51(5):205–8.

2690 Ball, J. 'Who wants a wages jungle?'. LM, May 1967, 49(5):209–12.

2691 Ballantine, W. 'Transport: an exercise in expediency'. LM, Apr. 1961, 43(4):163–7.

2692 Banyard, H.T. 'Trade unions in transition'. F, Dec. 1948, 164(984):385–9.

2693 Barou, N. *British trade unions.* Gollancz, 1947. xvi, 271pp.

2694 Barou, N. *Recent trends in British trade unions.* N.Y., League for Industrial Democracy, 1945. 31pp.

2695 Bates, L. 'Is it the end of the line?'. LM, Mar. 1962, 44(3):120–2.
A.E.U. railway workers.

2696 Bealey, F. and S. Parkinson. *Unions in prosperity.* Barrie and Rockliff (for Institute of Economic Affairs), 1960. 55p.

2697 Bean, R. 'Militancy, policy formation and membership opposition in the Electrical Trades Union, 1945–61'. PQ, Apr.–June 1965, 36(2):181–190.

2698 Behan, B. *Socialists and the trade unions.* Labour Review, 1958. 24pp.

2699 Bell, J.D.M. *Industrial unionism: a critical analysis.* Glasgow, University Press, 1949. 28pp.

2700 Bell, J.D.M. 'Stability of membership in trade unions'. SJPE, Mar. 1954,1(1):49–74.

2701 Besant, A. 'The trades union movement', *A selection of the social and political pamphlets of Annie Besant,* 29pp. New York, Kelley, 1970.

2702 Bidwell, S. 'Trade unions and government'. LM, Apr. 1969, 51(4):161–3.

2703 Birch, A.H. 'Structure of the British trade union movement'. MSS, Feb. 1957, 1–25.

2704 Birch, R. 'No automation without consultation'. LM, June 1956, 38(6):267–70.

2705 Birnbaum, B. 'Hands off the unions!'. LM, Mar. 1969, 51(3):115–16.

2706 Blackburn, R. and A. Cockburn, eds. *The incompatibles: trade union militancy and the consensus.* Penguin/New Left Review, 1967. 281pp.

2707 Blackburn, R.M. *Union character and social class: a study of white-collar unionism.* Batsford, 1967. 304pp.

2708 Blackburn, R.M. and K. Prandy. 'White-collar unionization: a conceptual framework'. BJS, June 1965, 16(2):111–22.

2709 Bond, R. 'Prices and incomes policy'. LM, Apr. 1967, 49(4):160–1.

2710 Bondfield, M. 'Welfare in distribution and domestic work'. F, Feb. 1945, 157(938):112–19.

2711 Bonnar, R. 'Give the railwaymen a fair deal'. LM, Dec. 1970, 52(12):545–548.

2712 Bonnar, R. 'Goodbye, Doctor Beeching'. LM, July 1965, 47(7):298–301.

2713 Bonnar, R. 'The great trainmen's robbery'. LM, Dec. 1965, 47(12):558–62.

2714 Bonnar, R. 'Our nationalised railways'. LM, June 1964, 46(6):255–8.

2715 Boon, E. 'Trade unions: hour of decision'. LM, June 1969, 51(6):260–2.

2716 Bottomley, A. *The use and abuse of trade unions.* Ampersand, 1963. 89pp.

2717 Bowman, D. 'The Beeching plan'. LM, Apr. 1963, 45(4):161–4.

2718 Bowman, D. 'Railway crisis: the truth'. LM, Dec. 1967, 49(12):545–8.

2719 Bowman, D. 'The railway warning signal'. LM, Mar. 1960, 42(3):118–22.

2720 Bowman, D. 'Storm over the railways'. LM, Jan. 1962, 44(1):28–31.

2721 Bowman, D. 'Trade union executives and wages'. LM, Mar. 1967, 49(3):109–12.

2722 Bowman, D. 'The wage rise that wasn't'. LM, June 1959, 41(6):270–2.

2723 Boyd-Carpenter, J. 'The closed shop and the closed mind'. TC, Oct. 1946, 140(836):191–6.

2724 Brantlinger, P. 'The case against trade unions in early Victorian fiction'. VS, Sept. 1969, 13(1):37–52.

2725 Bridges, G. 'Conferences: next round'. LM, July 1961, 43(7):327–9.

2726 Briginshaw, R.W. 'Intolerable'. LM, Sept. 1968, 50(9):396–8.
1964–70 anti-union policy.

2727 Briginshaw, R.W. 'Trade unions: hour of decision: Sogat E—Council statement'. LM, June 1969, 51(6):256–7.
On *In place of strife*.

2728 British Journal of Industrial Relations. Editorial: The Royal Commission on Trade Unions and Employers' Associations, 1965–1968: a summary of the report and recommendations. BJIR, Nov. 1968, 6(3):275–86.

2729 Brotherton, H. 'Trade unions know their business'. LM, Feb. 1958, 40(2):61–3.

2730 Brown, H.P. *The trade union and the common weal*. OUP for British Academy, 1967. ii, 14pp.

2731 Brown, K. 'Sub-postmasters . . . private traders and trade unionists'. BJIR, Mar. 1965, 3(1):31–45.

2732 Brown, M.B. 'The trade union question'. PQ, Apr.–June 1967, 38(2):156–64.

2733 Brown, M.B. and R. Harrison. 'Incomes policy—a reply'. NLR, May–June 1966, 37:86–94.
See nos.3109, 3110.

2734 Brown, R. and P. Brannen. 'Social relations and social perspectives amongst shipbuilding workers—a preliminary statement'. Two parts. SO, 1970. 4:71–84; 4:197–211.

2735 Buckman, P. 'Anatomy of a protest'. TC, 3, 1968, 177(1038):4–8.
Trade union activity at closing of GEC–AEI at Woolwich.

2736 Butler, D. and J. Freeman. 'Trade unions', *British political facts, 1900–18*, pp.206–20. Macmillan, 1969.

2737 Callaghan, J. *Whitleyism: a study of joint consultation in the civil service*. Fabian Society, 1953. 40pp.

2738 Campbell, J.R. *Hands off the trade unions*. Communist Party, 1965. 15pp.

2739 Campbell, J.R. 'Wage movement lessons'. LM, Feb. 1954, 36(2):77–81.

2740 Cannon, I.C. 'Ideology and occupational community: a study of compositors'. SO, 1967, 1:165–85.

2741 Carron, Sir W. 'Trade unions in industry'. DR, Summer 1963, 237(496):114–27.

2742 Central Office of Information. *Trade unions in Britain*. C.O.I. 1966. iv, 34pp.

2743 Chaloner, W.H. 'The British miners and the coal industry between the wars'. HT, June 1964. 14(6):418–26.

2744 Citrine, N.A. *Trade union law*. Stevens, 1960. xliv, 656pp.

2745 Clark, G. de N. 'Industrial law and the labour-only sub-contract'. MLR, Jan. 1967, 30(1):6–24.

2746 Clarke, D. *More about the trade unions*. Conservative Political Centre, 1950 (first pub. 1947). 31pp.

2747 Clegg, H.A. *Change and the unions*. Newman Neame, 1965. 15pp.

2748 Clegg, H.A. 'The Donovan Report and trade union history'. SSLH, Spring 1969, 18:12–13.

2749 Clegg, H.A. *Labour in nationalised industry*. Fabian Society, 1950. 40pp.

2750 Clegg, H.A. 'The Webbs as historians of trade unionism 1874–1894'. SSLH, Spring 1962, 4:8–9.

2751 Clegg, H.A., A. Fox and A.F. Thompson. *A history of British trade unions since 1889*. Vol. 1, 1889–1910. OUP/Clarendon, 1964. xi, 514pp.
    See no.3346.

2752 Clegg, H.A., A.J. Killick and R. Adams. *Trade union officers: a study of full-time officers, branch secretaries and shop stewards in British trade unions*. Oxford, Blackwell, 1961. xiii, 273pp.
    Based on an investigation into eighteen unions.

2753 Clements, R. *Glory without power: a study of trade unionism in our present society*. Barker, 1959. 143pp.

2754 Clements, R.V. 'British trade unions and popular economy 1850–75'. ECHR, Aug. 1961, 14(1):93–104.

2755 Clements, R.V. 'Trade unions and emigration, 1840–80'. PPS, Nov. 1955, 9(2):167–80.

2756 Coates, K. 'A.E.U. elections'. NLR, May–June 1964, 25:26–8.

2757 Coates, K. 'Incomes policy. 2. A strategy for the unions'. SR, 1965, 2:175–83.

2758 Coates, K. 'The state of the A.E.U.'. NLR, Mar.–Apr. 1967, 42:63–68.

2759 Cole, G.D.H. *Attempts at General Union: a study in British trade union history 1818–34*. Macmillan, 1953, viii, 218pp.

2760 Cole, G.D.H. *An introduction to trade unionism*. Allen and Unwin, 1953. 324pp.

2761 Cole, G.D.H., comp. *British trade unionism today: a survey*. Methuen, 1945. 591pp.
    Written with the collaboration of thirty trade union leaders and other experts.

2762 Cole, G.D.H. 'Some notes on British trade unionism in the third quarter of the nineteenth century', *Essays in economic history*, Vol. 3, pp. 202–21. Edited by E.M. Carus-Wilson. Arnold, 1962 (first pub. in International Review of Social History, Vol. 2, 1937).

2763 Cole, G.D.H. 'A study in legal repression (1789–1834)', *Persons and periods: studies,* pp.99–116. Penguin, 1945.
    Tolpuddle Martyrs.

2764 Cole, G.D.H. 'Trade unions and trade unionists in Britain today'. PQ, Jan.–Mar. 1949, 20(1):64–74.

2765 Cole, G.D.H. 'Trade unions, workers and production'. PQ, July-Sept. 1947, 18(3):250–60.

2766 Cole, G.D.H. *What is wrong with the trade unions?* Fabian Society, 1956. 28pp.

2767 Cole, J. 'The price of obstinacy; crises in the trade unions'. EN, July 1963, 21(1):56–64.

2768 Coleman, D.C. 'Combination of capital and labour in the English paper industry, 1789–1825'. E, Feb. 1954, 21(81):32–53.

2769 Collins, H. 'Karl Marx, the International and the British trade union movement'. SAS, Fall 1962, 26(4):400–21.

2770 Collins, H. *Trade unions today.* Muller, 1950. 141pp.

2771 Comerford, G. 'The miners' fight'. LM, June 1952, 34(6):275–7.

2772 Common Cause. *The political and industrial unholy alliance. Part One.* Common Cause Bulletin no.119, Spring 1968. 29pp.

2773 Communist Party. History Group. 'The working week'. OH, Winter 1958, 12:23pp.

2774 'Confed. Shipbuilders and engineers'. LM, Aug. 1962, 44(8):360–4.
    Confederation of Shipbuilding and Engineering Unions.

2775 Coombes, B.L. 'The miner and nationalization'. F, Mar. 1946, 159(951):187–91.

2776 Copland, J. 'Outlawed wage award for busmen'. LM, Mar. 1968, 50(3):116–18.

2777 Copps, J.A. 'The union in British socialist throught'. SEJ, July 1959, 26(1):50–7.

2778 Corfield, A. and E. McCullough. *Trade union branch officers' manual.* Chapman and Hall, 1964. viii, 184pp.

2779 Corina, J. *The Labour market.* Institute of Personnel Management, 1966. 35pp.

2780 Coulter, I. 'The trade unions', *The left: a symposium*, pp. 31–50 (*see* no.2595). Edited by G. Kaufman. Blond, 1966.

2781 Cowles, V. 'The trade unions', *No cause for alarm: a study of trends in England today*, pp.253–68. Hamilton, 1949 (*see* no.1549).

2782 Craig, J.B. 'We fight pit closures', LM, June 1959, 41(6):262–6.

2783 Crossbow. Editorial: 'Democracy and the unions'. C, Summer 1958, 1(4):5.

2784 Crossley, J.R . 'The Donovan Report: a case study in the poverty of historicism'. BJIR, July 1968, 6(2):204–19.

2785 Cyriax, G. 'How to make trade unions more responsible'. PQ, Oct.–Dec. 1961, 32(4):319–27.

2786 Cyriax, G. and R. Oakshott. *The bargainers: a survey of modern trade unionism*. Faber, 1960. 228pp.

2787 Daly, L. 'Protest and disturbance in the trade union movement'. PQ, Oct.–Dec. 1969, 40(4):447–53.

2788 Dalziel, R. 'The foundry workers'. LM, July 1962, 44(7):310–12.
A.U.F.W. conference.

2789 Davison, R.B. *Trade unions: a practical approach*. Longmans, 1961. v, 73pp.

2790 Dawson, K. and Peter Wall. *Trade unions*. OUP, 1969. i, 46pp.

2791 Delany, V.T.H. 'Immunity in tort and the Trades Disputes Act—a new limitation?'. MLR, July 1955, 18(4):338–43.

2792 [A Delegate]. 'A.E.U. National Committee'. LM, June 1965, 47(6):258–60.

2793 [A Delegate]. 'A.E.U. National Committee, 1966'. LM, June 1966, 48(6):272–4.

2794 [A Delegate]. 'Engineers' conference highlights'. LM, June 1964, 46(6):259–62.

A.E.U. conference.

2795 [A Delegate]. 'Engineers: what happened'. LM, June 1961, 43(6):260–262.

2796 [A Delegate]. 'The engineers'. LM, June 1962, 44(6):275–6.
A.E.U. conference.

2797 Doughty, G.H. *Keep the unions free: a statement on the Rookes v Barnard case*. D.A.T.A., ?1964. 20pp.
See no.3105.

2798 Doughty, G.H. 'Trade union structure and modern needs'. LM, June 1970, 52(2):267–70.

2799 Doughty, G.H. 'Trade unions and the law'. LM, May 1964, 46(5):205–206.

2800 Duffy, A.E.P. 'The eight hours movement in Britain, 1886–93'. MS, Sept. 1968, 36(3):203–22.

2801 Duffy, A.E.P. 'The eight hours movement in Britain, 1886–93'. MS, Dec. 1968, 36(4):345–63.

2802 Duffy, A.E.P. 'New unionism in Britain, 1889–90: a re-appraisal'. ECHR, Dec. 1961, 14(2):306–19.

2803 Dutt, R.P. 'Preparedness and the Labour movement'. LM, May 1958, 40(5):199–206.

2804 Dutt, R.P. 'Problems of trade unionism'. LM, Sept. 1963, 45(9):385–99.

2805 Dutt, R.P. 'Red Friday and after'. LM, Mar. 1960, 42(3):97–103.
National Union of Railwaymen.

2806 Dutt, R.P. 'Trade unions and politics'. LM, Dec. 1960, 42(12):536–41.

2807 Dutt, R.P. 'Trade unions and politics'. LM, Sept. 1967, 49(9):385–96.

2808 Dutt, R.P. 'Trade unions and the election'. LM, Sept. 1964, 46(9):385–98.

2809 Dutt, R.P. 'Trade unions, what now?'. LM, Sept. 1962, 44(9):385–400.

2810 Dutt, R.P. 'War on the unions'. LM, Feb. 1969, 51(2):49–60.

2811 Dutton, J.K. 'Neddy: the confidence trick'. LM, Dec. 1963, 45(12):543–5.

2812 Dykes, H. 'Trade unions: have we really got the answers?'. C, July–Sept. 1968, 11(44):32–4.

2813 Edelstein, J.D., M. Warner with W.F. Cooke. 'The pattern of opposition in British and American unions'. SO, 1970, 4:145–63.

2814 Elman, P. 'The beginnings of the Jewish trade union movement in England'. JHSE, 1951–2, 17:53–62.

2815 Elvin, G. 'The non-manual worker'. LM, Apr. 1961, 43(4):167–70.

2816 [Engineering correspondent]. 'The engineering wages movement'. LM, Dec. 1953, 35(12):547–51.

2817 England, B. *Trade union problems*. Labour Research Department, 1950. 127pp.

2818 Erickson, C. 'The encouragement of emigration by British trade unions, 1850–1900'. PPS, Dec. 1949, 3(3):248–73.

2819 Etheridge, D. 'After the ballot'. LM, June 1962, 44(6): 268–70.

2820 Evans, D.D. 'Change in the trade unions'. LM, Dec. 1962, 44(12):548–554.

2821 Evans, Sir Lincoln. 'Responsible trade unionism', *Right-turn: a symposium on the need to end the 'progressive' consensus in British thinking and policy*, pp.138–45. Edited by Dr. Rhodes Boyson. Churchill Press, 1970.

2822 Evans, Lloyd *British trade unionism 1850–1914*. Arnold, 1970, 64pp.

2823 A Fabian group. *The trade unions: on to 1980.* Fabian Society, 1967. 19pp.

2824 Fabian Society. *Labour: control and de-control—a report to the Fabian Economics Committee.* Fabian Society, 1945. 29pp.

2825 Fagan, H. 'The Tolpuddle Martyrs and the trade unions 1834', *The unsheathed sword: episodes in English history. Part 2. Champions of the workers,* pp.38–51. Lawrence and Wishart, 1959.

2826 Farrar, D.G. 'Trade unions: a challenge of the future'. LM, Mar. 1970, 52(3):126–8.

2827 Fay, S. *Measure for measure: reforming the trade unions.* Chatto, Knight, 1970. viii, 131pp.

2828 Feather, V. *The essence of trade unionism.* Bodley Head, 1963. 127pp.

2829 Feather, V. 'The Royal Commission's analysis: a trade union appraisal'. BJIR, Nov. 1968, 6(3):339–45.

2830 Fellows, A. 'The "closed shop" and its implications'. F, Nov. 1946, 160(959):316–21.

2831 'Fire-Dropper'. 'The footplatemen'. LM, July 1962, 44(7):308–10.
     A.S.L.E.F.

2832 Flanders, A. *British trade unionism.* Bureau of Current Affairs, 1948. 63pp.

2833 Flanders, A. *Trade unions.* Hutchinson, 1968 (first pub. 1952). 212pp.

2834 Flanders, A. *Trade unions and politics.* London Trades Council, 1961. 16pp.
     1860–1960 centenary lecture.

2835 Flanders, A. *Trade unions and the force of tradition.* Southampton, University, 1969. 24pp.
     16th Fawley Foundation lecture.

2836 Foster, J.R. 'Engineers' lesson in loyalty'. LM, June 1968, 50(6):254–7.

2837 Foulkes, F. 'Address to the electricians'. LM, Sept. 1961, 43(9):433–5.
     Presidential address to the Electrical Trades Union.

2838 Franks, W.F. 'New laws for new unionism'. C, Spring 1960, 3(11): 45–9.

2839 Fraser, W.H. 'Trade unionism', *Popular movements c.1830–1850,* pp.95–115. Edited by J.T. Ward. Macmillan, 1970.

2840 Frow, E. 'The right to work defended'. LM, June 1959, 41(6):267–70.

2841 Fryer, P. *Defend the ETU! Against Fleet Street and King Street.* The Author, 1958. 12pp.

2842 Fussell, G.E. *From Tolpuddle to T.U.C.: a centenary of farm-labourers' politics.* Slough, Windsor Press, 1948. 150pp.

2843 Galenson, W. 'The strength of unified trade unionism: Great Britain and Scandinavia', *Trade union democracy in western Europe,* pp.42–86. Berkeley, University of California Press, 1961.

2844 Garbati, I. 'British trade unionism in the mid-Victorian era'. UTQ, Oct. 1950, 20(1):69–84.

2845 Gard, E. *British trade unionism*. Methuen, 1970. 96pp.

2846 Gardner, J. 'Are wages high enough?'. LM, Aug. 1954, 36(8):347–51.

2847 Gardner, J. *Key questions for trade unionists*. Lawrence and Wishart, 1960. 72pp.

2848 Gardner, J. 'The metalworkers' wages'. LM, Aug. 1958, 40(8):352–6.

2849 Gardner, J. 'Trade union growth'. LM, Mar. 1963, 45(3):135–9.
     Review of no.3175.

2850 Gardner, J. 'War on the unions'. LM, Dec. 1957, 39(12):542–6.

2851 Gaskell, P. *Artisans and machinery*. Cass, 1968 (first pub. 1836). xv, 399pp.

2852 Gee, T. *Politics and the trade unions*. Signpost, 1945. 20pp.

2853 Giles, G.C.T. 'The teachers' lesson'. LM, Nov. 1961, 43(11):530–3.

2854 Gill, K. 'Hands off the unions'. LM, Mar. 1969, 51(3):117–18.

2855 Gillespie, F.E. *Labor and politics in England 1850–67*. Cass, 1966 (first pub. 1927). vii, 319pp.

2856 Goldthorpe, J.H.D., D. Lockwood, F. Bechhofer and J. Platt. 'The affluent worker and the thesis of embourgeoisement: some preliminary research findings'. SO, 1967, 1:11–31.

2857 Goldthorpe, J.D.H., D. Lockwood, F. Bechhofer and J. Platt. 'The worker and his union', *The affluent worker: industrial attitudes and behaviour*, pp.93–115. CUP, 1968.
     Luton is the setting for this survey.

2858 Gore, F.J. 'Crisis in civil air transport'. LM, Sept. 1961, 43(9):430–2.

2859 Graham, T. 'The clash in engineering'. LM, Mar. 1957, 39(3):108–11.

2860 Gregory, R. *The miners and British politics 1906–14*. OUP, 1968. xi, 207pp.
     See no.3217.

2861 Grice, F. 'The Tolpuddle Martyrs', *Rebels and fugitives*, pp.126–31. Batsford, 1963.

2862 Griffiths, B. 'Abdication of trade union rights'. LM, Jan. 1950, 32(1):23–5.

2863 Griffiths, B. 'Thou shall not muzzle the ox'. LM, Mar. 1950, 32(3):106–10.

2864 Grodin, J.R. *Union government and the law: British and American experience*. Los Angeles, University of California, 1961. vii, 209pp.

2865 Grunfeld, C. 'Donovan—the legal aspects'. BJIR, Nov. 1968, 6(3):316–29.

2866 Grunfeld, C. *Modern trade union law*. Sweet and Maxwell, 1966. xii, 517pp.

2867 Grunfeld, C. 'Political independence in British trade unions: some legal aspects'. BJIR, Feb. 1963, 1(1):23–42.

2868 Grunfeld, C. *Trade unions and the individual*. Fabian Society, 1957. 33pp.

2869 Grunfeld, C. *Trade unions and the individual in English law*. Institute of Personnel Management, 1963. 60pp.

2870 Gunther, R. *The future of the trade unions*. Industrial Educational and Research Foundation, 1968. 8pp.

2871 Guy, L.G. 'Trade unions and Vietnam'. LM, Feb. 1970, 52(2):68–71.

2872 Guy, L.G. 'Trade unions: our declaration of intent'. LM, Sept. 1966, 48(9):415–18.

2873 Gwyn, W.B. 'The Osborne Judgement', *Democracy and the cost of politics in Britain*, pp.178–205. Athlone Press, 1962.

2874 Halévy, E. 'The policy of social peace in England'. *The era of tyrannies: essays on socialism and war*, pp.82–122. Allen Lane, 1967.

2875 Halpin, K. 'Trade unions: hour of decision'. LM, June 1969, 51(6):253–6. *In place of strife.*

2876 Hannington, W. 'Sir Lincoln Evans and all that'. LM, July 1953, 35(7):305–10.

2877 Hannington, W. 'Storm warning for trade unionists'. LM, Mar. 1952, 34(3):111–15.

2878 Hannington, W. 'This fifteen per cent'. LM, Nov. 1953, 35(11):506–11.

2879 Hanson, C.G. 'The Royal Commission on trade unions, 1867–9'. NEG, Oct. 1969, 3:6.

2880 Harle, R. 'The role of trade unions in increasing productivity'. PQ, Jan.–Mar. 1956, 27(1):93–100.

2881 Harrison, M. *Trade unions and the Labour Party since 1945*. Allen and Unwin, 1960. 360pp.

2882 Hart, F. 'The boilermakers'. LM, July 1962, 44(7):306–8.

2883 Hart, F. 'Boilermakers' conference'. LM, July 1966, 48(7):333–6.

2884 Hart, P.E. and E.H.P. Brown. 'The size of trade unions: a study in the laws of aggregation'. EJ, Mar. 1957, 67(265):1–15.

2885 Hasbach, W. *A history of the English agricultural labourer*. Cass, 1966 (first pub. 1908). xvi, 470pp.

2886 Haxell, F. 'Trade union problems'. LM, July 1955, 37(7):309–14.

2887 Henderson, A.E. 'Engineers' package deal'. LM, Mar. 1965, 47(3):111–13.

2888 Hennessy, B. 'Trade unions and the British Labor Party'. APSR, Dec. 1955, 49(4):1050–66.

2889 Hickling, M.A. 'Restoring the protection of the Trades Dispute Act: some forgotten aspects'. MLR, Jan. 1966, 29(1):32–41.

2890 Hickling, M.A. 'Trade unions in disguise'. MLR, Nov. 1964, 27(6):625–42.

2891 Hill, E.J. 'Boilermaker speaks to unions'. LM, Aug. 1961, 43(8):366–9.

2892 Hill, E.J. 'A challenge to trade unionism'. LM, Jan. 1967, 49(1):14–15.

2893 Hill, E.J. 'The trade unions and the Labour government'. LM, Oct. 1963, 45(10):449–51.

2894 Hindell, K. 'Trade union membership'. PEP, 1962. pp.153–220*.
       *Vol. XXVIII, no.463 of the monthly broadsheets issued by PEP.

2895 Hinton, J. *Unions and strikes*. Sheed and Ward, 1968. 64pp.

2896 Hobley, L.F. *The trade union story*. Blackie, 1969. xii, 116pp.

2897 Hobsbawm, E.J. 'British gas-workers 1873–1914', *Labouring men: studies in the history of Labour*, pp.158–78 (*see* no.1191). Weidenfeld, 1968.

2898 Hobsbawm, E.J. 'General labour unions in Britain, 1889–1914', *Labouring men: studies in the history of Labour*, pp.179–203 (*see* no.1191). Weidenfeld, 1968.

2899 Hobsbawm, E.J. 'National unions on the waterside', *Labouring men: studies in the history of Labour*, pp.204–30 (*see* no.1191). Weidenfeld, 1968.

2900 Hobsbawm, E.J. 'Thoughts on the new trades unionism'. SSLH, Autumn 1966, 13:14–15.

2901 Hobsbawm, E.J. 'The tramping artisan', *Labouring men: studies in the history of Labour*, pp.34–63 (*see* no.1191). Weidenfeld, 1968.

2902 Hoffman, P.C. *They also serve: the story of the shop worker*. Porcupine, 1949. x, 257pp.

2903 Horner, A.L. 'Trade unions and communism'. LM, Feb. 1948, 30(2):41–8.

2904 Howarth, H. 'The engineers fight'. LM, July 1952, 34(7):317–19.

2905 Howarth, H. 'The engineers pay'. LM, July 1954, 36(7):314–17.

2906 Howarth, H. 'The right to work'. LM, Mar. 1959, 41(3):120–3.

2907 Huddleston, J. 'Trade unions in a technological society'. CNR, Nov. 1967, 211:251–9.

2908 Hudson, K. *Working to rule. Railway workshop rules: a study of industrial discipline*. Bath, Adams and Dart, 1970. 115pp.

2909 Hughes, J. 'British trade unionism in the sixties'. SR, 1966, 3:86–113.

2910 Hughes, J. *Change in the trade unions*. Fabian Society, 1964, 39pp.

2911 Hughes, J. 'An economic policy for Labour'. NLR, Mar.–Apr. 1964, 24:5–32.
       'the trade unions are the key to a socialist advance'.

2912 Humphreys, B.V. *Clerical unions in the civil service*. Oxford, Blackwell and Mott, 1958. xiv, 254pp.

2913 Hurworth, L. 'The railwaymen and common ownership'. LM, Feb. 1960, 42(2):78–9.

2914 Hutt, A. *British trade unionism: a short history*. Lawrence and Wishart, 1962 (first pub. 1941). 220pp.

2915 Hutt, A. 'The hours of labour'. MQ, Jan. 1955, 2(1):2–13.

2916 Hutt, R. 'Trade unions as friendly societies, 1912–52'. YB, Mar. 1955, 7(1):69–87.

2917 Hyndman, H.M. 'Socialism, trade unionism and political action'. MML, Oct.–Dec. 1966, 40:14–17.
    Previously unpublished article.

2918 Independent Labour Party. National Industrial Committee. *The changing structure of trade unions*. I.L.P., 1950. 25pp.

2919 Independent Tailors, Machinists, and Pressers Union. 'A voice from the aliens about the anti-alien resolution of the Cardiff Trades Union Congress (1895)'. SSLH, Spring 1966, 12:16–20.

2920 Industrial Research and Information Services Ltd. *Choosing the trade union official*. I.R.I.S., 1966. 16pp.

2921 Industrial Research and Information Services Ltd. *Ford in Britain: the company—the union—the agreement*. I.R.I.S., 1969. 22pp.

2922 Industrial Research and Information Services Ltd. *Voting in union elections*. I.R.I.S., 1968. 23pp.

2923 Inns of Court Conservative and Unionist Society. *A giant's strength: some thoughts on the constitutional and legal position of trade unions in England*. The Society, 1958. 86pp.

2924 International Labour Office. *The trade union situation in the United Kingdom. Report of a mission . . . .* Geneva, I.L.O., 1961. iv, 123pp.

2925 Jackson, T.A. 'The Tolpuddle Martyrs', *Trials of British freedom: being some studies in the history of the fight for democratic freedom in Britain*, pp.110–17 (*see* no.1193). Lawrence and Wishart, 1945.

2926 Jacobs, J. 'Trade unions—the fight back'. LM, Dec. 1970, 52(12):541–544.

2927 Jacobson, S. and W. Connor. *The Daily Mirror spotlight on trade unions*. Daily Mirror, 1950. 42pp.

2928 Jacobson, S. and W. Connor. 'The trade unions and Parliament'. PA, Autumn 1956, 9(4):470–7.

2929 James, G. 'Crisis on the rails'. LM, May 1958, 40(5):213–18.

2930 Jeffreys, J.B. *Trade unions in a Labour Britain*. Fabian Society, 1947. 13pp.

2931 Jenkins, C. and J.E. Mortimer. *British trade unions today*. Pergamon, 1965. vii, 125pp.

2932 Jenkins, C. and J.E. Mortimer. *The kind of laws the union ought to want*. Pergamon, 1968. viii, 184pp.

2933 Jenkins, H. 'International action: new actors' "method"'. TUA, Spring 1961, 2:23–6.

2934 Johnston, T.L. 'Public sector and white-collar bargaining'. SJPE, June 1970, 17(2):167–83.

2935 Jones, G. and M. Barnes. *Britain on borrowed time*. Penguin, 1967. 352pp.

2936 Jones, J. 'Peace and the trade unions'. LM, May 1970, 52(5):207–11.

2937 Jones, J. *Trade unionism in the seventies*. Transport and General Workers' Union, 1970. 10pp.

2938 Kahn-Freund, O. 'Trade unions, the law and society'. MLR, May 1970, 33(3):241–67.

2939 Kavanagh, A.M. 'Trade unions: hour of decision'. LM, June 1969, 51(6):258–9.
     In place of strife.

2940 Keeler, W.R.C. 'The Royal Commission's analysis: a management appraisal'. BJIR, Nov. 1968, 6(3):330–8.
     The Donovan Report.

2941 Kerrigan, P. 'Crisis in motors'. LM, Aug. 1956, 38(8):346–52.

2942 Kerrigan, P. 'The Easter conferences'. LM, May 1961, 43(5):210–14.

2943 Kerrigan, P. 'Fight back'. LM, June 1959, 41(6):273–6.

2944 Kerrigan, P. '49th AEU National Committee'. LM, June 1967, 49(6):273–6.

2945 Kerrigan, P. 'Tactics in the wage fight'. LM, Mar. 1954, 36(3):110–116.

2946 Kerrigan, P. 'Trade unionism in 1953'. LM, Jan. 1953, 35(1):13–18.

2947 Kerrigan, P. 'Trade unions and the Labour government'. LM, Dec. 1964, 46(12):548–51.

2948 Kerrigan, P. 'Unite and fight'. LM, Mar. 1962, 44(3):116–19.

2949 Kilroy-Silk, R. 'Trade union studies'. PS, Oct. 1968, 16(3):445–9.

2950 Kilroy-Silk, R. 'Trade unions and society; the Donovan Report'. PS, Mar. 1969, 17(1):95–101.

2951 King, J. 'The Donovan Report: back to fascism or forward to . . .?'. SP, Autumn 1968, 4:21–3.

2952 Kingsford, P.W. *Electrical engineers and workers*. Arnold, 1969. 268pp.

2953 Kingsford, P.W. *Engineers, inventors and workers*, Arnold, 1964. 272pp.

2954 Kingsford, P.W. 'Labour relations on the railways, 1835–75'. JTH, Nov. 1953, 1(2):65–81.

2955 Kitson, A.H. 'No paws on transport'. LM, Nov. 1961, 43(11):527–30.

1956 Knee, F. 'The revolt of Labour—40 years ago'. LM, June 1950, 32(6):275–9 (first pub. in Social Democrat, 15th November 1910).

1957 Knowles, K.G.J.C. and D.J. Robertson. 'Differences between the wages of skilled and unskilled workers, 1880–1950'. OUIS, Apr. 1951, 13(4):109–27.

1958 Lagenfelt, G. *The British trade union movement: a short account of its history and organisation.* Stockholm, Nordiska-Sprak-och-Kulturforlaget, 1952. 54pp.
Written for Swedish students of British trade unions.

1959 Lakeman, E. 'Balloting and the Electoral Reform Society'. TUA, Summer 1961, 3:129–35.

1960 Lane, P. *Trade unions.* Batsford, 1969. 96pp.

1961 Laski, H.J. *Trade unions in the new society.* Allen and Unwin, 1950. x, 182pp.

1962 Lean, G. 'Reluctant revolutionaries: the Tolpuddle Martyrs', *Brave men choose*, pp.70–86. Blandford, 1961.

1963 Leith, A. 'Defend the railways'. LM, May 1963, 45(5):210–12.

1964 Leith, A. 'Railwaymen take action'. LM, May 1962, 44(5):225–6.

1965 Lerner, S.W. *Breakaway unions and the small trade union.* Allen and Unwin, 1961. 210pp.

1966 Lewenhak, S., comp. *The early trade unions.* Jackdaw, 1966.
Reproductions of twelve contemporary documents, with six broadsheets on the history of trade unionism.

1967 Lincoln, J.A. *Journey to coercion: from Tolpuddle to Rookes v Barnard.* Institute of Economic Affairs, 1964. 78pp.

1968 Lincoln, J.A. *The restrictive society: a report on restrictive practices.* Allen and Unwin, 1967. 262pp.

1969 Lindley, J. 'Are dockers decasualised?'. LM, July 1961, 43(7):322–6.

1970 Lindley, J. 'Dockers and decasualisation'. LM, Aug. 1962, 44(8):355–60.

1971 Lloyd, D. 'Damages for wrong expulsion from a trade union—Bonsor v Musicians Union'. MLR, Mar. 1956, 19(2):121–35.

1972 Lobban, R.D. *The trade unions: a short history.* Macmillan, 1969. 64pp.

1973 Lockwood, D. 'Trade unionism', *The blackcoated worker: a study in class consciousness*, pp.135–98. Allen and Unwin, 1958.

1974 Loveless, G. *The victims of Whiggery.* Communist Party, 1969. 32pp.
Facsimile of pamphlet originally pub. by Central Dorchester Committee in 1837.

1975 Lowe, J. 'Trade unions and the future'. TC, Jan. 1951, 149(887), 27–32.

1976 Lynam, C.G. 'The trade unions and the feudal system'. QR, Apr. 1958, 296(616):146–55.

2977 McCarthy, W.E.J. *The closed shop in Britain*. Oxford, Blackwell, 1964. xii, 294pp.

2978 McCarthy, W.[E.J.]. *The future of the unions*. Fabian Society, 1962. 36pp.

2979 McCormick, B. 'Managerial unionism in the coal industry'. BJS, Dec. 1960, 11(4):356–69.

2980 McCormick, B. 'Trade union reaction to technological change in the construction industry'. YB, May 1964, 16(1):15–30.

2981 McCormick, B. and J.E. Williams. 'The miners and the eight-hour day, 1863–1910'. ECHR, Dec. 1959, 12(2):222–38.

2982 McCready, H.W. 'British Labour and the Royal Commission on Trade Unions, 1867–9'. UTQ, July 1955, 24(4):390–409.

2983 McDonald, D.F. *The state and the trade unions*. Macmillan, 1960. viii, 199pp.

2984 MacFarlane, J. 'Shipboard union representation in the British Merchant Navy'. IRSH, 1970, 15(1):1–18.

2985 McGahey, M. 'Action decides'. LM, July 1969, 51(7):302–4.

2986 McGahey, M. 'British miners in conference'. LM, Aug. 1966, 48(8):362–365.

2987 McGahey, M. 'The unions versus the Tories'. LM, Aug. 1970, 52(8):354–6.

2988 McGarvey, D. 'Britain's shipyards today'. LM, July 1958, 40(7):315–19.

2989 McGree, L. 'Battle for jobs'. LM, Jan. 1963, 45(1):16–19. Liverpool.

2990 McGree, L. 'The woodworkers'. LM, Aug. 1962, 44(8):364–5.

2991 Machen, J.R.A. 'The miners: a re-appraisal'. LM, Apr. 1958, 40(4):157–64.

2992 Mack, J.A. 'Trade union leadership'. PQ, Jan.–Mar. 1956, 27(1):71–81.

2993 Mack, J.A. 'Trade unions and the state'. SJPE, Feb. 1960, 7(1):47–64.

2994 McKaig, B. 'Women's work [in engineering]'. LM, Sept. 1962, 44(9):412–14.

2995 McKenna, F. '"Claymore" economics on the railways'. LM, April 1959, 41(4):162–4.

2996 McLean, A. 'Women's wages [in engineering]'. LM, Sept. 1962, 44(9):410–12.

2997 McLellan, N. 'When we come marching in'. LM, Nov. 1962, 44(11):497–500.

2998 Maden, M. 'Teacher militancy—a new phenomenon?'. LM, Jan. 1970, 52(1):26–9.

2999 Marsden, E. 'Trade unions—the next round'. LM, Aug. 1969, 51(8):354–356.

000 Martin, R. *Communism and the British trade unions 1924–33: a study of the National Minority Movement.* Oxford, Clarendon Press, 1969. xii, 209pp.

001 Martin, R. 'The National Minority Movement'. SSLH, Autumn 1968, 17:2–6.

002 Martin, R. 'Union democracy: an explanatory framework'. SO, 1968, 2:205–20.
   Amalgamated Engineering Union and National Union of Railwaymen.

003 May, S.V. 'The builders meet'. LM, Aug. 1964, 46(8):379–80.

004 May, S.V. 'Towards one building union'. LM, Mar. 1961, 43(3):118–19.

005 Maynard, J. 'The farmworkers [N.U.A.W.]'. LM, June 1962, 44(6):270–3.

006 Medd, P. 'Menace to individual liberty (The trade unions. 2)'. C, Summer 1958, 1(4):10–11.

007 Meyers, E. 'Nationalization, union structures and wages policy in the British coalmining industry'. SEJ, Apr. 1958, 34(4):421–33.

008 Mikardo, I. 'Trade unions in a full employment economy', *New Fabian essays,* pp.143–60 (*see* no.2437). Edited by R.H.S. Crossman. Turnstile, 1952.

009 Mills, S. 'The railwaymen'. LM, Aug. 1962, 44(6):366–7.
   National Union of Railwaymen.

010 Minchinton, W.E. *The British tinplate industry: a history.* Oxford, Clarendon Press, 1957, xvi, 286pp.

011 Moffatt, A. 'The miners' new fight'. LM, Dec. 1952, 34(12):546–50.

012 Mogridge, B. 'Militancy and inter-union rivalries in British shipping 1911–1929'. IRSH, 1961, 6(3):375–412.

013 Montagu, I. 'Poll or no poll'. LM, Apr. 1961, 43(4):170–2.

014 Moore, N. 'Trade unions and government'. LM, Apr. 1969, 51(4):174–5.

015 Mortimer, J.E. 'The case against joining the Common Market'. LM, Aug. 1961, 43(8):370–4.

016 Mortimer, J.E. 'The case for the forty hour week'. LM, July 1963, 45(7):314–18.

017 Mortimer, J.E. 'Incomes policy and the unions'. LM, Dec. 1964, 46(12):543–7.

018 Mortimer, J.E. 'The Prices and Incomes Bill'. LM, Apr. 1966, 48(4):158–61.

019 Mortimer, J.E. 'Some points for the Royal Commission on Trade Unions'. LM, Apr. 1965, 47(4):204–8.

020 Mortimer, J.E. 'The structure of the trade union movement'. SR, 1964, 1:175–91.

3021 Mortimer, J.E. 'The trouble with trade union journals'. TUA, Spring 1961, 2:115–26.

3022 Murry, J.M. 'Trade unions and the welfare state'. F, Jan. 1950, 167(997):8–13.

3023 Musson, A.E. 'The Webbs and their phasing of trade union development between the 1830's and the 1860's'. SSLH, Spring 1962, 4:6–8.

3024 National Liberals. Hastings Group. *Trade unions in a free society*. National Liberal Organisation, 1956. 72pp.

3025 National Union of Public Employees. *The challenge of new unionism: the case for industrial unionism as a dynamic solution to the problems facing trade unionists*. The Union, 1963. 28pp.

3026 Newton, J. 'A charter for women'. LM, Nov. 1963, 45(11):494–7.

3027 Newton, J. 'The great tragedy'. LM, Jan. 1961, 43(1):16–19.

3028 Nicholas, P. 'The motor industry inquiry'. LM, Jan. 1966, 48(1):20–3.

3029 Nicholson, J. 'Rail crisis—what next?'. LM, Mar. 1966, 48(3):112–15.

3030 Nicholson, J. 'Trade unions—hour of decision'. LM, June 1969, 51(6):262.

3031 Nolan, D. 'Equal pay 1910–1970'. LM, Mar. 1970, 52(3):128–30.

3032 O'Donovan, T. *Above the law? The case for a Royal Commission on trade unions*. Johnson, 1960. 86pp.

3033 O'Higgins, P. 'Trade Disputes Act, 1965'. CLJ, Apr. 1966, 24(1):34–5.

3034 O'Higgins, P. and M. Partington. 'Industrial conflicts: judicial attitudes'. MLR, Jan. 1969, 32(1):53–8.

3035 Oldbury, J. 'Unity on the rails'. LM, July 1959, 41(7):313–14.

3036 Oram, R.B. *The dockers' tragedy*. Hutchinson, 1970. xi, 196pp.

3037 Page, C. 'Equal pay—the fight in 1969'. LM, Jan. 1969, 51(1):40–2.

3038 Panter, B. 'Action decides'. LM, July 1969, 51(7):305–6.

3039 Parsons, O.H. *The Donovan Report; trade unions, strikes and negotiations*. Labour Research Department, 1968. 23pp.

3040 Parsons, O.H. *Trade unions hamstrung: the meaning of Rookes v Barnard*. Labour Research department, 1964. 24pp.

3041 Parsons, O.H. 'Trade unions under fire'. LM, May 1959, 41(5):233–7.

3042 Patterson, J.C. 'Nicky and the builders'. LM, June 1963, 45(6):258–61.

3043 Pattison, G. *An outline of trade union history: an introduction for young people and others*. Barrie and Rockcliff, 1962. 143pp.

3044 Paynter, W. *British trade unions and the problem of change*. Allen and Unwin, 1970. 172pp.

3045 Paynter, W. 'The coal crisis and the miner'. LM, Dec. 1958, 40(12):539–42.

3046 Paynter, W. 'The coal situation'. LM, Sept. 1961, 43(9):426–30.

3047 Paynter, W. 'Prices and incomes policy'. LM, Apr. 1967, 49(4):158–160.

3048 Paynter, W. 'The problem of automation'. LM, Aug. 1963, 45(8):349–53.

3049 Paynter, W. 'Trade unions and the government'. PQ, Oct.–Dec. 1970, 41(4):444–54.

3050 Pearce, B. *Some rank and file movements*. Labour Review, 1959. 40pp.

3051 Pearson, W. 'Trade unions—alert'. LM, Jan. 1952, 34(1):29–32.

3052 Pelling, H. *A history of British trade unionism*. Macmillan, 1966 (first pub. 1963). xii, 287pp.

3053 Pelling, H. 'The Knights of Labor in Britain, 1880–1901'. ECHR, Dec. 1956, 9(2):313–31.

3054 Pelling, H. 'The Labour unrest, 1911–14', *Popular politics and society in late Victorian Britain*, pp.147–64. Macmillan, 1968.

3055 Pelling, H. 'Trade unions, workers and the law', *Popular politics and society in late Victorian Britain*, pp.62–8. Macmillan, 1968.

3056 PEP. *British trade unionism: five studies by PEP*. PEP, 1955. xii, 199pp.

3057 Pickhard, A. 'What is a democratic trade union?'. NR, Spring 1958, 4:101–6.

3058 Pickstock, F. *British railways—the human problem*. Fabian Society, 1950. 37pp.

3059 Pike, E.R. '1914. Trade unions, welfare and the individual', *Living history: 1914*, pp.144–50. Edited by J. Canning. Odhams, 1967.

3060 Pike, E.R. 'Workers unite! Trade unions', *Human documents of the Victorian age (1850–75)*, pp.313–29. Allen and Unwin, 1967.

3061 Political Quarterly. 'Notes and comments: trade unions in a changing world'. PQ, Jan.–Mar. 1956, 27(1):1–5.

3062 Pollard, S. 'Trade union reactions to the economic crisis'. JCH, 1969, 4(4):101–15.

3063 Pollard, S. 'The trade unions and the crisis of the early 1930's'. NEG, Oct. 1968, 2:8–9.

3064 Pollard, S. 'Trade unions and the labour market, 1870–1914'. YB, May 1965, 27(1):98–112.

3065 Pollitt, H. *An open letter to a trade unionist*. Communist Party, 1951. 16pp.

3066 Pollitt, H. *Trade unionists—what next?* Communist Party, 1948. 16pp.

3067 Pollock, G. 'Employers and trade unions'. PQ, July–Sept. 17(3):237–249.

3068 Poole, H. 'Unions face a challenge'. LM, Mar. 1958, 40(3):111–13.

3069 Port, D. and R. Crombie. 'Closed shop'. PPA, Sept. 1947, 2(3):54–68.

3070 Porter, J.H. 'Industrial peace in the cotton trade 1875–1913'. YB, May 1967, 19(1):49–61.

3071 Price, J. *British trade unions*. Longmans, 1948 (first pub. 1942). 47pp.

3071a Pridgeon, C., S.J. *Opportunity for trade unionists*. Oxford, Catholic Social Guild, 1948. 162pp.

3072 Prince, W. 'New legislation on safety organisations'. LM, June 1970, 52(6):271–3.

3073 Pritt, D.N. 'The courts and the trade unions'. LM, Mar. 1964, 46(3):130–3.

3074 Pritt, D.N. *Law, class and society*. Book 1. *Employees, workers and trade unions*. 1970. 174pp. Book 2. *The apparatus of the law*. 1971. 127pp. Book 3. *Law and politics and law in the colonies*. 1971. 151pp. Book 4. *The substance of the law*. 1972. 189pp. Lawrence and Wishart.
'law and the legal system in relation to the class struggle'.

3075 Pritt, D.N. and R. Freeman. *The law versus the trade unions*. Lawrence and Wishart, 1958. 128pp.

3076 Purcell, H. 'Trade unions on the move'. LM, Aug. 1951, 33(8):367–9.

3077 Ramelson, B. *Keep the unions free*. Communist Party, 1969. 16pp.

3078 Rattenbury, O. *Flame of freedom: the romantic story of the Tolpuddle Martyrs*. The author, 1950 (first pub. 1931). 169pp.

3079 Rees, A. *The economics of trade unions*. Welwyn, Nisbet and CUP, 1962. xiii, 210pp.

3080 Reid, G.L. 'An economic comment on the Donovan Report'. BJIR, Nov. 1968, 6(3):303–15.

3081 Reid, J. 'Youths' campaign for jobs'. LM, Nov. 1963, 45(11):506–8.

3082 Rideout, R.W. 'The content of trade union disciplinary rules'. BJIR, July 1965, 3(2):153–63.

3083 Rideout, R.W. 'The content of trade union rules regulating admission'. BJIR, Mar. 1966, 4(1):77–89.

3084 Rideout, R.W. 'Protection of the right to work'. MLR, Mar. 1962, 25(2):137–48.

3085 Rideout, R.W. 'Responsible self-government in British trade unions'. BJIR, Mar. 1967, 5(1):74–86.

3086 Rideout, R.W. *The right to membership of a trade union*. Athlone Press, 1963. xliv, 243pp.

3087 Rideout, R.W. 'Trade unions: some social and legal problems. 1'. HR, Feb. 1964, 17(1):73–95.

3088 Rideout, R.W. 'Trade unions: some social and legal problems. 2'. HR, May 1964, 17(2):169–98.

3089 Rideout, R.W. *Trade unions: some social and legal problems.* Tavistock, 1964. 54pp.

3090 Rimlinger, G.V. 'The legitimation of protest: a comparative study in Labor history'. CSSH, Apr. 1960, 2(3):329–43.

3091 Roberts, B.C. *Trade union government and administration in Great Britain.* London School of Economics and Bell, 1956. viii, 570pp.

3092 Roberts, B.C. 'Trade unions and party politics'. CJ, Apr. 1953, 6(7):387–402.

3093 Roberts, B.C. *Trade unions in a free society: studies in the organisation of Labour in Britain and the U.S.A.* Hutchinson, Institute of Economic Affairs, 1962. 206pp.

3094 Roberts, B.C. *Trade unions in the new era.* International Pub. Co., 1947. 43pp.

3095 Roberts, B.C. 'Trade unions in the welfare state'. PQ, Jan.–Mar. 1956, 27(1):6–18.

3096 Roberts, Bryn. *As I see it.* National Union of Public Employees, 1957. x, 142pp.

3097 Roberts, Bryn. *Topical comments.* National Union of Public Employees, 1952. xii, 119pp.

3098 Roberts, E. 'How to fight back'. LM, Feb. 1969, 51(2):63–6.

3099 Roberts, E. 'Where do we stand now?'. LM, Jan. 1958, 40(1):22–7.

3100 Robertson, A. *The trade unions.* Hamilton, 1965. 122pp.

3101 Robertson, D.J. 'Trade unions and wage policy'. PQ, Jan.–Mar. 1956, 27(1):19–30.

3102 Robinson, O. 'Representation of the white-collar worker: the bank staff associations in Britain'. BJIR, Mar. 1969, 7(1):19–41.

3103 Robinson, O. 'White-collar bargaining—a case study in the private sector'. SJPE, Nov. 1967, 14(3):256–74.

3104 Rolph, C.H., comp. *All those in favour? An account of the High Court action against the Electrical Trades Union and its officers for ballot-rigging in the election of union officials (Byrne & Chapple v Foulkes and others, 1961). Prepared from the official court transcripts.* Deutsch, 1962. 255pp.

3105 Rookes, D. *Conspiracy.* Johnson, 1966. xiv, 287pp.
See nos.2797, 3184. Employment and dismissal by B.O.A.C., legal action against his trade union, D.A.T.A.

3106 Rothstein, A. 'Hyndman, trade unions and socialism'. MML, Oct.–Dec. 1966, 40:17–20.

3107 Routh, G. 'White-collar unions in the United Kingdom', *White-collar trade unions; contemporary developments in industrialized societies,* pp.165–204. Edited by A.F. Sturmthal. Urbana, University of Illinois, 1966.

3108 Rowe, R. 'British liberals and trade unionists'. CNR, Sept. 1961, 200:458–61.

3109 Rowthorne, B. 'A reply [to M.B. Brown and R. Harrison]'. NLR, May–June 1966, 37:94–5.
See no.2733.

3110 Rowthorne, B. 'The trap of an incomes policy'. NLR, Nov.–Dec. 1965, 34:3–11.
See no.2733.

3111 Roy, W. 'Membership participation in the National Union of Teachers'. BJIR, July 1964, 2(2):189–208.

3112 Samuels, H. *Trade union law*. Knight, 1966. xvii, 100pp.

3113 Sanderson, R. 'Modern conditions and the unions'. LM, June 1963, 45(6):271–3.

3114 Saville, J. 'Trade unions and free labour: the background to the Taff Vale decision', *Essays in Labour history*, pp.317–50 (*see* no.1179). Edited by A. Briggs and J. Saville, Macmillan, 1960.

3115 Saxena, S.K. *Nationalisation and industrial conflict: example of British coal-mining*. Hague, Nijhoff, 1955. viii, 185pp.

3116 Schidman, J. *British unions and economic planning*. Pennsylvania, Penn. State University, 1969. vi, 106pp.

3117 Scott, J.R. 'Engineers in the front line'. LM, Nov. 1952, 34(11):512–17.

3118 Scott, J.R. 'Some thoughts on engineering'. LM, June 1957, 39(6):255–8.

3119 Scott, J.R. 'Wages: the next step'. LM, Jan. 1954, 36(1):32–7.

3120 Scott, J.R. 'Wanted; a campaign'. LM, Mar. 1960, 42(3):111–14.

3121 Scott, T. 'Trade unions: hour of decision'. LM, June 1969, 51(6):263–6.

3122 Seabrook, D. 'Organising the unorganised'. LM, June 1961, 43(6):263–8.

3123 Selvin, D.F. 'Communications in trade unions: a study of union journals'. BJIR, Feb. 1963, 1(1):73–93.

3124 Sethur, F. 'Trade unionism and central planning in western Europe'. SEJ, Oct. 1955, 22(2):221–9.
Largely Great Britain.

3125 Shanks, M. 'Out-of-date structure' (The trade unions—1). C, Summer 1958, 1(4)8–9.

3126 Shanks, M. 'Politics and the trade unionist'. PQ, Jan.–Mar. 1959, 30(1):44–53.

3127 Shanley, J.R. 'Trade unionists and automation'. LM, Apr. 1964, 46(4):159–64.

3128 Sheffield Steel Workers' Group. *The steel industry in 1968*. Institute for Workers' Control?, ?1968. 7pp.

3129 Shell, K.L. 'Industrial democracy and the British Labor movement'. PSQ, Dec. 1957, 72(4):515–39.

3130 Sherman, L. 'Wageless trade unionists'. TUA, Winter 1960–61, 1:58–66.

3131 Simey, T.S. 'The problem of social change. The docks industry: a case study'. SOCR, Dec. 1956, 4(2):157–66.

3132 Simon, D. 'Master and servant', *Democracy and the Labour movement . . .*, pp.160–200 (*see* no.1215). Edited by J. Saville. Lawrence and Wishart, 1954.

3133 Smart, W.H. 'Public ownership of the construction industry'. LM, Aug. 1966, 48(8):370–2.

3134 Smillie, R.H. 'Crisis in transport'. LM, May 1959, 41(5):226–8.

3135 Smith, A. *The trade unions.* Oliver and Boyd, 1969. 119pp.

3136 Spence, A. 'On the sixtieth anniversary of the Osborne judgement'. MML, Oct–Dec. 1969, 52:13–15.

3137 Squire, L. 'Hands off the unions'. LM, Mar. 1969, 51(3):113–14.

3138 Stephenson, T.E. 'The changing role of local democracy. The trade union branch and its members'. SOCR, July 1957, 5(1):27–42.

3139 Stevens, W.C. 'Trade unions on the march'. LM, Oct. 1954, 36(10):459–62.

3140 Stewart, J.D. *British pressure groups: their role in relation to the House of Commons.* Oxford, Clarendon Press, 1958. xii, 273pp.
       Discusses the activities of several trade unions.

3141 Straus, H. *Trade unions and the law.* McCorquodale, ?1946. 78pp.

3142 Stuttard, G. *Work is hell: an anatomy of workplace clichés.* Macdonald, 1969. 126pp.

3143 Sweetingham, C.R. 'Wasted assets'. LM, May 1962, 44(5):222–4.

3144 Sykes, A.J.M. 'The approaching crisis in the trade unions'. QR, Oct. 1960, 298(626):383–95.

3145 Sykes, A.J.M. 'Attitudes to political affiliation in a printing trade union'. SJPE, June 1965, 12(2):161–79.

3146 Sykes, A.J.M. 'The cohesion of a trade union workshop organisation'. SO, 1967, 1:141–63.

3147 Sykes, A.J.M. 'Navvies: their work attitudes'. SO, 1969, 3:21–35.

3148 Sykes, A.J.M. 'Some differences in the attitudes of clerical and of manual workers'. SOCR, Nov. 1965, 13(3):297–310.

3149 Sykes, A.J.M. 'Trade-union workshop organization in the printing indus-try—the Chapel'. HR, Feb. 1960, 13(1):49–65.

3150 Sykes, A.J.M. 'Unity and restrictive practices in the British printing industry'. SOCR, Dec. 1960, 8(2):239–54.

3151 Teesdale, G. 'Incomes and prices: what now?'. LM, May 1966, 48(5):207–8.

3152 Thomas, A.R. 'Trade unions and government'. LM, Apr. 1969, 51(4):164–6.

3153 Thomas, R., ed. *An exercise in redeployment: the report of a trade union study group*. Pergamon, 1969. xiii, 266pp.

3154 Thomas, T.C. 'Trade union-member's remedy for wrongful expulsion'. CLJ, Nov. 1954, 12(2):162–5.

3155 Thomas, T.C. 'Trade unions and their members'. CLJ, Apr. 1956, 14(1):67–79.

3156 Thompson, E.P. 'English trade unionism and other Labour movements before 1790'. SSLH, Autumn 1968, 17:19–24.

3157 Topham, A.J. 'Incomes policy. 1. The background to the argument'. SR, 1965, 2:163–74.

3158 Torode, A.C. 'Managing a small union'. TUA, Spring 1961, 2:27–35.

3159 Torr, D. 'The miners' autubiography'. LM, Aug. 1949, 31(8):239–42. Review of no.3298.

3160 Tracey, H. *I am trade unionist*. Central Office of Information, 1952. 29pp. Prepared for the Colonial Office.

3161 Tracey, H. *The British trade union movement*. International Confederation of Free Trade Unions, 1955. 106pp.

3162 Tracey, H. *Trade unionism: its origins, growth and role in modern society*. Labour Party, 1952. 31pp.

3163 Trades Union Congress. *The evidence of the Trades Union Congress to the Royal Commission on trade unions and employers' associations*. Trades Union Congress, 1967 (first pub. 1966). ix, 202pp.

3164 Trades Union Congress. *A short history of British trade unionism*. T.U.C., 1947. 31pp.

3165 Trades Union Congress. *The story of the Dorchester labourers*. Trades Union Congress, 1966 (first pub. 1957). 16pp. Includes guide to the Old Crown Court, Dorchester and to the village of Tolpuddle.

3166 Trades Union Congress. *Trade unionism: the evidence of the Trades Union Congress to the Royal Commission on trades unions and employers' associations*. T.U.C., 1966. ix, 186pp.

3167 Trades Union Congress. *Two centuries of trade unionism*. T.U.C., 1953. 63pp.

3168 Trades Union Congress. *Women in the trade union movement*. T.U.C., 1955. 99pp.

3169 Tuckett, A. 'May Day and the engineers'. LM, May 1962, 44(5):211–14.

3170 Tuckett, A. 'Safeguard union rights'. LM, June 1964, 46(6):262–7.

3171 Turnbull, G. 'Labour in the industry', *A history of the calico printing industry of Great Britain*, pp.182–255. Altrincham, Sherratt, 1951.

3172 Turner, H.A. 'British trade union structure: a new approach?'. BJIR, July 1964, 2(2):165–81.

3173 Turner, H.A. 'The Donovan Report'. EJ, Mar. 1969, 79(313):1–10.

3174 Turner, H.A. 'The Royal Commission research papers'. BJIR, Nov. 1968, 6(3):346–59.

3175 Turner, H.A. 'Trade union growth, structure and policy: a comparative study of the cotton unions'. Allen and Unwin, 1962. 413pp.
     See no.2849.

3176 Turner, H.A. 'Trade union organization'. PQ, Jan.–Mar. 1956, 27(1):57–70.

3177 Turner, H.A. 'Trade unions, differentials and the levelling of wages'. MS, Sept. 1952, 20(3):227–82.

3178 Turner, J. 'The teachers' pay dispute'. LM, Sept. 1967, 49(9):422–6.

3179 Turner, M. 'Managers: the fight for security'. LM, Feb. 1969, 51(2):81–83.

3180 Turner, Samuels, M. *British trade unions*. Sampson Low, 1949. xii, 212pp.

3181 *United Kingdom First Annual Trades' Union Directory, 1861*. Gregg, 1968 (first pub. 1861). ii, 108pp.

3182 Usherwood, S. 'The Tolpuddle Martyrs, 1834–37: a case of human rights'. HT, Jan. 1968, 18(1):14–21.

3183 Van Den Bergh, T. 'The Osborne judgement (1906–9)', *The trade unions—what are they?*, pp.110–32. Pergamon, 1970.

3184 Van Den Bergh, T. 'Rookes v Barnard (1955–65)', *The trade unions—what are they?*, pp.133–47. Pergamon, 1970.
     See no.3105.

3185 Van Den Bergh, T. 'Taff Vale case (1901)', *The trade unions—what are they?*, pp.108–18. Pergamon, 1970.

3186 Van Den Bergh, T. 'Tolpuddle Martyrs', *The trade unions—what are they?*, pp.95–107. Pergamon, 1970.

3187 Van Den Bergh, T. *The trade unions—what are they?*, Pergamon, 1970. xviii, 261pp. (*see* nos.132, 169, 596, 1024, 1030, 3813–16).

3188 Vaughan, C. 'The state of the unions'. M, Nov. 1970, Second New Series 2(5):152–4.

3189 Vester, H. and A.H. Gardner. *Trade union law and practice*. Sweet and Maxwell, 1958. xxx, 300pp.

3190 Vester, H. and A.H. Gardner. *Trade unions and the law*. Methuen, 1955. vii, 120pp.

3191 Volker, D. 'NALGO's affiliation to the TUC'. BJIR, Mar. 1966, 4(1):59–76.

3192 'Vulcan', *pseud*. 'The Confed. and the right to work'. LM, Aug. 1963, 45(8):360–3.
    The Confederation of Shipbuilding and Engineering Unions.

3193 'Vulcan', *pseud*. 'Democracy in the unions'. LM, Mar. 1961, 43(3):113–17.

3194 'Vulcan', *pseud*. 'Men of metal on the move'. LM, June 1960, 42(6):259–261.

3195 'Vulcan', *pseud*. 'Wages curb on the rocks'. LM, Dec. 1963, 45(12):545–549.

3196 'Vulcan', *pseud*. 'What are we here for, Mr. Woodcock?'. LM, Apr. 1963, 45(4):174–9.

3197 Ward, J. 'The unions have a part' (3. An expanding society). C, New Year 1958, 1(2):18–19.

3198 Warman, B. 'Prices and incomes'. LM, Oct. 1969, 51(10):445–6.

3199 Warman, B. 'Shop stewards today'. LM, Feb. 1959, 41(2):71–5.

3200 Warman, B. 'Trade unions and government'. LM, Apr. 1969, 51(4):166–7, 173.

3201 Watters, F. 'Action decides'. LM, July 1969, 51(7):307–9.

3202 Weaver, H. 'A case for closer working'. LM, Sept. 1963, 45(9):400–2.

3203 Weaver, H. 'A case for nationalisation [of the building industry]'. LM, Feb. 1961, 43(2):65–9.

3204 Webb, S. and B. *The history of trade unionism*. Longmans Green, 1950 (first pub. 1894). xviii, 784pp.

3205 Wedderburn, K.W. 'The Bonsor affair: a post-script'. MLR, Mar. 1957, 20(2):105–23.

3206 Wedderburn, K.W. 'Trade union membership—validity of rules'. CLJ, Apr. 1964, 22(1):16–20.

3207 Welton, H. *The trade unions, the employers and the state*. Pall Mall, 1960. iv, 178pp.

3208 Whelan, J. 'Is there a future in mining?'. LM, May 1959, 41(5):226–8.

3209 Wigham, E. *Trade unions*. OUP, 1969 (first pub. 1956). 189pp.

3210 Wigham, E. *What's wrong with the unions?* Penguin, 1961. 234pp.

3211 Wigham, W.S. *The closed shop*. Independent Labour Party, 1947. 11pp.

3212 Wiles, P. 'Are trade unions necessary?'. EN, Sept. 1956, 7(3):5–11.

213 Williams, D. *The labour side of the motor industry and multi-national corporations*. Common Cause Bulletin no.124, Autumn 1969. 32pp.

214 Williams, D. *The labour side of the motor industry and multi-national corporations (Part 2)*. Common Cause Bulletin no.125, Winter 1969/70. 33pp.

215 Williams, F. *Magnificent journey: the rise of the trade unions*. Odhams, 1954. 448pp.

216 Williams, J.E. 'The political activities of a trade union, 1906–14'. IRSH, 1957, 2(1):1–21.

217 Williams, J.E. 'Politics in the coalfields'. SSLH, Autumn 1969, 19:39–42. Review of nos. 2860 and 3315.

218 Williamson, H. *The trade unions*. Heinemann, 1970. viii, 136pp.

219 Willis, R. 'A printer speaks to miners'. LM, Sept. 1959, 41(9):391–6.

220 Willis, R. 'The T.U.C. and planning'. LM, Feb. 1962, 44(2):62–4.

221 Willis, R. 'Turning points for trade unionists'. LM, Nov. 1960, 42(11):495–9.

222 Wilson, B. 'Not recognised'. LM, May 1959, 41(5):222–6.

223 Winchester, F.S. 'Wages, work and organisation'. LM, Jan. 1961, 43(1):19–22.

224 Wood, J. 'The miners fight back'. LM, Mar. 1959, 41(3):117–20.

225 Wood, W. 'Action against closures'. LM, Oct. 1963, 45(10):467–8. Beeching plan.

226 Woodcock, G. *The trade union movement and the government*. Leicester, University Press, 1968. 20pp.

227 Wootton, G. *Workers, unions and the state*. Routledge, 1966. xiii, 173pp.

228 Wright, R.W. 'Trade unions—the next road'. LM, Aug. 1969, 51(8):356–9.

229 Wright, T. *The great unwashed*. New York, Kelley, 1970 (first pub. 1868). xi, 292pp.

230 Wright, T. *Our new masters*. Cass, 1969 (first pub. 1873). ix, 392pp.

231 Wright, T. *Some habits and customs of the working classes*. New York, Kelley, 1967 (first pub. 1867). xi, 276pp.

232 Zweig, F. *Men in the pits*. Gollancz, 1948. vi, 177pp.

233 Zweig, F. *Productivity and trade unions*. Oxford, Blackwell, 1951. 240pp.

II LOCAL STUDIES

3234 Abrahamson, M.W. 'Trade Disputes Act—strict interpretation in Ireland'. MLR, Sept. 1961, 24(5):596–603.

3235 Aldcroft, D.H. 'Communication [on J.P.D. Dunbabin, 'The "Revolt of the Field"']' (*see* no.3251). PP, Apr. 1964, 27:109.

3236 Bell, J.D.M. *The strength of trade unionism in Scotland*. Glasgow, University Press, 1950. 48pp.

3237 Beyer, M. 'The Barbican participates'. LM, Apr. 1969, 51(4):176–7.

3238 Birch, A.H. 'Trade unions [in Glossop]', *Small-town politics: a study of political life in Glossop*, pp.167–75. OUP, 1959.

3239 Blake, F. 'Victims of Fords'. LM, June 1963, 45(6):261–3.

3240 Boyd, A. 'Double discrimination: Ireland's unions'. TUA, Spring 1961, 2:4–16.

3241 Brown, A.J.Y. 'Trade union policy in the Scots coalfields, 1855–85'. ECHR, Aug. 1953, 6(1):35–50.

3242 Chapman, D. 'The combination of hecklers in the east of Scotland, 1822 and 1827'. SHR, Oct. 1948, 27:158–64.

3243 Clarke, J.F. 'Labour shipbuilding on the north-east coast 1850–1900'. NEG, Oct. 1968, 2:3–7.

3244 Copland, J. 'Dundee moves'. LM, May 1969, 51(5):212–14.

3245 Darragh, J. 'Birmingham trade unions and coloured workers'. TUA, Summer 1961, 3:136–42.

3246 Davies, C.S., ed. *A history of Macclesfield*. Manchester, University Press (for Macclesfield Borough Council), 1961.
Trade unions, pp.188–98.

3247 Dennis, N., F. Henriques and C. Slaughter. *Coal is our life: an analysis of a Yorkshire mining community*. Tavistock, 1969 (first pub. 1956). 255pp.

3248 Dickinson, H. 'Lancashire fights back'. LM, May 1959, 41(5):219–22.

3249 Dunbabin, J.P.D. 'The incidence and organization of agricultural trades unionism in the 1870's'. AGHR, 1968, 16(2):114–41.

3250 Dunbabin, J.P.D. 'Labourers and farmers in the late nineteenth century—some changes'. SSLH, Autumn 1965, 11:6–9.

3251 Dunbabin, J.P.D. 'The "Revolt of the Field": the agricultural labourers' movement in the 1870's'. PP, Nov. 1963, 26:68–97.
See no.3235.

3252 Eldridge, J.E.T. 'Plant bargaining in steel: north east case studies'. SOCR, July 1965, 13(2):131–48.

3253 Evans, C. *Industrial and social history of Seven Sisters*. Cardiff, Cymric Fed. Press, 1964. viii, 182pp.

3254 Francis, H. 'Welsh miners and the Spanish Civil War'. JCH, 1970, 5(3):177–91.

3255 Giles, P.M. 'The felt-hatting industry, c.1500–1850 with particular reference to Lancashire and Cheshire'. LCAS, 1959, 69:104–32.

3256 Harraway, S. 'Fords—our stand'. LM, Apr. 1969, 51(4):178–80.

3257 Hebrew University. Circle for the history of the Jewish People. Institute for Research into Jewish Workers' Movements. *Jewish workers' unions in England, 1886–1890*. Jerusalem, The Institute, 1966. 84pp.
      Reproduces (Hebrew/English text) the rules of five small London-based Jewish trade unions.

3258 Hort, P. 'Farmers defence associations in Oxfordshire, 1872–4'. HST, May 1968, 1(1):63–70.

3259 Horn, P. 'Nineteenth century Naseby farm workers'. NPP, 1968/9, 4(3):167–73.

3260 Horn, P. 'Northamptonshire agricultural labourers and the quest for allotments—the 1870's'. NPP, 1971/2, 4(6):371–7.

3261 Houston, G. 'Farm labour in Scotland 1800–50'. SSLH, Autumn 1965, 11:10–13.

3262 Houston, G. 'Labour relations in Scottish agriculture before 1870'. AGHR, 1958, 6(1):27–41.

3263 Hunt, C.J. *The lead miners of the northern Pennines in the eighteenth and nineteenth centuries*. Manchester, University Press, 1970. ix, 282pp.

3264 Jones, E.J. '"Scotch cattle" and early trade unionism in Wales', *Industrial South Wales 1750–1914: essays in Welsh economic history*, pp.209–17. Edited by W.E. Minchinton. Cass, 1969.

3265 Lerner, S.W. 'The impact of Jewish immigration of 1880–1914 on the London clothing industry and trade unions'. SSLH, Spring 1966, 12:12–15.

3266 Lewis, E.D. *The Rhondda Valleys: a study in industrial development, 1800 to the present day*. Phoenix House, 1959. xiv, 312pp.
      Discusses South Wales Miners' Federation, Cambrian Miners' Association.

3267 Liverpool University. Department of Social Science. 'Dock workers and their trade union', *The dock worker: an analysis of conditions of employment in the Port of Manchester*, pp.115–43. Liverpool University Press, 1954. vii, 283pp.

3268 Lovell, J. *Stevedores and dockers: a study of trade unionism in the Port of London, 1870–1914*. Macmillan, 1969. 270pp.

3269 McClelland, A. 'The Mersey sound that Wilson doesn't like'. LM, May 1969, 51(5):208–11.

3270 Manley, E.R. *Meet the miner*. The author, 1947. 120pp.
      'a study of the Yorkshire miner at work, at home and in public life'.

3271 Morris, J.H. and L.J. Williams. 'The discharge note in the South Wales coal industry, 1841–98'. ECHR, Dec. 1957, 10(2):286–93.

3272 Odber, A.J. 'The origins of industrial peace: the manufactured iron trade of the north of England'. OEP, June 1951, 3(2):202–20.

3273 O'Higgins, R. 'Irish trade unions and politics, 1830–50'. HJ, 1961, 4(2):208–17.

3274 Owen, H. *The Staffordshire potter*. Bath, Kingsmead, 1970. viii, 357pp.

3275 Paterson, T.T. *Glasgow Limited: a case-study in industrial war and peace*. CUP, 1960. x, 243pp.

3276 Patterson, A.T. 'Trade union struggle and municipal controversies 1820–6', *Radical Leicester, a history of Leicester, 1780–1850*, pp.130–45. Leicester, University College, 1954.

3277 Pattison, G. 'Nineteenth-century dock labour in the Port of London'. MM, Aug. 1966, 52(3):263–79.

3278 Peacock, A.J. '"The Revolt of the Field" in East Anglia'. OH, Spring-Summer 1968, 49–50:38pp.

3279 Peacock, A.J. '"The Revolt of the Field" in East Anglia 1872–4'. NEG, Oct. 1967, 1:6–8.

3280 Pollard, S. *A history of labour in Sheffield*. Liverpool, University Press, 1959. xix, 372pp.
    Largely a history of the trade unions in the city.

3281 Russell, R.C., comp. *The 'Revolt of the Field' in Lincolnshire: the origins and early history of farm-workers' trade unions*. National Union of Agricultural Workers, Lincolnshire County Committee, 1956. 168pp.

3282 Shillman, B. *Trade unionism and trade disputes in Ireland*. Dublin, Dublin Press, 1960. 67pp.

3283 Simey, T.S., ed. *The dock worker: an analysis of conditions of employment in the Port of Manchester*. Liverpool, University Press, 1956. viii, 283pp.

3284 Thomis, M.I. 'The trade unions experiment of 1812–14', *Old Nottingham*, pp.173–88. Newton Abbot, David and Charles, 1968.

3285 Tunstall, J. *The fishermen*. MacGibbon and Kee, 1962. 294pp.

3286 Wallace, B. 'Redundancies in Belfast'. LM, Oct. 1966, 48(10):467–8.

3287 Williams, L.J. 'The new unionism in South Wales, 1889–92'. WH, Feb, 1963, 1(4):413–29.

III UNION HISTORIES

3288 Adams, F.R. 'From association to union: professional organization of Asylum Attendants, 1869–1919'. BJS, Mar. 1969, 2(1):11–26.

3289 Allen, E. *The Durham Miners' Association: a commemoration*. National Union of Mineworkers (Durham Area), 1969. 68pp.

3290 Allen, V.L. 'The National Union of Police and Prison Officers'. ECHR, Aug. 1958, 11(1):133–43.

3291 Amalgamated Engineering Union. *Celebration of the million membership and extension of general office* . . . . The Union, 1961. 40pp.
Cover title: 1811–1961. One hundred and fifty years progress. Over a million members.

3292 Amalgamated Engineering Union. *The story of the engineers.* The Union, 1951. 36pp.
Centenary souvenir.

3293 Amalgamated Union of Building Trade Workers. *The building workers' struggle: centenary souvenir.* The Union, ?1948. 36pp.

3294 Amalgamated Union of Engineering Workers. Enfield District Committee. *The first 80 years: some account to 1935 of the Enfield Lock Branch (founded 1855).* The District Committee, 1970. 20pp.

3295 Andrews, C.D. and G.C. Burger. *Progress report 1909–1959: the first fifty years in the history of the London County Council Staff Association.* The Association, 1959. 128pp.

3296 Arnot, R.P. 'Historiography ahoy!'. LM, Oct. 1967, 49(10):462–7.
Review of no.3400.

3297 Arnot, R.P. *A history of the Scottish miners from the earliest times.* Allen and Unwin, 1955. xiv, 455pp.
See no.3336.

3298 Arnot, R.P. *The miners: a history of the Miners' Federation of Great Britain 1889–1910.* Allen and Unwin, 1949, 409pp. (*see* no.3159).

3299 Arnot, R.P. *The miners: years of struggle. A history of the Miners' Federation of Great Britain (from 1910 onwards).* Allen and Unwin, 1953. 567pp.
See no.3335.

3300 Arnot, R.P. *The miners in crisis and war. A history of the Miners' Federation of Great Britain (from 1930 onwards).* Allen and Unwin, 1961. 451pp.
See no.3337.

3301 Arnot, R.P. *South Wales miners. Glowyr De Cymru: a history of the South Wales Miners' Federation (1898–1914).* Allen and Unwin, 1967. 390pp.

3302 Bagwell, P.S. 'Early attempts at national organization of the railwaymen, 1865–7'. JTH, Nov. 1957, 3(2):94–102.

3303 Bagwell, P.S. *The National Union of Railwaymen 1913–63: a half-century of industrial trade unionism.* The Union, 1963. 48pp.

3304 Bagwell, P.S. *The railwaymen: the history of the National Union of Railwaymen.* Allen and Unwin, 1963. 725pp.

3305 Barton, T.C. *A history of the Manchester Municipal Officers' Guild 1906–1956 (Branch of the National and Local Government Officers' Association).* Manchester, The Guild, 1956. vii, 61pp.

3306 Bassett-Vincent, C. *An authentic history of railway trade unionism*. Derby Printers, 1963 (first pub. 1902). 66pp.
Author was originator of the Amalgamated Society of Railway Servants.

3307 Belford, A.J. *Centenary handbook of the Educational Institute of Scotland*. Edinburgh, The Institute, 1946. vii, 430pp.

3308 Bending, H., ed. *Forty years: National Union of Scalemakers 1909–49*. The Union, 1949. 32pp.

3309 Bourne, R. and B. MacArthur. *The struggle for education 1870–1970: a pictorial history of popular education and the National Union of Teachers*. Schoolmaster, 1970. 128pp.

3310 Brown, K.D. 'The Trade Union Tariff Reform Association, 1904–13'. JBS, May 1970, 9(2):141–53.

3311 Buckley, K.D. *Trade unionism in Aberdeen 1878 to 1900*. Edinburgh, Oliver and Boyd for University of Aberdeen, 1955. xii, 201pp.

3312 Bundock, C.J. *The National Union of Journalists. A jubilee history 1907–57*. OUP for the Union, 1957. viii, 254pp.

3313 Bundock, C.J. *The story of the National Union of Printing, Bookbinding and Paper Workers*. OUP, 1959. xi, 589pp.

3314 Carter, J. 'One of the mammoths'. LM, May 1956, 38(5):227–30.
National Union of General and Municipal Workers.

3315 Challinor, R. and B. Ripley. *The Miners' Association: a trade union in the age of the Chartists*. Lawrence and Wishart, 1968. ii, 266pp.
See no.3217.

3316 Chalmers, J.M. *How we began: postal trade unionism 1870–1920*. Union of Post Office Workers, ?1965. 47pp.

3317 Chalmers, J.M. *Official recognition: the story of postal trade unionism*. Union of Post Office Workers, 1956. 52pp.

3318 Clegg, H.A. *General Union: a study of the National Union of General and Municipal Workers*. Oxford, Blackwell, 1954. xv, 358pp.

3319 Clegg, H.A. *General Union in a changing society: a short history of the National Union of General and Municipal Workers 1889–1964*. Oxford, Blackwell, 1964. xi, 226pp.
Commemorates the 75th anniversary of Union's founding.

3320 Communist Party. *United we stand: 100 years of struggle in the docks*. The Party, London District Committee, 1956. 32pp.
Issued in honour of the centenary of the birth of Tom Mann.

3321 Confederation of Health Service Employees. *1910–1960: fifty years of progress*. Banstead, The Confederation, 1960. ix, 24pp.

3322 Connelly, T.J. *The Woodworkers 1860–1960*. The Society, 1960. vii, 120pp.
History of the Amalgamated Society of Woodworkers.

3323 Cuthbert, N.H. *The Lace Makers' Society: a study of trade unionism in the British lace industry, 1760–1960*. The Amalgamated Society of Operative Lace Makers and Auxiliary Workers, 1960. xvi, 293pp.

3324 Edley, J. *A short history of the National Union of Gold, Silver and Allied Trades, to commemorate the fiftieth anniversary of the union*. Sheffield, The Union, 1961. 47pp.

3325 Edwards, H.T. *It was my privilege*. Denbigh, Gee, 1957. 90, viiipp.
   History of the Transport and General Workers' Union in North Wales.

3326 Electrical Trades Union. *The story of the E.T.U.: the official history of the Electrical Trades Union*. The Union, ?1952. ix, 266pp.

3327 England, J.W. *Midland Area 1908–1962: a short history (National Association of Colliery Overmen, Deputies and Shotfirers)*. Nottingham, The Association, 1962. 47pp.

3328 Evans, E.W. *The miners of South Wales*. Cardiff, University of Wales Press, 1961. x, 274pp.
   To 1912 national strike.

3329 Evans, G. 'Farm servants' unions in Aberdeenshire from 1870–1900'. SHR, Apr. 1952, 31(111):29–40.

3330 Fire Brigades Union. *The fifty-year march: FBU 1918–68*. The Union, 1968. 60pp.

3331 Fox, A. *A history of the National Union of Boot and Shoe Operatives, 1874–1957*. Oxford, Blackwell, 1958. viii, 684pp.

3332 French, J.O. *Plumbers in unity: history of the Plumbing Trades Union, 1865–1965*. The Union, ?1965. xi, 172pp.

3333 Furniture, Timber and Allied Trades Union. (History 1800–1951: a brochure issued to commemorate opening of new head office of union). The Union, 1951. 21pp.

3334 Fyrth, H.J. and H. Collins. *The foundry workers: a trade union history*. Manchester, Amalgamated Union of Foundry Workers, 1959. xii, 348pp.

3335 Gallacher, W. 'An epic story'. LM, May 1953, 35(5):227–31.
   Review of no.3299.

3336 Gallacher, W. 'Heroic story'. LM, Sept. 1955, 37(9):426–8.
   Review of no.3297.

3337 Gallacher, W. 'In crisis and war'. LM, Dec. 1961, 43(12):580–4.
   Review of no.3300.

3338 Gillespie, S.C. *A hundred years of progress: the record of the Scottish Typographical Association 1853–1952*. Glasgow, Maclehose for the Association, 1953. xv, 268pp.

3339 Golding, J. *75 years: a short history of the Post Office Engineering Union*. The Union, 1962. 64pp.

3340 Goldstein, J. *The government of British trade unions: a study of apathy and the democratic process in the Transport and General Workers' Union.* Allen and Unwin, 1952. 300pp.

3341 Griffin, A.R. *The miners of Nottinghamshire: a history of the Nottingham Miners' Association.** Vol. 1, 1881–1914. The Association, ?1955. xii, 212pp.
    *Now the Nottinghamshire Area of the National Union of Mineworkers.

3342 Griffin, A.R. *The miners of Nottinghamshire 1914–44: a history of the Nottinghamshire Miners' Unions.* Allen and Unwin, 1962. 323pp.

3343 Groves, R. *Sharpen the sickle! The history of the Farm Workers' Union.* Porcupine, 1949. 256pp.

3344 Gupta, P.S. 'Railway trade unionism in Britain, c.1880–1900'. ECHR, Apr. 1966, 19(1):124–53.

3345 Hilton, W.S. *Foes to tyranny: a history of the Amalgamated Union of Building Trade Workers.* The Union, 1963. 301pp.

3346 Hobsbawm, E.J. 'Trade union history'. ECHR, Aug. 1967, 20(2):358–364.
    Review of no.2751.

3347 Hopwood, E. *A history of the Lancashire cotton industry and the Amalgamated Weavers' Association.* Manchester, the Association, 1969. xiii, 199pp.

3348 Howe, E. *The London bookbinders 1780–1806.* Dropmore, 1950. ii, 182pp.

3349 Howe, E., ed. *The London compositor: documents relating to wages, working conditions, and customs of the London printing trade 1785–1900.* OUP for the Bibliographical Society, 1947. 528pp.

3350 Howe, E. *The typecasters.* The Monotype Corporation, 1955. 40pp.
    Privately printed for presentation to The Monotype Casters' and Typefounders' Society.

3351 Howe, E. and J. Child. *The Society of London Bookbinders, 1780–1951.* Sylvan, 1952. 288pp.

3352 Howe, E. and H.E. Waite. *The London Society of Compositors (re-established 1848): a centenary history.* Cassell, 1948. xvi, 359pp.

3353 Howe, G.W. *Jubilee of the National Union of Press Telegraphists 1909–1959.* The Union, 1959. 44pp.

3354 Hughes, F. *By hand and brain: the story of the Clerical and Administrative Workers' Union.* Lawrence and Wishart for the Union, 1953. 150pp.

3355 Irish Transport and General Workers' Union. *Fifty years of Liberty Hall. The golden jubilee of the Irish Transport and General Workers' Union, 1909–59.* Dublin, The Union, 1959. 96pp.

3356 Jefferys, J.B. *The story of the engineers 1800–1945.* Lawrence and Wishart, 1946. vi, 301pp.

3357 Judge, A. *The first fifty years: the story of the Police Federation*. The Federation, 1968. vi, 140pp.

3358 Kidd, A.T., comp. *History of the Tin-plate Workers and Sheet Metal Workers and Braziers Societies*. The Society, 1949. vii, 334pp.

3359 Liberty Magazine. *Special commemorative issue to celebrate the golden jubilee of the Irish Transport and General Workers Union (1909–1959)*. Dublin, Liberty Magazine, May 1959. 96pp.

3360 MacDermott, T.A. 'National Labour Federation (1886–1892?)'. NEG, Oct. 1969, 3:24–6.

3361 Machin, F. *The Yorkshire miners: a history*. Vol. 1. Barnsley, National Union of Mineworkers (Yorkshire Area), 1958. xi, 496pp.
   To 1881.

3362 McKillop, N. *The lighted flame: a history of the Associated Society of Locomotive Engineers and Firemen*. Nelson, 1950. xiii, 402pp.

3363 Manzer, R.A. *Teachers and politics: the role of the National Union of Teachers in the making of national educational policy in England and Wales since 1944*. Manchester, University Press, 1970. xi, 164pp.

3364 Michael, W.J. 'A modern amalgamation in process'. LM, July 1960, 42(7):328–30.
   Associated Blacksmiths' Forge and Smithy Workers' Society and United Society of Boilermakers, Shipbuilders and Structural Workers.

3365 Moran, J. *NATSOPA, seventy-five years: the National Society of Operative Printers and Assistants (1889–1964)*. Heinemann for NATSOPA, 1964. ix, 160pp.

3366 Morgan, J.E. *A village workers' council—and what it accomplished, being a short history of the Lady Windsor Lodge, South Wales Miners' Federation*. Pontypridd, Celtic Press, 1950. vi, 75pp.

3367 Mortimer, J.E. *A history of the Association of Engineering and Shipbuilding Draughtsmen*. The Association, 1960. xi, 489pp.

3368 Morton, B., ed. *Action 1919–69: a record of the growth of the National Association of Schoolmasters*. The Association, 1969. 30pp.

3369 Murie, A. *The carpet weavers of Kidderminster*. Power Loom Carpet Weavers' and Textile Workers' Association, 1966. 18pp.

3370 Musson, A.E. *The Typographical Association, origins and history up to 1949*. Cumberlege, 1954. ix, 487pp.

3371 National Association of Head Teachers. *The first fifty years: jubilee volume of the National Association of Head Teachers*. University of London Press, 1947. xvi, 219pp.

3372 National Union of General and Municipal Workers. *Sixty years*. The Union, 1949. vi, 98pp.
   Souvenir brochure, 1889–1949.

3373 National Union of Seamen. *The story of the seamen: a short history of the National Union of Seamen*. The Union, 1964. 48pp.

3374 National Union of Vehicle Builders. *A short history of the National Union of Vehicle Builders to commemorate the 125th anniversary of the Union, 1834–1959*. The Union, 1959. 43pp.

3375 Newman, B. *Yours for action*. The Union, 1953. viii, 196pp.
      History of the Civil Service Clerical Association.

3376 Newman, J.R. *The N.A.O.P. heritage: a short historical review of the growth and development of the National Association of Operative Plasterers 1860–1960*. The Association, 1960. viii, 180pp.

3377 Oliver, W.H. 'The Consolidated Trades' Union of 1834'. ECHR, Aug. 1964, 17(1):77–95.

3378 Owen, J. *Ironmen: a short history of the union from 1878 to 1953*. Middlesbrough, National Union of Blastfurnacemen, Ore Miners, Coke Workers and Kindred Trades, 1953. 48pp.

3379 Perkin, H. *Key profession: the history of the Association of University Teachers*. Routledge, 1969. viii, 268pp.

3380 Pierotti, A.M. *The story of the National Union of Women Teachers*. The Union, 1963. iv, 88pp.

3381 Printing and Kindred Trades Federation. *Sixty years of service: Printing and Kindred Trades Federation*. The Federation, 1961. 31pp.
      1901–61.

3382 Pugh, Sir A. *Men of steel: a chronicle of eighty-eight years of trade unionism in the British iron and steel industry*. The Confederation, 1951. xiv, 624pp.
      The Iron and Steel Trades Confederation.

3383 Radford, F.H. *"Fetch the engine . . .": the official history of the Fire Brigades Union*. The Union, 1951. 192pp.

3384 Railway Clerks Association. *50 years: a brief review of the work of the Railway Clerks Association*. The Union, 1947. 16pp.
      Period: 1897–1947.

3385 Ravensdale, J.R. 'The China Clay Labourers' Union'. HST 1968, 1(1):51–62.

3386 Reynolds, J. *The letter press printers of Bradford: a short history of the Bradford Graphical Society**. Bradford, National Graphical Association, Bradford Branch, 1970. 40pp.
      *formerly Bradford Typographical Society.
      'To commemorate the 150th anniversary of the establishment of TU principles of combination amongst the Journeymen Printers of Bradford'.

3387 Rowles, G.E. *The "Line" is on: a centenary souvenir of the London Society of Compositors 1848–1948*. The Society, 1948. 116pp.

3388 Roy, W. *The Teachers' Union: aspects of policy and organisation in the National Union of Teachers, 1950–1966.* Schoolmaster Publishing Co., 1968. xv, 183pp.

3389 Schaffer, G. *Light and liberty: sixty years of the Electrical Trades Union.* The Union, 1949. viii, 94pp.

3390 Shane, T.E.H., *pseud. Passed for press: a centenary history of the Association of Correctors of the Press.* Association, 1954. 63pp.
　　　Period: 1854–1954.

3391 Simpson, A.B. *The Educational Institute of Scotland 1847—1947.* Edinburgh, The Institute, 1947. 40pp.

3392 Singleton, F. 'The Saddleworth Union, 1827–30'. SSLH, Autumn 1962, 5:33–6.

3393 Spoor, A. *White-collar union: sixty years of Nalgo.* Heinemann, 1967. xi, 625pp.
　　　Period: 1905–65.

3394 Sprague, K., comp. *Unity, strength, progress: the story of the Transport and General Workers' Union.* The Union, 1967. 40pp.

3395 Stewart, M. and L. Hunter. *The needle is threaded: 'the history of an industry'.* Heinemann/Newman Neame, 1964. x, 241pp.
　　　History of the National Union of Tailors and Garment Workers and development of the tailoring industry.

3396 Swift, J. *History of the Dublin bakers and others.* Dublin, Irish Bakers, Confectioners and Allied Workers Union, 1948. 383pp.

3397 Taylor, A.J. 'The Miners' Association of Great Britain and Ireland, 1842–8: a study in the problem of integration'. E, Feb. 1955, 22(85):45–60.

3398 Tropp, A. *The school teachers: growth of the teaching profession in England and Wales from 1800 to the present day.* Heinemann, 1957. viii, 286pp.

3399 Trory, E. *The sacred band.* Brighton, Crabtree, 1946. 128pp.
　　　Centenary celebrations of the Brighton 1st Branch of the A.E.U.

3400 Tuckett, A. *The Scottish carter: the history of the Scottish Horse and Motormen's Association 1898–1964.* Allen and Unwin, 1967. 448pp.
　　　See no.3296.

3401 United Patternmakers Association. *75 years agrowing! A brief account of the history and development of the United Patternmakers Association.* The Association, 1947. 55pp.
　　　Period: 1872–1947.

3402 Williams, J.E. *The Derbyshire miners: a study in industrial and social history.* Allen and Unwin, 1962. 933pp.

Rank and file movements, workers' control

3403 Alexander, K.J.W. and C.L. Jenkins. *Fairfields: a study of industrial change.* Lane, 1970. 286pp.
'Fairfields (Glasgow) Ltd., a shipyard in Govan was created by a unique combination of government, trade-union and private enterprise capital.'

3404 Arnot, R.P. 'Shopkeepers, shop stewards and shop lifters'. LM, Jan. 1969, 51(1):33–5.

3405 Butt, D. 'Workers' control'. NLR, July–Aug. 1961, 10:24–33.

3406 Chalmers, J.M., I. Mikardo and G.D.H. Cole. *Consultation or joint management? A contribution to the discussion of industrial democracy.* Fabian Society, 1949. 28pp.

3407 Cliff, A. and C. Barker. *Incomes policy, legislation and shop stewards.* London Industrial Shop Stewards Defence Committee, 1966. 136pp.

3408 Coates, K. and A.J. Topham, eds. *Workers' control: a book of readings and witnesses for workers' control.* Panther, 1970 (first pub. 1968). xl, 464pp.

3409 Crosland, A. 'What does the worker want?'. EN, Feb. 1959, 12(2):10–15.

3410 Dinning, N. 'In defence of shop stewards'. LM, Nov. 1959, 41(11):508–11.

3411 Goodman, J.F.B. and T.G. Whittingham. *Shop stewards in British industry.* McGraw-Hill, 1969. xiv, 256pp.

3412 Gossman, L. *Industrial management—the socialist way.* Fabian Society, 1949. 28pp.

3413 Graham, J. *Socialism and workers' councils.* Independent Labour Party, 1957. 12pp.

3414 Guinan, M. 'The industrial vanguard'. LM, May 1960, 42(3):114–15.

3415 Harrison, R. 'Retreat from industrial democracy'. NLR, July–Aug. 1960, 4:32–8.

3416 Hinton, J.S. 'The shop stewards' movement in the First World War'. SSLH, Autumn 1966, 13:4–7.

3417 Industrial Research and Information Services Ltd. *Shop stewards.* I.R.I.S., 1968. 28pp.

3418 Lerner, S.W. and J. Bescoby. 'Shop steward combine committees in the British engineering industry'. BJIR, July 1966, 4(2):154–64.

3419 Lerner, S.W. and J. Marquand. 'Regional variations in earnings, demand for labour and shop stewards' combined committees in the British engineering industry'. MS, Sept. 1963, 31(3):261–96.

3420 Macfarlane, J. 'Shipboard union representation in the British merchant navy'. IRSH, 1970, 15(1):1–18.

3421 Marsh, A.I. and E.E. Coker. 'Shop steward organization in the engineering industry'. BJIR, June 1963, 1(2):170–90.

3422 Moore, W. 'Sheffield shop stewards in the First World War'. OH, Summer 1960, 18:18pp.

3423 Murphy, J.T. 'Are the workers ready to control industry?'. F, May 1948, 163(977):341–6.

3424 Parker, S.R. and J.M. Bynner. 'Correlational analysis of data obtained from a survey of shop stewards'. HR, Aug. 1970, 23(4):345–59.

3425 Pribićevic, B. *The shop stewards' movement and workers' control 1910–22.* Oxford, Blackwell, 1959. xii, 179pp.

3426 Reckitt, M.B. *Industry and democracy; the triumph of workers' control: an historical outline.* League for Workers' Control, 1952. 16pp.

3427 Ross, N.S. 'Joint consultation and workers' control'. PQ, Jan–Mar. 1956, 27(1):82–92.

3428 Scanlon, H. *The way forward for workers' control.* Nottingham, Institute for Workers Control, 1968. 10pp.

3429 Scott, J.R. 'The salt of the earth'. LM, Jan. 1960, 42(1):17–21.

3430 Scott, W.H. *Industrial democracy: a revaluation.* Liverpool, University Press, 1955. 40pp.

3431 Sturmthal, A. 'Nationalization and workers control in Britain and France'. JPE, Feb. 1953, 61(1):43–79.

3432 Sykes, A.J.M. 'The shop stewards' place in industry'. QR, Jan. 1960, 298(623):8–16.

3433 Tocher, J.W. 'The shop steward's job'. LM, Aug. 1959, 41(1):348–50.

3434 Topham, A.(J.). 'Shop stewards and workers' control'. NLR, Mar.–June 1964, 25:3–16.

3435 White, E. *Workers control?* Fabian Society, 1951. 31pp.

Trades Union Congress

3436 Allen, V.L. 'The centenary of the British Trades Union Congress 1868–1968'. SR, 1968, 5:231–52.

3437 Allen, V.L. 'The reorganization of the Trades Union Congress, 1918–27'. BJS, Mar. 1960, 11(1):24–43.

3438 Allison, G. 'Bridlington Congress'. LM, Oct. 1949, 31(10):301–5.

3439 Allison, G. 'The October T.U.C.'. LM, Oct. 1946, 28(10):304–7.

3440 Anderson, J.R.L. 'The powers of Transport House', *Who runs Britain?*, pp.30–5. Contract, 1949.

3441 Atkinson, N. 'From Brighton to Blackpool'. LM, Oct. 1970, 52(10):444–7.

3442 Ball, J. 'Pay, the government and the unions'. LM, Oct. 1968, 50(10):466–8.

3443 Birch, L., ed. *The history of the T.U.C. 1868–1968: a pictorial survey of a social revolution*. T.U.C., 1968. 159pp.

3444 Bond, R. 'T.U.C. lessons for Labour'. LM, Oct. 1965, 47(10):446–50.

3445 Bowman, D. 'Impressions of the Scottish Trades Union Congress 1967'. LM, June 1967, 49(6):270–3.

3446 Bowman, D. 'The T.U.C. leadership'. LM, May 1961, 43(5):215–21. Review of no. 3489.

3447 Bowman, D. 'T.U.C. review reviewed'. LM, Mar. 1968, 50(3):113–116.

3448 Campbell, J.R. 'The T.U.C. and the government'. LM, Sept. 1945, 27(9):274–8.

3449 Davies, D.I. 'The politics of the T.U.C.'s colonial policy'. PQ, Jan.–Mar. 1964, 35(1):23–34.

3450 Drain, G. 'Politics and the T.U.C.'. TUA, Summer 1961, 3:46–53.

3451 Dutt, R.P. 'From Brighton to Scarborough'. LM, Oct. 1967, 49(10):433–44.

3452 Elger, W. *50 years of progress: the building of the Scottish Trades Union Congress: 1897–1947*. Scottish Trades Union Congress, General Council, 1947. 40pp.

3453 [An English delegate]. 'The Scottish T.U.C.'. LM, June 1962, 44(6):273–275.

3454 Frow, E. and M. Katanka. *1868, year of the unions: a documentary history*. Katanka, 1968. 184pp.

3455 Frow, R. and E. 'The first Trades Union Congress'. MML, Apr.–June 1968, 46:8–12.

3456 Gardner, J. 'Trades Union Congress 1952'. LM, Sept. 1952, 34(9):396–401.

3457 Hamlin, R. 'Docker's view of the T.U.C.'. LM, Sept. 1970, 52(9):404–6.

3458 Harrison, R. 'Practical, capable men'. NR, Autumn 1958, 6:105–19. Review of no.3487.

3459 Hart, F. 'Problems before the T.U.C.'. LM, Aug. 1961, 43(8):374–82.

3460 Haxell, F. 'T.U.C. programme'. LM, Oct. 1956, 38(10):470–2.

3461 Hill, E.J. 'Wages and the planning council'. LM, Mar. 1962, 44(8):113–115.

3462 Horner, J. 'Behind the potted plants at Southport'. LM, Oct. 1955, 37(10):447–51.

3463 Horner, J. 'Clash at the T.U.C.'. LM, Oct. 1953, 35(10):463–6.

3464 Horner, J. 'Margate T.U.C.'. LM, Oct. 1952, 34(10):450–9.

3465 Horner, J. 'The Southport T.U.C.'. LM, Oct. 1947, 29(10):299–303.

3466 Hughes, J. *The T.U.C.: a plan for the 1970's.* Fabian Society, 1969. 37pp.

3467 Hutchinson, H. 'TUC'. TC, Oct. 1956, 160(956):302–7.

3468 Hutt, A. 'The TUC's century'. LM, June 1968, 50(6):257–60.

3469 Kavanagh, P. 'TUC youth lobby'. LM, Sept. 1970, 52(9):423–5.

3470 Kerrigan, P. 'TUC prospects'. LM, Sept. 1969, 51(9):397–9.

3471 Lerner, S.W. 'The T.U.C. jurisdictional dispute settlement, 1924–57'. MS, Sept. 1958, 26(3):222–40.

3472 Lockett, R.C. 'T.U.C.: racial discrimination'. LM, Oct. 1967, 49(10:4.

3473 Lovell, J. and B.C. Roberts. *A short history of the T.U.C.* Macmillan, 1968. 200pp.

3474 Lyons, R. 'TUC prospects'. LM, Sept. 1969, 51(9):402–6.

3475 Marx Memorial Library. Quarterly Bulletin. 'On the centenary of the T.U.C.'. MML, Oct.–Dec. 1968, 48:13–16.

3476 Moffatt, A. 'This Trades Union Congress'. LM, Oct. 1961, 43(10):471–478.

3477 Mortimer, J.E. 'Changing the General Council'. TUA, Winter 1960,1:12–29.

3478 Mortimer, J.E. 'Trades Union Congress, 1958'. LM, Oct. 1958, 40(10):473–6.

3479 Musson, A.E. *The Congress of 1868: the origins and establishment of the Trades Union Congress.* T.U.C., 1968 (first pub. 1955). 48pp.

3480 Newton, J. 'The aim behind the planning council'. LM, Apr. 1962, 44(4):169–72.

3481 Pollitt, H. 'After the Brighton T.U.C.'. LM, Dec. 1946, 28(12):360–372.

3482 Pollitt, H. 'The Brighton TUC'. LM, Oct. 1950, 32(10):442–9.

3483 Pollitt, H. 'The Margate conference'. LM, Oct. 1948, 30(10):298–303.

3484 Quaestor, *pseud.* 'The left at Blackpool'. LM, Oct. 1951, 33(10):467–74.

3485 Renshaw, P. 'The origins of the Trades Union Congress'. HT, July 1968, 18(7):456–63.

3486 Rice, E. 'TUC prospects'. LM, Sept. 1969, 51(9):400–2.

3487 Roberts, B.C. *The Trades Union Congress: 1868–1921*. Allen and Unwin, 1958. 408pp.
    See no.3458.

3488 Roberts, Bryn. *At the T.U.C.: resolutions, speeches, comments*. National Union of Public Employees, 1947. vi, 344p.

3489 Roberts, Bryn. *The price of the T.U.C. leadership*. Allen and Unwin, 1961. 148pp.
    See no.3446.

3490 Roberts, E. 'TUC—the trade unionists' defence'. LM, Sept. 1970, 52(9):400–3.

3491 Sinclair, B. 'Irish Congress of Trade Unions'. LM, Sept. 1970, 52(9):410–15.

3492 Spence, A. 'Year of the unions'. MML, July–Sept. 1968, 47:9–13.

3493 Taylor, S. 'T.U.C.: Congress in revolt'. LM, Oct. 1967, 49(10):447–8.

3494 Trades Union Congress. *ABC of the TUC*. T.U.C., 1954. 24pp.

3495 Trades Union Congress. *Report of proceedings of the annual Trades Union Congress, 1945 to date*. T.U.C., 1945–

3496 'Vulcan', *pseud*. 'The General Council [of the TUC] and the shop stewards'. LM, Feb. 1960, 42(2):64–8.

3497 'Vulcan', *pseud*. 'Have we the leadership we deserve?'. LM, Sept. 1960, 42(9):404–7.

3498 Weiner, H.E. *British Labour and public ownership*. Stevens, 1960. xii, 111pp.

3499 Wetherby, T. 'This T.U.C. set-up'. LM, Nov. 1959, 41(11):495–500.

3500 Winterton, E.M. 'Rising tide at Blackpool'. LM, Oct. 1957, 39(10):453–8.

3501 Winterton, E.M. 'T.U.C.; the election and class struggle'. LM, Oct. 1964, 46(10):458–64.

Strikes, disputes, disturbances

3502 Alderson, F. *View north: a long look at northern England*. Newton Abbot, David and Charles, 1968.
    Strike, pp.147–68.

3503 Ambrose, M. 'The printers' dispute'. LM, July 1970, 52(7):314–16.

3504 Arnison, J. *The million pound strike*. Lawrence and Wishart, 1970. 85pp.
      Roberts-Arundel works in Stockport, 1967–8.

3505 Arnot, R.P. 'Class strategy'. LM, May 1957, 39(5):193–206.

3506 Barker, C. *The Pilkington strike*. International Socialists, 1970. 24pp.

3507 Barr, J. 'Clydeside in action'. LM, May 1969, 51(5):224–6.

3508 Bernard, W.N. 'Victory of the Derby bank managers'. TUA, Spring 1961,
      2:36–42.

3509 Bescoby, J. and H.A. Turner. 'An analysis of post-war labour disputes in
      the British car-manufacturing firms'. MS, May 1961, 29(2):133–60.

3510 Blumler, J.G. and A.J. Ewbank. 'Trade unionists, the mass media and the
      unofficial strikes'. BJIR, May 1970, 8(1):32–54.

3511 Bovill, E.W. 'Captain Swing', *English country life, 1780–1830*, pp.28–45.
      OUP, 1962.

3512 Bowman, D. 'The British Railways Board takes to the air'. LM, Aug.
      1968, 50(8):356–8.

3513 Bowman, D. 'The right to strike'. LM, May 1964, 46(5):207.

3514 Bowman, D. 'The signals go red'. LM, Nov. 1962, 44(11):493–6.
      N.U.R. strike, 3rd Oct. 1962.

3515 Brunner, E. 'The origins of industrial peace: the case of the British book
      and shoe industry'. OEP, June 1949, 1(2):247–59.
      1895 dispute.

3516 Buchan, W. 'Scottish teachers revolt'. NLR, July–Aug. 1961, 10:64–6.

3517 Burgess, K. 'Technological change and the 1852 lock-out in the British
      engineering industry'. IRSH, 1969, 14(2):215–36.

3518 Cameron, G.C. 'Post-war strikes in the north-east shipbuilding and ship-
      repairing industry 1946–61'. BJIR, Mar. 1964, 2(1):1–22.

3519 Campbell, J.R. 'Seamen and the state'. LM, July 1966, 48(7):305–9.

3520 Cavanagh, J. 'The London tally clerks'. TUA, Autumn–Winter 1961,
      4:118–24.

3521 Clarke, R.O. 'The dispute in the British engineering industry 1897–98: an
      evaluation'. E, May 1957, 24(94):128–37.

3522 Clegg, H.A. 'Strikes'. PQ, Jan.–Mar. 1956, 27(1):31–43.

3523 Clegg, H.A. and R. Adams. *The employers' challenge: a study of the national
      shipbuilding and engineering disputes of 1957*. Oxford, Blackwell, 1957. viii,
      179pp.

3524 Coates, K. 'The right to strike'. NLR, Mar.–Apr. 1964, 24:58–61.

3525 Cohen, J. '1919: year of revolt, a brief survey of the British scene 50 years
      ago'. MML, Jan.–Mar. 1969, 49:8–11.

3526 Committee on Trades' Societies. [Report on] *Trades' societies and strikes.* New York, Kelley, 1968 (first pub. 1860). xxiii, 651pp.
    Committee appointed by the National Association for the Promotion of Social Science.

3527 Cottle, P. 'The stone masons of the Law Courts'. MML, Apr.–June 1968, 46:16–18.

3528 Davies, V.E. *The Rebecca riots.* Cardiff, University of Wales Press, 1961. 88pp.
    For 11–13 year–olds. Welsh/English parallel text.

3529 Divine, D. *Mutiny at Invergordon.* Macdonald, 1970. 259pp.

3530 Dutt, R.P. '1. Strike strategy? 2. Class and party'. LM, June 1958, 40(6):241–57.

3531 Dutt, R.P. 'Strikes and votes'. LM, Dec. 1969, 51(12):529–40.

3532 Eldridge, J.E.T. *Industrial disputes: essays in the sociology of industrial relations.* Routledge, 1968. x, 277pp.
    Discusses strikes, shop stewards.

3533 Eldridge, J.E.T. and G.C. Cameron. 'Unofficial strikes: some objections considered'. BJS, Mar. 1964, 15(1):19–37.

3534 Evans, David. *Labour strife in the South Wales coalfield 1910–11: a historical and critical record of the Mid-Rhondda, Aberdare Valley and other strikes.* Cardiff, Cymric Fed. Press, 1963 (first pub. 1911). viii, 257pp.

3535 Forchheimer, K. 'Some international aspects of the strike movement'. OUIS, Jan. 1948, 10(1):9–24.

3536 Forchheimer, K. 'Some international aspects of the strike movement; the results of labour disputes'. OUIS, Sept. 1948, 10(9):294–304.

3537 Forchheimer, K. 'Some international aspects of the strike movement; the effectiveness of large and of long strikes, with a specific reference to Sweden'. OUIS, Sept. 1949, 11(9):279–86.

3538 Galambos, P. and E.W. Evans. 'A reply' [to no.3571]. OUIS, Nov. 1966, 28(4):283–4.

3539 Galambos, P. and E.W. Evans. 'Work stoppages in the United Kingdom, 1951–64: a quantitative study'. OUIS, Feb. 1966, 28(1):33–57.

3540 Gannaway, F. 'Printers, police and picketing'. LM, Sept. 1959, 41(9):397–400.

3541 Gardner, J. 'Why these strikes?'. LM, Jan. 1946, 28(1):23–6.

3542 Glasgow District Trades Council. *Calton Weavers' Memorial 1787: the first recorded industrial strike in the history of Glasgow.* Glasgow, Trades Council, 1957. 12pp.

3543 Golby, J.M. 'Public order and private unrest: a study of the 1842 riots in Shropshire'. BHJ, 1967–8, 11:157–69.

3544 Griffiths, T. *The teachers strike (1969–70)*. National Union of Teachers, 1970. 29pp.

3545 Hannington, W. 'Industrial revolt'. LM, Apr. 1951, 33(4):166–71.

3546 Hardy, G. 'Seamen's struggles'. LM, Oct. 1960, 42(10):464–7. 1911 and 1925.

3547 Henderson, S. 'The dockers and Mr. Deakin'. LM, Dec. 1954, 36(12):554–8.

3548 Hikins, H.R. 'The Liverpool General Transport Strike 1911'. HSLC, 1962, 113:169–95.

3549 Hinton, J. *Unions and strikes*. Sheed and Ward, 1968. 64pp.

3550 Hobsbawm, E.J. and G. Rudé. *Captain Swing*. Lawrence and Wishart, 1969. 384pp.
     See no.3590.

3551 Hodgins, C. and J. Prescott. *Not wanted on voyage: the seamen's reply, June 1966*. Hull, National Union of Seamen, Hull Dispute Committee, 1966. 21pp.

3552 Horn, P. 'The Evenley strike in 1867'. NPP, 1966–7, 4(1):47–50.

3553 Horner, A.L. 'The right to strike'. LM, Aug. 1955, 37(8):352–4.

3554 Hughes, J. 'The rise of the militants'. TUA, Winter 1960–1, 1:45–57.

3555 Humberstone, T.L. *"Battle of Trafalgar Square"*. Ridgill Trout, 1948. 24pp. Commemorative pamphlet for Bloody Sunday. Short biographies of R.B. Cunninghame Graham and John Burns.

3556 Hunt, C.J. 'Strikes and industrial disturbances', *The lead miners of the Northern Pennines in the eighteenth and nineteenth centuries*, pp.122–37. Manchester, University Press, 1970.

3557 Industrial Research and Information Services Ltd. *Darkness over dockland: an assessment of the London and Liverpool dock strikes*. I.R.I.S., 1967. 27pp.

3558 Industrial Research and Information Services Ltd. *Mischief on the building sites (Cameron Inquiry into disputes on Barbican and Horseferry Road sites)*. I.R.I.S., 1967. 32pp.

3559 Industrial Research and Information Services Ltd. *Strikes in Britain*. I.R.I.S., 1968. 24pp.

3560 Jackson, T.A. 'The socialists—and the riots of 1866–7', *Trials of British freedom: being some studies in the history of the fight for democratic freedom in Britain*, pp.165–72 (*see* no.1193). Lawrence and Wishart 1945.

3561 Jenkins, C. 'BOAC: the anatomy of a strike: political interference in a nationalised industry'. ULR, Spring 1959, 1(6):30–4.

3562 Jenkins, H. 'The Equity strike'. TUA, Summer 1962, 5:31–41.

3563 Jones, D.J.V. 'The Carmarthen riots of 1831'. WH, Dec. 1968, 4(2):129–42.

3564 Jones, D.J.V. 'Law enforcement and popular disturbances in Wales 1793–1835'. JMH, Dec. 1970, 42(4):496–523.

3565 Jones, D.J.V. 'The Merthyr riots of 1800: a study in attitudes'. BCS, May 1969, 23(2):166–79.

3566 Jones, D.J.V. 'The Merthyr riots of 1831'. WH, Dec. 1966, 3(2):173–205.

3567 Kay, H. 'The seamen's strike'. M, July–Aug. 1966, 36(1/2):34–9.

3568 Knowles, K.G.J.C. 'The post-war dock strikes'. PQ, July–Sept. 1951, 22(3):266–90.

3569 Knowles, K.G.J.C. 'Strike-proneness and its determinants'. AJS, Nov. 1954, 60(3):213–29.

3570 Knowles, K.G.J.C. *Strikes, a study in industrial conflict: with special reference to British experience between 1911 and 1947.* Oxford, Blackwell, 1952. xiv, 330pp.

3571 Knowles, K.G.J.C. 'Work stoppages in the United Kingdom: a comment'. OUIS, Feb. 1966, 28(1):59–62.
     See no.3538.

3572 Lloyd, E. 'How we began the fight'. LM, Apr. 1952, 34(4):159–63.
     South Wales mineworkers.

3573 McCarthy, W.E.J. 'The nature of Britain's strike problem. A re-assessment of arguments in the Donovan Report and a reply to H.A. Turner'. BJIR, July 1970, 8(2):224–36.
     See no.3610.

3574 McCarthy, W.E.J. 'The reasons given for striking: an analysis of official statistics, 1945–1957'. OUIS, Feb. 1959, 21(1):17–29.

3575 McCord, N. 'The seamen's strike of 1815 in north-east England'. ECHR, Apr. 1968, 21(1):127–43.

3576 McCord, N. and D.E. Brewster. 'Some labour troubles of the 1790's in north-east England'. IRSH, 1968, 13(3):366–83.

3577 McKelvey, J.T. *Dock labor disputes in Great Britain: a study in the persistence of industrial unrest.* New York, Cornell University, New York State School of Industrial and Labor Relations, 1953. vi, 61pp.

3578 McLaren, D. 'My first strike'. LM, Oct. 1960, 42(10):467–9.

3579 Mahon, J. 'Lessons of the dispute'. LM, Oct. 1959, 41(10):458–63.
     Printers' seven weeks' strike.

3580 Mahon, J. and D. Goodwin. 'London, the battlefield'. LM, July 1958, 40(7):320–5.
     Busmen's strike, May–June.

3581 Methane, D.C.F., *pseud.* 'Inside the Frigidaire strike'. TUA, Spring 1961, 2:65–76.

3582 Michaelson, D.A. 'The right to strike'. LM, Jan. 1951, 33(1):33–6.

3583 Micklewright, F.H.A. 'From within the teachers' strike'. LM, Feb. 1970, 52(2):87–90.

3584 Midwinter, E.C. *Law and order in early Victorian Lancashire*. York, St. Anthony's Press, 1968. 42pp.

3585 Oram, R.B. 'The Great Strike of 1889: the fight for the "Dockers' Tanner"'. HT, Aug. 1964, 14(8):532–41.

3586 Parsons, O.H. *The Donovan Report: trade unions, strikes and negotiations*. Labour Research Department, 1968. 24pp.

3587 Parsons, O.H. *Strikes and trade unions: Government White Paper explained*. Labour Research Department, 1969. 20pp.

3588 Pattison, G. 'The coopers' strike at the West India Dock, 1821'. MM, May 1969, 55(2):163–84.

3589 Peacock, A.J. *Bread or blood: a study of the agrarian riots in East Anglia in 1816*. Foreword by E.P. Thompson. Gollancz, 1964. 191pp.

3590 Peacock, A.J. 'Review of Captain Swing'. SSLH, Spring 1969, 18:64–6.
    Review of no.3550.

3591 Pencavel, J.H. 'An investigation into industrial strike activity in Britain'. E, Aug. 1970, 37(147):239–56.

3592 Phelan, S. 'This strike was unofficial'. LM, Dec. 1959, 41(12):541–3.
    Railway restaurant car staff's strike.

3593 Porter, J.H. 'The Northampton Arbitration Board and the shoe industry dispute of 1887'. NPP, 1968–9, 4(3):149–54.

3594 Pritt, D.N. 'The right to strike'. LM, July 1951, 33(7):301–10.

3595 Quaestor, *pseud*. 'What means this strike?'. LM, Aug. 1949, 31(8):255–231.
    London dock strike, July 1949.

3596 Reynolds, G.W. and A. Judge. *The night the police went on strike*. Weidenfeld, ?1968. 246pp.
    1918 strike, its aftermath and the case of John Syme.

3597 Robson, H.H. 'The papers of Henry Havelock Robson (1858–1929)—Durham colliery engineman'. NEG, Oct. 1969, 3:27–33.
    Contemporary account by a branch secretary of one of the unions involved in the Durham coal lock-out of 1892.

3598 Rose, A.G. 'The Plug Riots of 1842 in Lancashire and Cheshire'. LCAS, 1957, 67:75–112.

3599 Rowe, D.J. 'The strikes of the Tyneside Keelmen in 1809 and 1819'. IRSH, 1968, 13(1):58–75.

3600 Rudé, G. 'The study of popular disturbances in the "pre-industrial" age'. HS, May 1963, 10(40):457–69.

3600a Rudé, G. 'Captain Swing' and 'Rebecca's daughter', *The crowd in history: a study of popular disturbances in France and England. 1730–1848*, pp.149–63. New York, John Wiley, 1964.

3601 Singleton, F. 'Captain Swing in East Anglia'. SSLH, Spring 1964, 8:13–15.

3602 Sires, R.V. 'Labour unrest in England, 1910–14'. JEH, Sept. 1955, 15(3):246–66.

3603 Slaughter, C. 'The strike of the Yorkshire mineworkers in May 1955'. SOCR, Dec. 1958, 6(2):241–59.

3604 Smith, H.L. and V. Nash. *The story of the dockers' strike, told by two East Londoners*. Bath, Chivers, 1970 (first pub. 1889). 190pp.

3605 Stafford, A. *A match to fire the Thames*. Hodder, 1961. 219pp.
    Match girls' strike of 1888 and dock strike of 1889.

3606 Swann, J.M. 'A sequel to the shoe industry dispute of 1887'. NPP, 1969–70, 4(4):247–8.

3607 Tuckett, A. 'Press Lords and strikes'. LM, May 1955, 37(5):224–9.

3608 Turner, G. *The car makers*. Penguin, 1964. 270pp.

3609 Turner, H.A. 'The Crossley strike'. MS, Sept. 1950, 18(3):179–216.

3610 Turner, H.A. *Is Britain really strike-prone? A review of the incidence, character and costs of industrial conflict*. CUP, 1969. 48pp.
    See no.3573.

3611 Turner, H.A. *The trend of strikes*. Leeds, University Press, 1963. 21pp.

3612 Turner, H.A. and J. Bescoby, 'Strikes, redundancy and the demand cycle in the motor car industry'. OUIS, May 1961, 23(2):179–85.

3613 Wedderburn, K.W. 'Intimidation and the right to strike'. MLR, May 1964, 27(3):257–81.

3614 Wedderburn, K.W. 'The right to threaten strikes'. MLR, Sept. 1961, 24(5):572–91.

3615 Wedderburn, K.W. 'The right to threaten strikes—2'. MLR, Sept. 1962, 25(5):513–30.

3616 Weller, K. and E. Stanton. *What happened at Fords*. Solidarity, 1967. 27pp.

3617 Wellisz, S. 'Strikes in coal-mining'. BJS, Dec. 1953, 4(4):346–66.

3618 Whiteley, R. 'Lock-out, 1967'. LM, July 1967, 49(7):322–4.
    Shipbuilding Employers Federation.

3619 Williams, D. *The Rebecca Riots: a study in agrarian discontent*. Cardiff, University of Wales Press, 1955. xi, 377pp.

3620 Williams, G.A. 'The Merthyr riots: settling the account'. NLW, Winter 1959, 11(2):124–41.

3621 Wright, R.W. 'Dollar dispute: Roberts Arundel, Stockport'. LM, Aug. 1967, 49(8):374–5.

The General Strike

I GENERAL

3622 Arnot, R.P. 'The General Strike, 1926'. LM, May 1956, 38(5):215–21.

3623 Brown, T. *The British General Strike*. Syndicalist Workers Federation, 1961 (first pub. 1942). 15pp.

3624 Brown, T. *The social General Strike*. A.F.B. [i.e. Anarchist Federation of Britain], 1948. 15pp.

3625 Bull, T. 'The theory of the General Strike'. SP, Autumn 1968, 4:13–15.

3626 Cantor, N.F. 'The General Strike in Britain', *The age of protest: dissent and rebellion in the twentieth century*, pp.89–106. Allen and Unwin, 1970.

3627 Citrine, Lord. *Men and work*, pp.129–219 [Vol. 1 of autobiography]. Hutchinson, 1964.
General Strike when Lord Citrine was Secretary of the T.U.C.

3628 Clegg, H.A. 'Some consequences of the General Strike'. MSS, Jan. 1954, 1953–54:1–29.

3629 Cootes, R.J. *The General Strike (1926)*. Longmans, 1966. ix, 85pp.

3630 Crook, W.H. *Communism and the General Strike*. Hamden, Connecticut, Shoe String Press, 1960. xiii, 483pp.

3631 Graves, R. and A. Hodge. 'Revolution again averted, 1926', *The long week-end: a social history of Great Britain 1918–1939*, pp.150–70. Allen and Unwin, 1950 (first pub. 1940).

3632 Hughes, M., comp. *Cartoons from the General Strike*. Evelyn, Adams and Mackay, 1968. 72pp.

3633 James, R.R., ed. 'The General Strike 1926', *Memoirs of a Conservative, J.C.C. Davidson's memoirs and papers, 1910–37*, pp.226–61. Weidenfeld, 1969.

3634 Klugman, J. *History of the Communist Party of Great Britain: Vol. 2, 1925–7: The General Strike*. Lawrence and Wishart, 1969. 373pp.
See no.3638.

3635 Labour Monthly. 'A council of action—40 years ago'. LM, June 1966, 48(6):269–71.

3636 Labour Monthly. 'General Strike, May 1926'. LM, May 1966, 48(5):215–18.

3637 Labour Monthly. 'Memory of the General Strike'. LM, June 1951, 33(6):277–83.
Selections from Labour Monthly June 1926.

3638 Mason, A. 'The General Strike'. SSLH, Spring 1970, 20:45–9.
Review of no.3634.

3639 Mason, A. 'The government and the General Strike, 1926'. IRSH, 1969, 14(1):1–21.

3640 Millar, J.P.M. 'The 1926 General Strike and the N.C.L.C.'. SSLH, Spring 1970, 20:41–5.

3641 Montgomery, J. 'The General Strike', *The twenties*, pp.138–49. Allen and Unwin, 1970.

3642 Mortimer, J.E. '13 days that produced The British Worker'. TUA, Summer 1961, 3:72–81.

3643 Mowat, C.L. 'Dead centre: the General Strike and after, 1925–1929', *Britain between the wars 1918–1940*, pp.284–352. Methuen, 1968 (first pub. 1955).

3644 Mowat, C.L. *The General Strike, 1926*. Arnold, 1969. 64pp.

3645 Murray, J. *The General Strike of 1926: a history*. Lawrence and Wishart, 1951. 208pp.

3646 Shefftz, M.C. 'The Trades Disputes and Trade Union Act of 1927: the aftermath of the General Strike'. RP, July 1967, 29(3):387–406.

3647 Sitwell, O. 'The General Strike', *Laughter in the next room: being the fourth volume of Left hand, right hand!*, pp.199–243. Macmillan, 1949.

3648 Stalin, J.V. 'The General Strike, 1926. 1'. LM, Apr. 1953, 35(4):169–74.

3649 Stalin, J.V. 'The General Strike, 1926. 2'. LM, May 1953, 35(5):232–4. Speech of 8th June 1926.

3650 Symons, J. *The General Strike: a historical portrait*. Cresset Press, 1957. xi, 259pp.

II LOCAL STUDIES

3651 Baines, D.E. and R. Bean. 'The General Strike on Merseyside, 1926', *Liverpool and Merseyside: essays in the economy and social history of the port and its hinterland*, pp.239–75. Edited by J.E. Harris. Cass, 1969.

3652 Communist Party. History Group. 'The General Strike in the north-east'. OH, Summer 1961, 22:19pp.

3653 Feeney, J. 'General Strike in Middlesbrough'. NEG, Oct. 1970, 4:22–4.

3654 Hyman, R. *Oxford workers in the Great Strike*. Oxford, Centre for Socialist Education, Oxford Branch, 1966. 8pp.

3655 Leonard, J.W. 'The North Eastern Daily Gazette and the General Strike'. NEG, Oct. 1970, 4:19–22.

3656 Mason, A. *The General Strike in the north east*. Hull, The University, 1970. vi, 116pp.

3657 Mason, A. 'The General Strike on Teesside'. NEG, Oct. 1970, 4:17–19.

3658 Peck, J.A. *The miners' strike in South Yorkshire, 1926.* Sheffield, University Institute of Education, 1970. 28pp.

3659 Stephenson, J. 'General Strike in Middlesbrough'. NEG, Oct. 1970, 4:25–32.

Trades councils

3660 Barnsby, G. *The origins of the Wolverhampton Trades Council.* Wolverhampton, Bilston and District Trades Council, 1965. 16pp.
Cover title: 1865—Centenary year—1965.

3661 Bather, L. 'Manchester and Salford Trades Council from 1880'. SSLH, Spring 1963, 6:13–16.

3662 Birch, A.H. 'Glossop Trades Council', *Small-town politics: a study of political life in Glossop*, pp.169–75. OUP, 1959.

3663 Bolton and District United Trades Council. *Centenary brochure and directory: 1866–1966.* Bolton, Trades Council, 1966. 43pp.

3664 Brighton, Hove and District Trades Council. *The history of 60 years: 1890–1950.* Brighton, Trades Council, 1950. 19pp.

3665 Clinton, A. 'Trades Councils during the First World War'. IRSH, 1970, 15(2):202–34.

3666 Corbett, J. *The Birmingham Trades Council 1866–1966.* Lawrence and Wishart, 1966, 192pp. (*see* no.3683).

3667 Fraser, W.H. 'Edinburgh Trades Council Minutes 1859–1873'. SSLH, Autumn 1969, 19:35–9.
Review of no.3674.

3668 Fraser, W.H. 'Scottish trades councils in the nineteenth century'. SSLH, Spring 1967, 14:11.

3669 Grant, B. 'Trades Councils 1860–1914'. LHN, Summer 1957, 3(4):160–5.

3670 Hall, P.P. *Seventy-five years of achievement: the history of the Blackpool Trades Council 1891–1966.* Blackpool, Trades Council, 1966. 108pp.

3671 Hall, P.P. *Sixty years of achievement: the history of the Blackpool Trades Council 1891–1951.* Blackpool, Trades Council, 1951. 116pp.

3672 Hamling, W. *A short history of the Liverpool Trades' Council 1848–1948.* Liverpool, Trades Council and Labour Party, ?1948. 47pp.

3673 Johnston, J. 'Glasgow's Trades Council and the Polaris base'. TUA, Summer 1961, 3:54–60.

3674 MacDougall, I., ed. *The minutes of the Edinburgh Trades Council 1859–1873*. Edinburgh, Scottish Historical Society, 1968. xliv, 412pp.
See no.3667.

3675 MacKinven, H. *Edinburgh and District Trades Council Centenary 1859–1959*. Edinburgh, the Trades Council, 1959.
92nd Annual Report for the year ending 31st December 1958, pp.25–64.

3676 McShane, H. *Glasgow District Trades Council. Centenary brochure 1858–1958: a hundred years of progress*. Foreword by Emanuel Shinwell. Glasgow, District Trades Council, 1958. 41pp.

3677 Mendelson, J. and others. *Sheffield Trades and Labour Council 1858 to 1958*. Sheffield, Trades and Labour Council, 1958. 105pp.
Other contributors: Wm. Owen, Sidney Pollard, V.M. Thornes.

3678 Oldham Trades and Labour Council. *Centenary 1867–1967*. Oldham, Trades Council, ?1967. 80pp.

3679 Peterborough and District Trades Council. *Diamond jubilee 1899–1959*. Peterborough, Trades Council, ?1959. 24pp.

3680 Pontypridd Trades Council and Labour Party. *Action, struggle, achievement: a history of the Labour Party and trade union movement in Pontypridd, compiled from the minute books*. Pontypridd, Trades Council and Labour Party, ?1948. 56pp.
1898–1948.

3681 Pope, R. and F.W.A. Skerritt. *Struggle: Ipswich and District Trades Council 1885–1969*. Ipswich, Trades Council, 1969. iv, 43pp.

3682 Rawtenstall Borough Trades' Council. *50th anniversary (1902–1952)*. Rawtenstall, Trades Council, 1952, 35pp.

3683 Saville, J. 'Trades Councils and the Labour movement to 1900'. SSLH, Spring 1967, 14:29–34.
Review of no.3666 and an unpublished thesis, 'The Labour movement in Hull, 1870–1900', by Raymond Brown.

3684 Stonelake, E. *Aberdare Trades and Labour Council. Jubilee souvenir 1900–1950*. Aberdare, Trades and Labour Council, ?1950. 28pp.

3685 Tate, G. *London Trades Council, 1850–1950: a history*. Lawrence and Wishart for the London Trades Council, 1950. viii, 160pp.

3686 Williams, G.M. *London Trades Council 1860–1960: a hundred years of protest and progress*. Trades Council, 1960. 32pp.

Co-operation

The Co-operative movement

3687 Allen, A. *The co-operative story*. Manchester, Co-operative Union, 1953. 69pp.
For young readers.

3688 Bailey, J. *The British co-operative movement*. Hutchinson, 1960. 180pp.

3689 Bailey, J. *The co-operative movement*. Labour Party, 1952. 31pp.

3690 Banks, J.A. and G.N. Ostergaard. *Co-operative democracy: a study of the democratic process in certain retail co-operative societies*. Loughborough, Co-operative Union, 1955. 72pp.

3691 Barou, N., ed. *The co-operative movement in Labour Britain*. Gollancz, 1948. 143pp.

3692 Bonner, A. *British co-operation: the history, principles and organisation of the British co-operative movement*. Manchester, Co-operative Union, 1961. vii, 540pp.

3693 Bonner, A. *Lessons of Rochdale co-operation*. London Co-operative Society, 1945. 33pp.

3694 Carberry, T.F. *Consumers in politics: a history and general review of the Co-operative Party*. Manchester, University Press, 1969. vii, 276pp.

3695 Cole, G.D.H. *The British co-operative movement in a socialist society*. Allen and Unwin, 1951. 168pp.
Written for the Fabian Society.

3696 Cole, G.D.H. *A century of co-operation*. Allen and Unwin for the Co-operative Union, 1947. viii, 428pp.

3697 Cole, G.D.H. *The Co-ops and Labour*. London Co-operative Society Education Committee, 1945. 24pp.

3698 Co-operative Union. *Co-operative Party Report to the Annual Conference, 1945–*. Co-operative Union for the Co-operative Party, 1945–.

3699 Co-operative Union. *Report of the annual Co-operative Congress, 1945–*. Co-operative Union, 1945–.

3700 Digby, M. *Co-operation: what it means and how it works*. Longmans, Green, 1947. 96pp.

3701 Digby, M. 'Co-operation in Great Britain', *Essays in Jewish sociology, Labour and co-operation in memory of Dr. Noah Barou 1889–1955*, pp.139–50. Edited by H.F. Infield, Yoseloff, 1962.

3702 Dodds, E. 'The Co-op Commission' [Hugh Gaitskell report]. LM, Oct. 1958, 40(10):470–2.

3703 Dunman, J. 'Consumers' co-operatives and the future'. LM, Oct. 1970, 52(10):458–62.

3704 Flanagan, D. *1869–1969: a centenary story of the Co-operative Union of Great Britain and Ireland*. Manchester, Co-operative Union, 1969. viii, 152pp.

3705 Greer, P. *Co-operatives: the British achievement*. New York, Harper, 1955. xv, 171pp.

3706 Groombridge, B. *The future of auxiliaries: a postscript*. Loughborough, Co-operative Union, 1963. 50pp.

3707 Lazell, D. *Consumers and the community: a study guide on the application of the Rochdale principles to modern consumer problems*. Loughborough, Co-operative Union, Education Dept., 1961. v, 34pp.

3708 Leonard, R.L. 'The Co-ops in politics', *The left: a symposium*, pp.51–73 (*see* no.2595). Edited by G. Kaufman. Blond, 1966.

3709 MacKenzie, W.J.M. and C. Arditti. 'Co-operative politics in a Lancashire constituency'. PS, June 1954, 2(2):112–27.

3710 Marx Memorial Library. Quarterly Bulletin. 'Early co-operative societies and early trades unions'. MML, Oct.–Dec. 1958, 8:8–11.

3711 Musson, A.E. 'The ideology of early co-operation in Lancashire and Cheshire'. LCAS for 1958, 68(1959):117–38.

3712 Oliver, W.H. 'The Labour exchange phase of the co-operative movement'. OEP, Oct. 1958, 10(3):355–67.

3713 Ostergaard, G.N. 'Parties in co-operative government'. PS, Oct. 1958, 6(3):197–219.

3714 Ostergaard, G.N. and A.N. Halsey. *Power in co-operatives: a study of the internal politics in British retail societies*. Oxford, Blackwell, 1965. xvi, 249pp.

3715 Parkinson, C.N. 'The co-operative movement', *Left luggage: from Marx to Wilson*, pp.175–82. Murray, 1967.

3716 Pollard, S. *The co-operatives at the crossroads*. Fabian Society, 1965. 44pp.

3717 Pollard, S. 'Nineteenth-century co-operation: from community building to shopkeeping', *Essays in Labour history*, pp.74–112 (*see* no.1179). Edited by A. Briggs and J. Saville. Macmillan, 1960.

3718 Reeves, J. 'The co-operatives at the crossroads'. LM, Oct. 1956, 38(10):465–9.

3719 Rhodes, G.W. *Co-operative-Labour relations 1900–62*. Loughborough, Co-operative Union, 1962. 122pp.

3720 Royal Arsenal Co-operative Society. *The co-operative way*. The Society, 1956. 64pp.

3721 Shea, P. *'Times past': paragraphs on the history of the Co-operative Party*. Co-operative Union, 1955. 40pp.

3722 Smith, B. and G.N. Ostergaard. *Constitutional relations between the Labour and Co-operative parties: an historical review*. Hansard Society, 1960. 32pp.

3723 Stephenson, T.E. 'The role of principles in a democratic organisation'. PS, Oct. 1964, 12(3):327–40.

3724 Topham, E. and J.A. Hough. *The co-operative movement in Britain*. Longmans for the British Council, 1948. 52pp.

3725 Youngjohns, B.J. *Co-operation and the state 1814–1914*. Loughborough, Co-operative Union, Education Dept., 1954. 72pp.

Co-operative society histories

3726 Ammanford Co-operative Society. *Fifty years of service and progress; jubilee souvenir, 1900–1950*. Ammanford, The Society, 1950. 37pp.

3727 Bacup Co-operative Society. *100 years of co-operation*. Bacup, The Society, 1947. 24pp.
   Cover title: Centenary 1847–1947. Souvenir programme.

3728 Barnie, D. *Seventy five years' co-operation in Oxford and district*. Reading, C.W.S., 1947. 36pp.
   1872–1947.

3729 Barnsley British Co-operative Society. [Cover title] *A century of service 1862–1962*. Manchester, C.P.S., 1962. 42pp.

3730 Barnsley British Co-operative Society. [Cover title] *Souvenir brochure of ninety years of progress . . . 1862–1952*. 1952. 14pp.

3731 Bennett, I.G., ed. *Centenary year: Cramlington District Co-operative Society: 1861–1961*. Manchester, C.P.S., 1961. 32pp.

3732 Berry, T.C. *A century of co-operation*. Prestwich, The Society, 1961. 32pp.
   Cover title: Centenary year 1861–1961: Prestwich Co-operative Society.

3733 Bishop Auckland Co-operative Society. *Into the second century, Bishop Auckland Co-operative Centenary, May 26th 1960*. Manchester, C.P.S., 1960. i, 25pp.
   1860–1960.

3734 Bolton Co-operative Society. *Into the second century*. Bolton, The Society, 1959. 26pp.

3735 Bonner, A. *The Rochdale Equitable Pioneers' Society: an illustrated souvenir.* Manchester, Co-operative Union, 1967. 32pp.

3736 Boydell, D. *Centenary story: a hundred years of co-operation in Derby.* Manchester, Co-operative Press, 1950. 125pp.

3737 Bozeat Co-operative Society. *A century of co-operation in Bozeat.* Wallaston, The Society, 1964. 8pp.
    1864–1964.

3738 Brelstaff, W.D. *Seventy-five years: a brief history of the Guisborough Provident Industrial Society.* Pelaw-on-Tyne, The Society, 1948. 27 leaves.
    1873–1948.

3739 Briscoe, R. *Centenary history: a hundred years of co-operation in Plymouth.* Manchester, Co-operative Press, 1960. 176pp.
    1860–1960.

3740 Brown, W.H. *Eastleigh co-operation: on the permanent way 1892–1948.* Eastleigh, The Society, 1949. vi, 54pp.

3741 Brown, W.H. *Hepworth's hundred years of co-operative adventure.* Hepworth, Hepworth Industrial Society, 1948. 59pp.

3742 Brown, W.H. *Heywood's co-operative centenary 1850–1950.* Heywood, Heywood Industrial Co-operative Society, 1950. 63pp.

3743 Brown, W.H. *Mansfield's co-operative advance 1864–1950.* Mansfield, Mansfield, Sutton and District Co-operative Society, 1950. 78pp.

3744 Brown, W.H. *Newmarket's co-operative jubilee history 1899–1949.* Newmarket, Newmarket Co-operative Society, 1949. 38pp.

3745 Brown, W.H. *Winchester's co-operative golden jubilee 1900–1950.* Winchester, Winchester and District Industrial Co-operative Society, 1950. 71pp.

3746 Bury District Co-operative Society. *Centenary 1856–1956.* Bury, The Society, 1956. 14pp.

3747 Cainscross and Ebley Co-operative Society. *A century of service, 1863–1963.* Manchester, C.P.S., 1963. 18pp.

3748 Cairns, A. G. *The co-operative movement in Blairgowrie and district.* Blairgowrie, The Society, 1967. 39pp.

3749 Calthorpe, W.W., A.M. Smith and W. Law. *100 UP! Centenary history of Colchester and East Essex Co-operative Society.* Reading, C.W.S., 1961. 48pp.
    1861–1961.

3750 Carluke Co-operative Society. *History of the Carluke Co-operative Society Ltd.: a souvenir of the celebration of the 100th anniversary of the founding of the Society, 1862–1962.* Carluke, The Society, 1962. 24pp.

3751 Cefn and District Co-operative Society. *Jubilee souvenir 1901–1951.* Rhosymedre, Wrexham, The Society, 1951. 13pp.

3752 Chelmsford Star Co-operative Industrial Society. *Century star: the story of the Chelmsford Star Co-operative Industrial Society Ltd.* Chelmsford, The Society, 1967. 32pp.
  1867–1967.

3753 Close Hill Industrial and Provident Co-operative Society. *A century of co-operative endeavour 1847–1947.* Close Hill, The Society, 1947. 30pp.

3754 Codd, L. *Acorn to oak—a short history of Guildford and District Co-operative Society.* Guildford, The Society, 1948. 22pp.

3755 Cowlairs Co-operative Society. *75th anniversary: Cowlairs Co-operative Society Ltd.: a short history of seventy five years of service and progress, 1881–1956.* Cowlairs, The Society, 1956. 32pp.

3756 Failsworth Industrial Co-operative Society. *Centenary 1859–1959.* Manchester, The Society, 1959. 24pp.

3757 Flanagan, D. *Centenary souvenir of Middleton and Tonge Industrial Society: 1850–1950.* Middleton, The Society, 1950. 24pp.

3758 Flanagan, D. *Co-operation in Halifax.* Halifax, The Society, 1951. 24pp.
  Cover title: Path of progress; Halifax Co-operative Society centenary, 1851–1951.

3759 Flanagan, D. *Something to remember; our centenary of co-operation 1856–1956.* Brighouse, The Society, 1956. 16pp.

3760 Flanagan, D. *Triumph at Leek: the centenary story of Leek and Moorlands Co-operative Society.* Manchester, C.W.S., 1959. 18pp.
  1859–1959.

3761 Gibbs, T.D. and A. Cooper, comps. *The history of the Runcorn and Widnes Co-operative Society Ltd.* Runcorn, The Society, 1962. 20pp.
  1862–1962.

3762 Gloucester Co-operative Industrial Society. *The history 1860 to 1960.* Manchester, C.P.S., 1960. 23pp.

3763 Gordon, T.C. *History of Alva Co-operative Bazaar Society Ltd.* Alva, The Society, 1948. viii, 112pp.

3764 Gorlas Co-operative Society Ltd. *1909–1959: fifty years of service and progress.* Gorlas, Llanelli, The Society, 1959. 20pp.

3765 Gregory, N.H. *A century's progress: 100 years of co-operation in Hebden Bridge.* Todmorden, Bentley, 1948. 24pp.

3766 Gregory, N.H. *A century's progress; one hundred years of co-operation in Littleborough.* Littleborough, The Society, 1950. 28pp.
  Littleborough Co-operative Society of Industry Ltd., 1850–1950.

3767 Hazell, W. *The gleaming vision: being the history of the Ynysbwl Co-operative Society, 1889–1954.* Pontypridd, The Society, 1954. 156pp.

3768 Hazell, W. *Jubilee time in Tredegar: 1901–1951*. Tredegar, The Society, 1951. 40pp.
Tredegar Industrial and Provident Society.

3769 Hendry, K.A. *St. Blazey and District Co-operative Society. 100th balance sheet and extracts from the early history of the Society, 1902–1952*. Reading, C.W.S., 1952. 20pp.

3770 Hill, C., comp. *One hundred years of progress. 1864–1964*. Airedale, The Society, 1964. 12pp.
Airedale Co-operative Society.

3771 Hill, T. *Rise and progress of Newmilns Co-operative Society, 1856—1956*. Newmilns, The Society, 1956. 24pp.

3772 Hobson, W.G. *One hundred years of village co-operation, 1856–1956*. Greenfield, The Society, 1957. 56pp.
Greenfield Co-operative Society.

3773 Hodgkinson, A.E. *The great adventure*. Halstead, Halstead Industrial Co-operative Society, 1960. 63pp.

3774 Hulse, K. *A century of service 1867–1967*. Coventry, The Society, 1967. 51pp.
Coventry and District Co-operative Society.

3775 Hunt, W.D. *The story of the century 1861–1961: Dunfermline Co-operative Society Ltd*. Dunfermline, The Society, 1961. 61pp.

3776 Hyde, H. *Co-operation in the peaceful valley, 1860–1960*. Manchester, CP.S., 1960. 25pp.
Darwen Industrial Co-operative Society.

3777 Ipswich Co-operative Society. *A history of East Anglia's largest retailers*. Reading, C.W.S., 1968. 32pp.
1868–1968: a century of service; the success story of Ipswich Co-operative Society.

3778 Jones, B.I., ed. *Taibach and Port Talbot Co-operative Society: jubilee 1902–1952*. Stockport, C.W.S., 1952. 40pp.

3779 Jones, P., comp. *Co-operative story at Stalybridge: 100 years of progress*. Manchester, C.P.S., 1959. 26pp.
Stalybridge Good Intent Industrial Co-operative Society 1859–1959.

3780 Keighley and Skipton District Co-operative Society. *A century of co-operation in Keighley 1860–1960*. Keighley, The Society, 1960. 11pp.

3781 Kilnhurst Co-operative Society. *Centenary handbook and souvenir: 1860–1960*. Kilnhurst, The Society, 1960. 16pp.

3782 Lambert, A.E., comp. *Ashton-under-Lyne Working Men's Co-operative Society Ltd.: Centenary, 1857–1957*. Ashton, The Society, 1957. 33pp.

3783 Laws, H. *Forty years with the Co-op: recollections and reflections*. Southampton, The Society, 1948. 119pp.
Southampton Co-operative Society.

3784 Lawson, W.E. *A history of Clydebank Co-operative Society Ltd.* Glasgow, S.C.W.S., 1948. 106pp.

3785 Lawson, W.E. *One hundred years of co-operation: the history of the St. Cuthbert's Co-operative Association 1859–1959.* Manchester, Co-operative Press, 1959. vii, 71pp.

3786 Leach, C. *Decision and destiny: the story of one hundred years of co-operation in Warrington.* Warrington, C.W.S., 1960. 80pp.
   Warrington Co-operative Society, 1860–1960.

3787 Leeman, F.W. *Co-operation in Nottingham: a history of one hundred years of Nottingham Co-operative Society.* Nottingham, The Society, 1963. xiii, 176pp.

3788 Lockwood, A. *Co-operation in the Thames Valley.* Reading, C.W.S., 1949. 134pp.
   Reading Industrial Co-operative Society.

3789 McAlpine, D. *A hundred years of service: a history of Portobello Co-operative Society Ltd., 1864–1964.* Glasgow, S.C.W.S., 1964. 32pp.

3790 MacAskill, J. *A century of co-operation 1860–1960.* Stafford, Stafford and Stone Co-operative Society, 1960. 40pp.

3791 McWhirter, J. *History of the Barrhead Co-operative Society Ltd. 1861–1961.* Barrhead, The Society, 1962. 88pp.
   Vol. III, *The Long View, 1937–1961* (previous vols. pub. 1911 and 1937).

3792 Marshall, S. *History of co-operative development (Hull and district).* Manchester, Co-operative Press, 1951. 146pp.

3793 Martin, G. *Ninety not out: the history of the Uddingston Co-operative Society, 1861–1951.* Uddingston, The Society, 1952. 62pp.

3794 Newbiggin District Industrial and Provident Society. *One hundred years of co-operation, 1863–1963.* Pelaw-on-Tyne, The Society, 1963. 32pp.

3795 North Shields Co-operative Society Ltd. *Into the second century.* Manchester, Co-operative Press, 1960. 30pp.

3796 Oldham Equitable Co-operative Society Ltd. *and* Oldham Industrial Co-operative Society Ltd. *Co-operation in Oldham, 1850–1950: souvenir of the centenary of the Equitable and Industrial Co-operative Societies.* Manchester, C.W.S. Publications Dept., 1950. 64pp.

3797 Parkstone and Bournemouth Co-operative Society. *Greetings and good wishes to the delegates to the International Co-operative Alliance Congress, Bournemouth 1963; a brief sketch of Parkstone and Bournemouth Co-operative Society Ltd.* Bournemouth, The Society, 1963. 16pp.

3798 Pendleton Co-operative and Industrial Society. *Pendleton's Pride: 100 years of progress 1860–1960: commemorative booklet.* Manchester, The Society, 1960. 26pp.

3799 Peters, J. and others. *Dalton-in-Furness Co-operative Society, 1861–1961: 100 years of progress.* Dalton-in-Furness, The Society, 1961. 9pp.

3800 Port Glasgow United Co-operative Society Ltd. *Co-operation in Port Glasgow.* Glasgow, The Society, 1961. 8pp.
    Centenary brochure 1861–1961.

3801 Ripley Co-operative Society Ltd. *Centenary 1860–1960: a hundred years of progress.* Manchester, 1960. 24pp.

3802 Royton Industrial Co-operative Society Ltd. *Co-operative story at Royton: a hundred years of progress, 1857–1957.* Manchester, C.P.S., 1957. 16pp.

3803 Rugby Industrial and Provident Co-operative Society. *The history 1862 to 1962.* Manchester, 1962. 27pp.

3804 Russell, M.J. *The development of Enfield Highway Co-operative Society 1945–1955, with special reference to employment of capital.* The Society, 1958. 62pp.

3805 St. Albans Co-operative Society Ltd. *Jubilee souvenir, 1902–1952: fifty years of service in St. Albans.* Reading, C.W.S., 1952. 21pp.

3806 Sandall, B. and A. Chappell. *A brief history of the Congleton Society: 100 years of progress.* Stockport, C.W.S., 1960. 24pp.
    1860–1960.

3807 Selkirk Co-operative Society. *A century of co-operation: published to mark the centenary of the Society 1846–1946.* Selkirk, The Society, 1946. 15pp.

3808 Settle Co-operative Society. *A hundred years of Settle Co-op.* Settle, The Society, 1961. 13pp.
    1861–1961.

3809 Sheehan, J. *A centenary: a brief history of the Society.* Manchester, C.W.S., 1957. 16pp.
    Eccles and District Co-operative Society, 1857–1957.

3810 Smith, T. *Seventy years of service: the story of the Birmingham Co-operative Society, 1881–1951.* Birmingham, Birmingham Printers, 1951. 63pp.

3811 Southampton Co-operative Society Ltd. *Sixty years of progress, 1887–1947.* Southampton, The Society, 1947. 19pp.

3812 Stockport Co-operative Society. *The history 1860 to 1960.* Manchester, C.P.S., 1960. 24pp.

3813 Strathaven Co-operative Society. *Centenary report and balance sheet, 10th September 1968.* Glasgow, S.C.W.S., 1968. 16pp.
    1868–1968.

3814 Taylor, G.A. *From acorn to oak: Part II, being the history of the Walsall and District Co-operative Society Ltd., 1936–1961. Prepared on the occasion of the 75th anniversary of the Society, 1961.* Birmingham, Birmingham Printers, 1961. xvi, 164pp.

3815 Topham, P. *Seventy-five years of co-operative progress: a history of the Worcester Co-operative Society Ltd.* Stockport, C.W.S., 1956. 125pp.

816 Torquay Co-operative Society. *Sixty years of co-operation in Torquay 1890–1950.* Torquay, The Society, 1950. 19pp.

817 Treorchy Workmen's Industrial Co-operative Society Ltd. *A century of co-operative service.* Treorchy, The Society, 1968. 16pp.

818 Twelves, A. *Jubilee history of the Colwyn Bay and Llandudno Junction Co-operative Society, 1902–1952.* Colwyn Bay, The Society, 1952. 24pp.

819 Vickrage, H.M. *Blackley's co-operative centenary.* Blackley, Co-operative Retail Services Ltd., 1961. 10pp.
      1861–1961.

820 Vickrage, H.M. *Seventy five years of co-operative endeavour 1875–1950: a brief history of the Ten Acres and Stirchley Co-operative Society Ltd.* Stockport, C.W.S., 1950. 24pp.

821 Vickrage, H.M. *Seventy five years of co-operative endeavour: a history of Ten Acres and Stirchley Co-operative Society Ltd.* Stockport, C.W.S., 1951. 246.
      1875–1950.

822 Wakefield, W.A.S. *1866–1966: 100 years of progress. A centenary souvenir of the success story of Kettering Industrial Co-operative Society.* Kettering, The Society, 1966. 43pp.

823 Wall, Percy. *"You inherit!" Abergavenny and District Co-operative Society on occasion of their Golden Jubilee.* Cardiff, The Society, 1960. 24pp.

824 Walsall and District Co-operative Society. *Seventy fifth anniversary . . . 1886–1961.* Manchester, C.P.S., 1961. 51pp.

825 Warrington Co-operative Society. *This is your heritage: a record of one hundred years of successful trading in Warrington.* Warrington, C.W.S., 1960. 24pp.
      1860–1960.

826 Worksop Co-operative Society. *Centenary 1867–1967: one hundred years of progress.* Worksop, The Society, 1967. 22pp.

827 Wright, W.B. *A souvenir written in commemoration of the completion of seventy-five years of co-operative effort in Northampton, 1870–1945.* Northampton, The Society, 1945. 181pp.

Co-operative commercial, industrial and manufacturing societies

828 Derby Printers Ltd. *Sixty years 1900–1960.* Derby, The Printers, 1960. 12pp.

829 Digby, M. *Agricultural co-operation in Great Britain.* Crosby Lockwood, 1949. xv, 108pp.

3830 Digby, M. *Co-operative land use: the challenge to traditional co-operation.* Oxford, Blackwell, 1963. iv, 84pp.

3831 Flanagan, D. *The gleaming record: 50 years.* United Co-operative Laundries Association, 1962. 25pp.

3832 Garnett, R.G. *A century of co-operative insurance.* Allen and Unwin, 1968. x, 324pp.

3833 Garnett, R.G. 'A housing association for New Lanark'. LHN, Summer 1964, 6(4):118–20.

3834 Jeffreys, J.B. *Retail trading in Britain 1850–1950.* CUP, 1954. xvii, 497pp.

3835 Kettering Co-operative Boot and Manufacturing Society. *60th anniversary: 1888–1948.* Kettering, The Society, 1948. 32pp.

3836 Roberts, W.V. *A half-century of co-operative partnership 1899–1949.* Wigston, Wigston Co-operative Hosiers, 1949. 75pp.

3837 Scottish Labour History Society. 'New Lanark: Robert Owen's village'. SSLH, Autumn 1963, 7:35–6.

3838 Smith, T. *Fifty years of printing: a history of the Birmingham Printers Ltd.* Birmingham, The Printers, 1952. ix, 102pp.

Index

Index

Anderson, J.R.L.   3440
Anderson, M.   1
Anderson, Mosa   744–5
Anderson, P.   1173, 1276, 1500, 2580
Andrews, C.D.   3295
Andrews, E.   35
Andrews, W.H.   36
Angell, N.   37
Annan, Lord   1160
Anti-Poor Law movement   2216
Applegarth, R.   38–9.
Arch, J.   40–1, 923
Arditti, C.   3709
Armstrong, G.   1174
Armytage, W.H.G.   429, 646, 724–5, 765, 1441–3, 2370
Arnison, J.   3504
Arnold, G.L.   2433, 2581
Arnot, R.P.   16–17, 36, 42–3, 211, 449, 649–52, 889, 897, 933, 1020, 1094, 1501–3, 2161, 2466–7, 2546, 2679–84, 3159, 3296–3301, 3335–7, 3404, 3505, 3622
Arundel, H.   546
Ashby, A.W.   41
Ashe, G.   775
Ashley, Sir W.   44
Ashraf, P.M. Kemp. *See* Kemp-Ashraf, P.M.
Ashton, T.S.   1001
Ashton-under-Lyne Working Men's Co-operative Society   3782
Aspinall, A.   2
Associated Blacksmiths' Forge and Smithy Workers' Society   3364
Associated Society of Locomotive Engineers and Firemen   2831, 3362
Association of Correctors of the Press   3390
Association of Engineering and Ship-building Craftsmen   3367
Association of University Teachers   3379
Asylum attendants   3288
Atkins, A.H.   1133
Atkinson, N.   3441
Attlee, C.R.   45–69, 1504–5, 1995, 2064
Attwood, T.   70–4
Aveling, E.   2230
Awbery, S.   1825

B., J.   1505
Backstrom, P.N.   1220, 2371

Bacup Co-operative Society   3727
Bagwell, P.S.   3302–4
Bailey, J.   2468, 3688–9
Bailey, S.K.   212
Bain, G.S.   2685–6
Baines, D.E.   3651
Baird, J.   1506
Ball, F.C.   1036
Ball, J.   2104, 2687–90, 3442
Ballantine, W.   2691
Balmer, T.   1996
Balogh, T.   1507–8
Bamford, S.   75–9
Banbury   1846
Banks, J.A.   101, 3690
Banks, O.   101
Banyard, H.T.   2692
Barbican, The   3237
Barker, B.   1826
Barker, C.   3407, 3506
Barker, G.F.R.   277, 307, 388
Barker, J.   80–1
Barker, R.   2274
Barker, T.   82–4
Barnes, G.N.   85
Barnes, H.   2606
Barnes, L.   1605
Barnes, M.   2935
Barnes, R.   2372
Barnett, C.   1444
Barnie, D.   3728
Barnsby, G.   1445, 2162–3, 3660
Barnsley British Co-operative Society   3729–30
Barons Court, 1964 election   1931
Barou, N.   86, 2693–4, 3691
Barr, Rev. J.   87–8
Barr, J.   3507
Barratt, M.   584
Barrhead Co-operative Society   3791
Barrow, L.   135, 1175
Barrow-in-Furness Labour Party   1841
Barry, M.M.   89
Barton, T.C.   3305
Bassett, R.   1984
Bassett-Vincent, C.   3306
Bates, L.   2695
Bateson, F.W.   1277
Bath   1467
Bather, L.   3661
Baylen, J.O.   934
Bayliss, F.J.   2275

222